TO EACH
ITS OWN
MEANING

An Introduction

To Each

to Biblical Criticisms

Its Own

and Their

Meaning

Application

STEPHEN R. HAYNES AND
STEVEN L. MCKENZIE, EDITORS

Westminster/John Knox Press
Louisville, Kentucky

Book design by Susan E. Jackson

First edition

Published by Westminster/John Knox Press
Louisville, Kentucky

This book is printed on acid-free paper that meets the American National Standards Institute Z39.48 standard. ∞

PRINTED IN THE UNITED STATES OF AMERICA

9   8   7   6   5   4   3   2   1

Library of Congress Cataloging-in-Publication Data

To each its own meaning : an introduction to biblical criticisms and
their applications / edited by Stephen R. Haynes, Steven L.
McKenzie. — 1st ed.
        p.   cm.
    ISBN 0-664-25236-2 (pbk. : alk. paper)

    1. Bible—Criticism, interpretation, etc.—Methodology.
I. Haynes, Stephen R.   II. McKenzie, Steven L., 1953–
BS511.2.T64   1993
220.6—dc20   92-26563

*To our wives, Natalie and Vilma
and to our daughters, Christiana,
Christina, and Bonnie.*

THE CHIEF CUPBEARER TOLD PHARAOH, "TODAY I REMEMBER MY SINS. WHEN PHARAOH WAS ANGRY WITH HIS SERVANTS AND IMPRISONED ME AND THE CHIEF BAKER IN THE HOUSE OF THE CHIEF OF THE BODYGUARD, HE AND I DREAMT DREAMS ON THE SAME NIGHT, EACH DREAM WITH ITS OWN MEANING. A HEBREW LAD, SERVANT TO THE CHIEF OF THE BODYGUARD, WAS THERE WITH US, AND WHEN WE TOLD HIM OUR DREAMS HE INTERPRETED THEM FOR US, GIVING *TO EACH ITS OWN MEANING.*"

—Genesis 41:9–12, editor's translation

CONTENTS

CONTRIBUTORS

Introduction
    Stephen R. Haynes and Steven L. McKenzie
    Rhodes College, Memphis, Tennessee

Reading the Bible Historically: The Historian's Approach
    J. Maxwell Miller
    Candler School of Theology, Emory University, Atlanta, Georgia

Source Criticism
    Pauline A. Viviano
    Loyola University of Chicago, Chicago, Illinois

Tradition-Historical Criticism
    Robert A. Di Vito
    Loyola University of Chicago, Chicago, Illinois

Form Criticism
    Martin J. Buss
    Emory University, Atlanta, Georgia

Redaction Criticism
    Gail Paterson Corrington
    Rhodes College, Memphis, Tennessee

Social-Scientific Criticism
    Dale B. Martin
    Duke University, Durham, North Carolina

Canonical Criticism
    Mary C. Callaway
    Fordham University, Bronx, New York

Rhetorical Criticism
    Yehoshua Gitay
    University of Capetown, Capetown, South Africa

Structural Criticism
  Daniel Patte
  Vanderbilt University, Nashville, Tennessee

Narrative Criticism
  David M. Gunn
  Columbia Theological Seminary, Decatur, Georgia

Reader-Response Criticism
  Edgar V. McKnight
  Furman University, Greenville, South Carolina

Poststructuralist Criticism
  William A. Beardslee
  Process and Faith Center, Claremont University, Claremont, California

Reading the Bible Ideologically: Feminist Criticism
  Danna Nolan Fewell
  Southern Methodist University, Dallas, Texas

INTRODUCTION

"EVERYONE INTERPRETS THE BIBLE IN THEIR OWN WAY."

THIS sentiment is often expressed during informal discussions on the nature of the Bible and the beliefs to which it gives rise. And the statement contains an element of truth. Different people certainly come away from the Bible with different understandings; no two people see it exactly the same way. Furthermore, the plethora of competing critical methods utilized by biblical scholars, often aimed at the very same texts, gives popular credence to the notion that, indeed, "everyone interprets the Bible in their own way." After all, if the "experts" cannot agree on how the Bible should be read, what hope is there for the rest of us in discovering meaning there?

But the statement above is also misleading because it implies that there is no common ground for understanding the Bible, no way of evaluating a given interpretation, and that one person's guess about the meaning of a passage is as good as another's. Yet biblical scholars, who study the text professionally, work on the assumption that some interpretations of biblical texts are "better" than others. Still, the average reader of the Bible remains largely unaware of the techniques employed by professional biblical critics to arrive at meaningful interpretations. The distance from biblical scholarship felt by even the educated nonspecialist is exacerbated by two other factors. First, biblical scholars too often write only for one another, and thus their work is often filled with technical jargon. Second, while long on theoretical justification, their published writings tend to be short on practical demonstration.

The present volume seeks to address this state of affairs by introducing the most important methods of biblical criticism with special attention to the way in which they can be applied to specific biblical texts. Although theoretical questions are not ignored by the authors who have contributed these chapters, each has made a concerted effort to demonstrate how his or her method is actually applied, targeting the reader who is not an expert: the student, educated members of the clergy, and the nonspecialist who teaches the Bible.

1

Not surprisingly, the frustrating experiences of the editors are what is behind the conception of this volume. The idea for such a book was born in part
from the struggles of an advanced graduate student trying to apply biblical
criticism to the task of bringing the Bible to life for undergraduates. It did not
take long to realize that these students were only likely to show interest in
biblical criticism if its value could be demonstrated in action—if they could be
convinced, that is, that biblical criticism sheds light upon texts that appear
difficult or incomprehensible. When the graduate student became a fledgling
college professor, he gained a new colleague who was trained as a biblical
scholar and who made a living teaching introductory Bible classes. The biblical
scholar had experienced his own frustrations in teaching the Bible to undergraduates. Among them was his inability to find an up-to-date text for a course
introducing critical methods for understanding the Bible. After many discussions, the nonspecialist and the specialist joined forces to plan and edit this
volume.

Despite our differences, then, we editors are united by the common, and
often frustrating, experience of trying to show students how scholarship sheds
light on the meaning of the Bible and thus helps bring it alive. Specifically, we
share dismay at how little of what is written in the field of biblical scholarship
addresses our goals for this volume. These goals are (1) to offer an up-to-date
presentation of the principal methods of critical biblical study, including their
assumptions and objectives; (2) to make the information about these methods
readily accessible to students and other nonspecialists; and (3) to show biblical
criticism in action by demonstrating how particular methods may be imple-
mented in the interpretation and explication of specific texts. The surprising
ease with which we were able to interest the editors at Westminster/John Knox
Press in our idea for a text that addressed these goals told us we were not alone
in our perceptions of this gap in biblical scholarship.

The Current Shape of Biblical Studies

As editors we are hopeful that our markedly different approaches to the
Bible are an additional factor that will distinguish this book. One of us has
training in hermeneutics and literary theory and approaches biblical criticism
from a "literary," and thus relatively nontraditional, posture. The other is
trained in the techniques of modern biblical criticism and approaches the Bible
primarily according to the more traditional "historical-critical method."

Significantly, our differing backgrounds and orientations are representative
of an important division within biblical criticism itself. Increasingly over the
last twenty years the hegemony of historical methods for interpreting the Bible
has been challenged by biblical critics unhappy with either the results or the
very assumptions of historical-critical scholarship. The division between criti-

cal methods that adhere to a historical paradigm for understanding texts and those that embrace a literary paradigm has been well documented in recent literature and is referred to in several of the chapters of this book. We offer here only a few comments on this critical split, and the way it is reflected in the book's organization.

One fundamental disagreement between "historical" and "literary" methods of biblical criticism is found in their assumptions about the relationship between texts and history. This disagreement can be expressed in simple terms by saying that historical methods such as source criticism, form criticism, tradition-historical criticism, and redaction criticism emphasize the historical, archaeological, or literary *backgrounds* or roots of a text, and the development of the text *through time.* Thus historical-critical methods are sometimes referred to as "diachronic." On the other hand, literary methods like structuralist criticism, narrative criticism, reader-response criticism, and poststructuralist criticism tend to focus on the *text itself* in its final form (however the final form might have been achieved), the relationships between a variety of textual elements (both surface and deep), and the interaction between texts and *readers.*

One methodological example of this difference in focus between historical and literary approaches may be particularly helpful to keep in mind while using this volume. Historically oriented biblical critics tend to regard an author's intention in writing as important for construing what a text meant originally, as well as what it means now. Scholars who depart from historical approaches in favor of more literary readings, however, often view authorial intention as irretrievable, or irrelevant to the interpretive process altogether. The latter even invoke the term "intentional fallacy" to argue that assumptions related to the author of an ancient text and his or her intentions are always dubious.

While we hope the preceding has been helpful in communicating the distinction between historical and literary methods in general, we also realize that it is in some ways misleading. For easy distinctions break down even in an introductory text like this, where authors attempt to describe their methods in the simplest terms. For one thing, many scholars utilize a combination of historical and literary approaches in working with texts. Even scholars who think of themselves as theoretical purists (whether of the historical or literary variety) will often utilize insights from "the other side" when they prove illuminating. Also, some critical methods—social-scientific criticism, canonical criticism, and rhetorical criticism, for instance—simply do not fit easily under the rubrics "historical" or "literary." As the chapters that describe these critical methods demonstrate, they are in some ways typically "historical" and in others more characteristically "literary."

Finally, the literary/historical distinction becomes problematical when scholars use traditional (historical) methods in nontraditional ways. For instance, Martin Buss, in his chapter on form criticism, describes a critical method that developed early in this century as part of the historical-critical paradigm in biblical studies. However, Buss elaborates and applies the method in fresh ways unanticipated by form criticism's pioneers. Buss also calls attention to the implicit relationship between philosophical orientations and forms of social organization. Thus form criticism as introduced and applied by Buss reminds us that we are not to think of historical methods as stale holdovers from an earlier era that are necessarily blind to their own social location.

Yehoshua Gitay's chapter on rhetorical criticism provides another example of the way in which facile distinctions fail to do justice to the present state of biblical scholarship. The term "rhetorical criticism" is often used to describe close attention to stylistic and ideological elements in a text. Such scholarship is "literary" in its attention to the final form of a text and the interrelationships of textual elements. On the other hand, what Gitay introduces under the heading "rhetorical criticism" involves scrutiny of an author's persuasive intention as revealed in the rhetoric employed. While Gitay's rhetorical-critical approach does pay attention to the relation of textual elements (a trait of the more literary type of rhetorical criticism), its emphasis on recapturing an original "rhetorical situation" between author and audience places it within the domain of the historical paradigm.

The reader will recognize a comparable plurality of views *within* the confines of particular methods in other chapters—especially those on canonical criticism by Mary Callaway and social-scientific criticism by Dale Martin. These chapters also have in common with Gitay's on rhetorical criticism a continuation and revision of the historical paradigm. Together, these three chapters comprise the second section of the book, which we have chosen to call "the tradition expanded."

As one example of how the distinction between the historical and literary paradigms can actually become secondary for biblical studies, we include a chapter on feminist criticism by Danna Nolan Fewell. While Fewell's own orientation to the biblical text is "literary," this should not lead the reader to suppose that all feminist critics of the Bible have eschewed the historical-critical method. That this is not the case is clear from the works of feminist historical critics cited in Fewell's chapter, as well as the feminist concerns of scholars like Gail Corrington (author of the chapter on redaction criticism), whose research falls within the historical paradigm.

Fewell's chapter is titled "Reading the Bible Ideologically: Feminist Criticism," a phrase referring to the fact that feminist criticism is one example of "ideological criticism"—a practice that is growing in importance and influence in biblical studies. But ideological critique is found throughout this volume— for example, in the articles by Buss, William Beardslee, and David Gunn. In his discussion of narrative criticism, the latter forays into both feminist and poststructuralist criticism.

In many parts of the book, disagreement over the importance of historical investigation for understanding the biblical text is evident. For Daniel Patte, Gunn, Edgar McKnight, and Beardslee (authors of the chapters on structural criticism, narrative criticism, reader-response criticism, and poststructuralist criticism, respectively), the relationship between biblical texts and their historical origins or accuracy is of purely secondary importance, if it is considered at all. Conversely, for Pauline Viviano and Robert Di Vito (who introduce "historical" methods in section one), in addition to Buss and Corrington, historical questions are central, especially those concerning the development of texts through time. These larger assumptions regarding the relationship of history and biblical criticism are implicit throughout the book but are discussed explicitly in J. Maxwell Miller's introductory chapter, "Reading the Bible Historically: The Historian's Approach."

The Contributors

As editors, we have sought to maintain a balance in a number of areas: between theory and application, usefulness for students and teachers, and, as should be clear by now, sympathy for historical and nonhistorical approaches to the Bible. Especially on the final point, such balance is rare in works by one author, and even in edited works, which often originate from one person or a group of persons with a similar critical orientation. The balance we have tried to achieve in this volume is evident in the nearly equal space devoted to "historical" and "literary" methods. But it has also been present in the process of editing itself, during which questions "from both sides" were directed strenuously at each chapter as the book took shape. In this sense, our respective weaknesses became strengths, as one of us was always able to articulate "dumb questions" the other had overlooked entirely. It also seems to us a sign of balance that, despite our friendship, we consistently disagreed on points of methodology raised in this book from start to finish.

We have also sought to achieve diversity, if not total balance, in the identities and backgrounds of our contributors. Four are women and nine are men. Seven are Hebrew Bible/Old Testament scholars, and six work primarily in New Testament. Three are from Roman Catholic backgrounds, one is Jewish, and nine represent a variety of Protestant denominations. Six of our contributors teach in seminaries or graduate divinity schools, while seven teach in college or university departments of religion. Seven are well established in their academic careers, while six are younger scholars who have yet to make their greatest contributions to biblical scholarship.

Again in the interest of balance, some younger scholars were assigned chap-

ters on more traditional methods, while more established scholars were asked
to write chapters on newer methods. This was done in order to challenge the
common misconception that literary and ideological methods are utilized only
by the youngest generation of biblical critics, and that only those out of touch
with current trends still practice historical methods of biblical criticism. The
reality within the field of biblical studies is rather different. While it is finding
increasing acceptance among important scholars, the literary paradigm has yet
to make historical-critical investigation of the Bible obsolete. This book, therefore, challenges both the *evolutionary* picture of modern biblical criticism—
according to which literary and ideological methods represent a movement out
of a primitive stage of biblical criticism—and the *de-evolutionary* picture—in
which literary criticism symbolizes a fall from the critical paradise in which
confidence in objective certainties once reigned.

Although we have tried to produce a work that is both inclusive and ecu-
menical, some perspectives (for instance, Roman Catholic, Jewish, and feminist) are not represented according to their importance in the field of biblical
studies at the present moment. It is important to understand that this book is
not organized according to ideological *perspective* but according to critical
method. This accounts for our inclusion of the standard methods of criticism
while excluding, for example, various liberationist readings of the Bible that
are extremely influential in the current scholarly milieu. On the other hand,
liberationist *perspectives* have been formative for many of our authors, some of
whom are clearly engaged in the kind of ideological criticism described in the
book's final chapter.

Perhaps the most rewarding aspect of editing a volume like this one is that
nearly every chapter has provided its own "a-ha" experiences. On several oc-
casions in the process of reading and rereading these articles, we shared moments of revelation as a particular method was placed neatly within its
intellectual or historical context or was applied to a passage in illuminating
ways. We are grateful to the contributors for giving us these experiences and
for enhancing our grasp of the methods they present. We are confident this
book will prove helpful to others, partly because we believe it will have many
readers like ourselves—those who, whether they are students or teachers, will
benefit from observing practitioners of these methods as they explain and apply them.

Chapter Format

While the chapters in this book reflect differences in style as well as content, a general format has guided the writing of each chapter. This format was
specified by the editors and was followed (more or less closely) by each of the
contributors. The proposed chapter format was outlined in five parts and sent

to each contributor as a general guide for her or his writing. With variations depending on the style of individual contributors and the methods they present, then, each chapter addresses five sets of issues:

1. Definition of the method, important terms and concepts, history of its development, assumptions made about the relationship of text and history, prospects for the future

2. The method in relation to others discussed in this book

3. The method in action, with reference to a particular text in either Genesis or Luke-Acts

4. The drawbacks of the method

5. Suggested reading for those who wish to pursue the method further

The Contribution

We believe that two aspects of this book's uniqueness lie in what we as editors asked each of the contributors to do. First, the critical method being dealt with is to be not only described, both in its own terms and in relation to other methods and intellectual currents, but also demonstrated in working with a particular text. In fact, this practical dimension generally takes up a quarter to a third of each chapter. Second, each contributor is asked to assess honestly the shortcomings of the critical method, suggesting the kind of texts on which it may not yield results.

Part of our format prescription found in point 1 above deserves further comment. A concern in our own discussions across the divide that separates historical from literary approaches to the Bible has been whether textual meaning is to be found "behind" a text (that is, in the historical events or sources that underlie it), "in" the text (that is, in the interaction of elements and structures that emerge in a close reading of the text in its final form), or "in front of" the text (that is, in the construction of meaning that takes place in the interaction between text and reader). It was not our expectation that this question would receive a definitive answer in the book. We only sought to provide a forum for each author to address it and provide his or her own version of an answer. The editors' attempt at an inclusive view would be that the best biblical criticism does not confidently announce what a text "means" but humbly assures us that the text can be "meaningful" by demonstrating one or more possible, if not convincing, meanings. This dialogical strategy suggests that we believe mutual enlightenment is in fact attainable through dialogue. This is at least our hope, and we pause to make it explicit because it is taken for granted less and less in scholarly circles. The balanced, dialogical format we have chosen also makes us hopeful that strawpersons will be more easily identifiable, as each method is described in detail by a practitioner.

This book itself has arisen from a dialogue between two persons who were raised in conservative Christian traditions, lost their precritical naiveté through engagement with critical study of the Bible, and found reorientation to this sacred text in different ways. While we are experienced enough to realize that rapprochement between the competing methodologies described here will not be easy, we remain naive enough to believe this is a legitimate goal, one toward which this book will, we hope, contribute.

PART ONE
TRADITIONAL METHODS
OF BIBLICAL CRITICISM

1

READING THE BIBLE HISTORICALLY: THE HISTORIAN'S APPROACH

J. Maxwell Miller

History and Historical Methodology

ALTHOUGH "history" is a much-used term, it is not easily defined. Is history the sum total of past people and events? Or does it include only those people and events whose memory is preserved in written records? The available written evidence from ancient times is uneven in coverage, with some peoples and periods better represented than others. Moreover, the ancient documents provide very selective kinds of information. This information often is ambivalent, and sometimes the ancient sources make unbelievable or conflicting claims. Would it be more accurate, then, to say that history is the past as understood by historians, based on their analysis and interpretation of the available evidence but not necessarily identical with the claims made by ancient documents? What if the historians disagree? And does history belong to the professional historians anyhow? Perhaps history should be equated instead with the common consensus notions about the past held by the general public. These notions might be influenced by what professional historians say as well as by other factors, such as prevailing political, social, and religious attitudes. For that matter, are not professional historians themselves deeply influenced by prevailing attitudes?

It may be said, in any case, that historians seek to understand the human past and that they depend heavily on written sources for their information. Heavy reliance on written evidence is perhaps the main distinguishing characteristic of historical research as compared with other disciplines that also seek to understand the human past. This does not mean, of course, that contemporary historians concentrate solely on written evidence or that historical research is conducted independently of other disciplines. Contemporary scholars exploring the history of ancient Israel find themselves necessarily involved, for example, in Palestinian archaeology and sociology.

Historians seek objectivity. They are interested in discovering and reporting what really happened in the past, as opposed to collecting and passing on
fanciful stories, writing "docudramas," or producing "revisionist" accounts of
the past for propagandistic or ideological purposes. However, complete objectivity is a goal never reached. The historian's own presuppositions, ideology,
and attitudes inevitably influence his or her research and reporting. Perhaps it
is not an overstatement to say that any history book reveals as much about its
author as it does about the period of time treated. If so, then a proper definition of history would suggest that it consists neither of the totality of past
people and events on the one hand, nor of what we contemporaries know (or
think we know) about the past on the other, but of an ongoing conversation
between the past and the present. As we humans, individually and collectively, seek to understand the present, we naturally look to the past for bear-
ings. At the same time, we constantly revise our understanding of the past in
light of current developments, understandings, and attitudes.

Basic to modern historiography is the principle of "analogy." Historians
assume, consciously or unconsciously, that the past is analogous to the present and that one human society is analogous to another. Thus a historian's
understanding of present reality serves as an overriding guide for evaluating
evidence and interpreting the past, and the cultural patterns of a better-
known society may be used as a guide for clarifying those of a lesser-known
society. As an example of how this works in modern treatments of ancient
Israelite history, note that the Bible presupposes a dynamic natural world
into which God intrudes overtly upon human affairs from time to time. It is a
world with waters rolling back so that the Israelites can escape Pharaoh's
army, a world of burning bushes and floating ax heads. God hands down laws
on Mount Sinai and sends angels to defend Jerusalem against the massive
Assyrian army. Modern Western historians tend to perceive the world as
being more orderly, however, and one of the standard tenets of modern
historiography is that a natural explanation for a given historical phenomenon or event is preferable to an explanation that involves overt divine intervention. When speculating about the "actual historical events" behind the
biblical account of Israel's past, therefore, what historians often do, in effect,
is bring the biblical story into line with reality as we moderns perceive it.
Surely the Assyrian army was not routed by angels, because angels, if they
exist at all, do not play this sort of role in the world as we experience it.
What other "more reasonable" explanation might there be for the rout of
the Assyrians—"more reasonable" in the sense that it is more in keeping
with our modern Western perception of reality? Possibly a plague broke out
among the Assyrian troops, or maybe the narrator of the biblical account
embellished the report. Either of these possibilities would be analogous to
the world as we perceive it. But angels are not. In effect, then, the modern

historian offers explanations that do not involve miracles or "God talk" for historical developments reported in the Bible.

The analogy principle also is at work when historians draw upon knowledge of other societies, ancient and modern, in attempts to clarify aspects of Israelite and early Christian history. The Bible reports the names of court officials who served under David and Solomon, for example, but does not describe the duties of these various officials. Historians, assuming that the royal court in Jerusalem would have been similar to other royal courts of the day, search the records of neighboring kingdoms for information regarding the duties and responsibilities of such officials.

Another example pertains to the chronological data provided in the Bible for each of the Israelite and Judean kings following Solomon. Specifically, each king's accession to the throne is dated relative to the reign of his contemporary on the other throne; and also the length of each king's reign is recorded. The following verses are typical.

> In the twentieth year of King Jeroboam of Israel Asa began to reign over Judah; he reigned forty-one years in Jerusalem. (1 Kings 15:9)

> Nadab son of Jeroboam began to reign over Israel in the second year of King Asa of Judah; he reigned over Israel two years. (1 Kings 15:25)

> In the third year of King Asa of Judah, Baasha son of Ahijah began to reign over all Israel at Tirzah; he reigned twenty-four years. (1 Kings 15:33)

However, the figures provided do not always "add up." This may be due in part to copyists's mistakes in the transmission of the ancient manuscripts. But there are also other factors to be considered in view of the records of other ancient Middle Eastern kingdoms. It is known, for example, that some of these records presuppose a fall-to-fall calendar year while others presuppose a spring-to-spring calendar year. Some designate as the first year of a king's reign the year during which he ascended to the throne; others count only his first full year (i.e., the first full fall-to-fall or spring-to-spring year, depending on the calendar used). The possibility arises, therefore, on analogy with the practices of neighboring peoples, that the two Hebrew kingdoms, Israel and Judah, used separate and different calendars, employed different methods of reckoning their respective kings' reigns, and may even have changed calendars or methods of reckoning at one time or another. One or more of these factors may explain why the biblical figures seem to be internally inconsistent. It is hardly surprising, moreover, in view of the confusing biblical figures and the various factors to be taken into account, that historians rarely agree on exact dates for the Israelite and Judean kings.

Other than this principle of analogy, which is basic also to the other approaches treated in this volume, there is no specific methodology for historical research. Rather, the historian might be compared to an investigative lawyer who searches out and examines whatever evidence is available and relevant to a particular case, employs whatever techniques and methods of analysis apply to the evidence (often relying on the opinion of specialists), constructs a hypothetical scenario as to what probably happened, and then presents the case for this scenario to other historians and the public. The last step is as important as the first. The leading historians who have been able to influence academic and public opinion regarding the past have not only been outstanding scholars who demonstrated amazing coverage, competence, and creativity in research, but have also been able to present their ideas in an understandable and convincing fashion. Thus history is a search for "what really happened," but it is also what the historians can convince us really happened.

The Bible as History

The opening books of the Hebrew Bible, Genesis through 2 Kings, present a narrative account of people and events that extends from creation to the end of the Judean monarchy. Another sequence of books, 1–2 Chronicles, Ezra, and Nehemiah, presents an overlapping account that begins with Adam and concludes with Nehemiah's activities in Jerusalem under Persian rule. The so-called prophetical books (Isaiah, Jeremiah, Ezekiel, Hosea, etc.) make numerous references to national and international circumstances. The first part of the book of Daniel (chapters 1–6) describes events that supposedly occurred in the Babylonian court while Daniel and other Jews were exiled there. The latter part (chapters 7–12) reports a dream-vision that organizes world history into a sequence of four great empires and anticipates the culmination of history during the fourth. The Gospel of Luke dates Jesus' birth in relation to Roman history (Luke 2:1), and all four of the Gospels narrate episodes in Jesus' ministry in what the reader is left to suppose is an essentially chronological sequence. The book of Acts describes the emergence of Christianity from the immediate aftermath of Jesus' crucifixion to Paul's arrival in Rome for trial. Finally, the book of Revelation reports dream-visions similar to those of the book of Daniel and also presupposing a schematic view of history.

In short, the biblical writers were very conscious of history, and the Bible itself may be looked upon as largely historical in format and content. It is not history written for the sake of history, of course, and not history of the sort one would read in a modern history book. One might argue, in fact, that the biblical writers were more akin to contemporary theologians than to historians. Nevertheless, the theological messages that the biblical writers sought to convey are so thoroughly intermeshed with their perceptions of history that it is difficult to separate one from the other. The Bible itself, in other words, confronts us with history and raises historical questions that are difficult to ignore. It is only natural, therefore, that biblical scholarship through the ages has involved attention to historical matters.

Reflected to some degree in earlier biblical research, but becoming especially intense during the twentieth century, are differences of opinion regarding the trustworthiness and accuracy of the Bible as a source of historical information. At one extreme are those who, usually on theological grounds, insist that the Bible is literally accurate in all historical details, including the chronological data provided in Genesis–2 Kings that place the creation of the world approximately 6000 years ago. Historical research for those who hold this extreme position involves harmonizing the information provided in different parts of the Bible—for example, the overlapping accounts of Genesis–2 Kings and 1 Chronicles–Nehemiah—and interpreting evidence from extrabiblical sources (other ancient documents and archaeology) to fit. Apparent contradictions within the Bible are viewed as being only "apparent," usually the result of the modern reader's failure to understand all of the surrounding circumstances. Conflicts between the Bible and extrabiblical sources also are explained away in one way or another.

At the opposite extreme are those who regard the biblical accounts as being so theologically and nationalistically tendentious and composed of such a hodgepodge of literary genera (myths, legends, etc.) that, except where extrabiblical sources shed some light, any attempt to reconstruct the history of ancient Israel is fruitless. This extreme is sometimes stated or implied by scholars who take essentially ahistorical approaches to the text, such as structuralist, narrative, or reader-response criticisms (see especially Part 3 of this volume).

However, it is very difficult to hold consistently to either of these extreme positions. The first, that of unwavering confidence in the historical accuracy of the biblical materials, is difficult to maintain in view of (1) the obvious tension between the dynamic and theocentric view of nature and history presupposed by the biblical writers and the more "scientific" or positivistic approach to reality that characterizes modern Western thought, (2) the mental gymnastics required to harmonize some of the apparent contradictions within the biblical narratives and to bring extrabiblical evidence into line, and (3) the results of close analysis of the biblical materials in accordance with source criticism, form criticism, tradition history, and other historical-critical methods.

As for the second position, that of extreme skepticism, it can hardly be doubted that there was an ancient Israel, that Israel had a history, or that the Bible is somehow relevant for understanding that history. Indeed, the very existence of the Bible, regardless of what one makes of its historical claims, is an undeniable item of historical evidence pointing to ancient Israel. It is difficult, moreover, regardless of the theory behind one's methodology, to approach an ancient document totally free of the influence of notions regarding the historical context from which it emerged. This is especially true with the Bible, which, as indicated above, is overtly attentive to history and makes such forceful historical claims. Close attention to the wording of their comments, therefore, often reveals that scholars who seem to take totally ahistorical approaches to the biblical materials nevertheless work with presuppositions regarding the history of ancient Israel that influence their overall understanding of the Bible if not their individual research.

Most biblical scholars, therefore, fall somewhere between the two extremes described above. On the one hand, they proceed in confidence that the Bible preserves authentic historical memory. On the other hand, they recognize that the Bible is not a monolithic document, that its different voices reflect different perceptions of ancient Israel's history, that these perceptions usually are heavily influenced by theological and nationalistic interests, and that some of the biblical materials were not intended to be read as literal history in the first place. The historian's task, therefore, is to separate the authentic historical memory from its highly theological and often legendary context.

Naturally, there is a wide range of views even within this middle ground between the extreme positions, with some scholars tending to place greater confidence in the historical accuracy of the biblical materials regardless of the theological, nationalistic, or legendary overtones and others tending to place less confidence in them. To see how this works out on a passage-by-passage basis, one might compare the *NIV Study Bible* (1985) with *The New Oxford Annotated Bible* (1991). The commentary and explanatory notes of the former were prepared by scholars who, although not biblical literalists, tend to take the biblical accounts of Israel's past as essentially historically accurate. Those of the latter were prepared by scholars who tend to be much more cautious on the matter.

Biblical Scholarship and the Study of Ancient Israelite History

Biblical scholarship and the study of ancient Israelite history are integrally related. On the one hand, most of our information about the history of ancient Israel prior to Roman times comes from the Bible. There are, to be sure, certain other ancient written sources and an ever-increasing amount of archaeological data to take into account. As will become apparent below, however, these extrabiblical sources are useful primarily in that they shed light on the general cultural, social, and international circumstances of biblical times. Usually they tell us very little specifically about the people and events of Israelite history, except when interpreted in light of the biblical record. On the other hand, as observed above, analysis of biblical literature generally involves some knowledge of (or at least some notions about) the history of ancient Israel. This is particularly true insofar as the analysis is historical-critical in approach. Historical-critical analysis (including such specialized approaches as source criticism, form criticism, tradition-historical criticism and redaction criticism) seeks to determine the historical contexts out of which the various biblical materials emerged, and what changes occurred in these materials as they were transmitted from ancient times to the present. Even to speculate on such matters presupposes some knowledge of the history of biblical times.

It is not surprising, therefore, that modern histories of ancient Israel typically have been written by scholars also deeply involved in biblical research, and that their application of historical-critical methodology to the biblical materials has significantly influenced their treatments of Israelite history. This is noticeable especially when one compares histories of Israel written during the nineteenth century. H. H. Milman's *History of the Jews* (1829) represents the emerging spirit of critical biblical scholarship during the first half of the century. H. G. A. Ewald's *Geschichte des Volkes Israel bis Christus* (1843–1855)[1] was based on a systematic source analysis of the Pentateuch, although not yet the classical "documentary hypothesis." While recognizing that the biblical traditions derive from a much later time than the period they describe and include imaginative elements, Ewald went to great lengths to explain that these traditions nevertheless preserve historical memory. He never clearly committed himself on what, if any, historical memory is preserved in the opening chapters of Genesis (which describe creation, the great flood, and the spread of population following the Tower of Babel episode), but he regarded the patriarchs (Abraham, Isaac, Jacob) as personifications of tribal groups. Ewald was also noncommittal regarding the specific circumstances of the exodus but believed that it was a historical event in connection with which Moses inaugurated a Hebrew monotheistic theocracy that set the direction for the future of Israelite history.

Julius Wellhausen, so closely identified with the documentary hypothesis in its classical form, spelled out the radical implications of this and other late nineteenth-century historical-critical developments in his compelling *Prolegomena zur Geschichte Israels* (1878).[2] Since, according to the documentary hypothesis, none of the four sources that compose the Pentateuch predates the Israelite monarchy, neither these individual sources nor the Pentateuch as a whole is trustworthy for reconstructing history prior to that time. According to the hypothesis, moreover, the "Priestly" source, which accounts for the bulk of the narrative and legal instructions associated with Moses, actually reflects circumstances at the end of Judah's history, the time of the Babylonian exile and following. In Wellhausen's treatment of Israel's history, therefore, Moses becomes a very shadowy and virtually unknown figure, and the characteristic features of the Mosaic era as presented in the Pentateuch (monotheism, a highly developed priesthood, elaborate legal and cultic practices, etc.) are seen instead as characteristic of exilic and postexilic times.

During the present century, as other historical-critical methodologies (especially form criticism, tradition history, and redaction criticism) have added their voices to source criticism, usually it has not been a question of whether treatments of Israelite history should presuppose a historical-critical approach to the Bible but of how much emphasis to place on the results of the analysis of the biblical literature itself as opposed to those of Palestinian archaeology or sociological models. This is illustrated by two widely used histories of Israel that were written during the 1950s and became very influential during the 1960s and 1970s—Martin Noth's *Geschichte Israels* (1950)[3] and John Bright's *A History of Israel* (1959).

Noth was one of the pioneers of tradition history, published comprehensive studies of the Pentateuch and the Deuteronomistic History,[4] and agreed with Wellhausen's conclusion that the Pentateuchal account of Israel's origins is an artificial literary construct composed largely of legendary materials. Thus Noth's history of Israel does not treat the patriarchs as historical figures, nor does he regard the exodus from Egypt or the conquest of Canaan as historical events. Drawing instead upon the sociological theories of Max Weber, the creative ideas of his teacher Albrecht Alt, clues from his own extensive tradition-historical studies of the Pentateuch, and what he thought were close parallels between early Israelite society and that of ancient Greek and Italian tribal leagues (known as amphictyonies), Noth argued that the ancestors of Israel probably were seminomads who ranged between the desert fringe and Canaan in search of pasture until they gradually settled down and took up agriculture. In stages, for which Noth believed there are clues in the Pentateuchal traditions, these tribal settlers formed an amphictyonic cultic league. Finally, under Saul and David, there emerged the Israelite monarchy, and it was only with the expansion of this monarchy under David that it is appropriate to speak of an Israelite conquest of Canaan.

Bright, while not ignoring the implications of historical-critical analysis, was inclined to give the biblical presentation of Israel's origins the benefit of the doubt except where it seemed to be in serious conflict with extrabiblical evidence. Also, he was much influenced by the ideas of his teacher W. F. Albright, who had been one of the pioneers in Palestinian archaeology and had advanced some rather appealing correlations between the biblical account of Israel's origins and archaeology. Thus Bright's *History* began with the patriarchs and followed the biblical outline fairly closely from that point on. Following Albright, he saw these as historical figures who lived approximately 2000 B.C.E. and probably were associated with Amorite movements that were believed to have been under way at the time. The exodus from Egypt occurred during the reign of Ramses II (ca. 1304–1237 B.C.E.), and the Israelite conquest of Canaan, which occurred near the close of the thirteenth century, was reflected in the pattern of city destructions that brought the Late Bronze Age to an end in Palestine.

While Noth's and Bright's histories of Israel still are widely read, the 1970s witnessed a decided shift in the discussion. This is reflected, for example, in a series of essays by an international team of scholars published under the title *Israelite and Judean History* (Hayes and Miller, 1977). Before turning our attention to recent developments in this discussion, however, some observations are in order regarding epigraphy, archaeology, and sociology.

Epigraphical Evidence

In its broadest sense, epigraphy is the study of written documents recovered from ancient times. Over the past two centuries, thousands of such documents have been recovered and numerous languages of the peoples of the ancient Middle East deciphered. Among the major developments are the decipherment, beginning in 1822, of Egyptian hieroglyphic writing; the decipherment, beginning in 1846, of the cuneiform scripts of several Mesopotamian languages; the discovery in 1887, in the el-Amarna district of Egypt, of correspondence between Egypt and various Syro-Palestinian rulers during the late fifteenth–early fourteenth centuries B.C.E.; the decipherment in 1915 of royal Hittite archives discovered at Boghazköy (ancient Hattusas) in central Turkey; the discovery in 1929 at Ras Shamra (ancient Ugarit) on the Syrian coast of a mid-fourteenth- to early twelfth-century B.C.E. archive of Canaanite documents, including mythical texts concerning the Canaanite god, Baal; the discovery, beginning in 1947, in caves along the northwest shore of the Dead Sea, of Hebrew documents from the first centuries B.C.E. and C.E., including manuscript fragments of most of the books of the Hebrew Bible; and finally, in 1975, the discovery at Tell Mardikh in Syria of royal archives of the ancient city of Ebla.

The recovery and decipherment of extrabiblical documents from the ancient Middle East understandably has had a major impact on biblical studies. The Israelites are not mentioned very often in these documents, however, which probably is to be explained on two grounds. First, epigraphical evidence from ancient Palestine is meager compared to the extensive archives that have been discovered in Egypt, Mesopotamia, Syria, and Asia Minor. Second, the Israelites rarely played a significant role in international affairs outside of Palestine, so that there was little occasion for them to be mentioned in the documents from ancient Egypt, Mesopotamia, and so forth.

A hieroglyphic inscription from the reign of Merneptah, an Egyptian pharaoh of dynasty XIX (thirteenth century B.C.E.), provides the earliest epigraphical reference to "Israel." Unfortunately, we learn very little about Israel from this inscription, and no other such references turn up in the epigraphical sources for the next three and a half centuries, until the time of Omri and Ahab in the ninth century B.C.E. This means that none of the characters or events that appear earlier than Omri and Ahab in the biblical narrative (Abraham, Isaac, Jacob, Joseph, Moses, the exodus from Egypt, Joshua, the conquest of Canaan, Saul, David, Solomon, etc.) are mentioned in any ancient sources outside the Bible. Another Egyptian inscription from the tenth century reports Pharaoh Sheshonk's military campaign into Palestine, an event that is mentioned also in 1 Kings 14:25–28 (where he is called Shishak). But while Sheshonk claims to have conquered some cities in Palestine, some of which presumably belonged at that time to the separate kingdoms of Israel and Judah, his inscription is conspicuously silent regarding these kingdoms.

Israel (the northern kingdom) seems to have enjoyed a brief period of national strength during the reigns of Omri and Ahab in the ninth century. But Assyria was beginning to expand westward during the same century and continued to grow in strength and to dominate much of the ancient Middle East for the next two centuries. Thus several kings of Israel and Judah are mentioned in the records of the Assyrian kings as having been subjugated by them or having paid tribute to them. Since these Assyrian rulers can be dated fairly securely, the points of contact between their records and the biblical account serve as valuable benchmarks for working out the chronology of the Israelite and Judean kings. With the collapse of Assyria and the rise of Babylon, the Palestinian kingdoms (including Judah) that had survived Assyrian domination fell into Babylonian hands. One of the Babylonian Chronicles reports Nebuchadrezzar's conquest of Jerusalem in March of 597 B.C.E., and King Jehoiachin of Judah is mentioned in Babylonian lists of exiles in Babylon during Nebuchadrezzar's reign (604–561).

Of the epigraphical evidence from Palestine that pertains to the time of the Israelite and Judean monarchies, the following items are especially noteworthy. The *Mesha Inscription* reports the accomplishments of Mesha, king of Moab in the ninth century B.C.E. Mesha boasts that he rid Moab of Israelite domination and identifies Omri as the Israelite king who subjugated Moab in the first place. Mesha himself figures in the narrative of 2 Kings 3:4–28. The *Siloam Inscription* commemorates the completion of a tunnel hewed out of solid rock for the purpose of transferring water from the Gihon Spring to the Siloam Pool in Jerusalem. Most scholars associate it with Hezekiah (cf. 2 Kings 20:20; 2 Chron. 32:30), although no king is mentioned by name on the surviving, legible portion of the inscription. Groups of *ostraca* (inscribed pottery fragments) from the ruins of several ancient cities in Israel and Judah contain administrative records and military correspondence.

There are no specific references to either the province of Samaria or Judah in surviving records of the Persian rulers (who succeeded the Babylonians as masters of Syria-Palestine in 539 B.C.E.) or of the Ptolemaic and Seleucid rulers who dominated Syria-Palestine following Alexander the Great's conquest of the East. For the period following Alexander, the writings of Josephus, a Jewish historian in the latter half of the first century C.E., become our chief source of information for Samaritan and Judean affairs. Other Greek and Roman writers add further details and perspectives on the history of Palestine following Alexander. Also, occasional papyrus and manuscript discoveries from this time are useful for historical research. Included among these are the Dead Sea Scrolls, which provide insight into a Jewish sect around the time of the emergence of Christianity in the first centuries B.C.E. and C.E.

Archaeological Evidence

Artifactual evidence—that is, material remains of the sort usually associated with archaeology (city and village ruins, architectural remains, remnants of tools, potsherds, etc.)—is to be distinguished from epigraphical evidence, even though artifacts occasionally bear written messages (ostraca, scarabs, seal impressions, etc.), and many of the epigraphical texts discussed above were discovered in the course of archaeological excavations. With systematic analysis of the artifactual evidence surviving in a given area, archaeologists can learn a great deal about the settlement patterns and life-styles of the people who lived there in times past. Since artifactual evidence typically is nonverbal, however, it usually is neither ethnic-specific nor very useful for clarifying matters of historical detail. If the people who lived in the cities, used the tools, and produced the pottery are to be identified in terms of their ethnic identity, in other words, or if any details are to be known about specific individuals and events of their history, the artifactual record must be coordinated with and interpreted in the light of written sources. The following is an example of how this works in the case of Palestinian archaeology and Israelite history.

Palestinian archaeologists recognize the end of the thirteenth century as a time of transition between two major cultural phases—that is, the end of the Late Bronze Age (ca. 1550–1200 B.C.E.) and the beginning of the Iron Age (ca. 1200–332 B.C.E.). Among the changes that marked the transition was the appearance of numerous Early Iron Age villages in the central Palestinian hill country, an area that had been only sparsely settled during the Late Bronze Age. Nothing has been discovered in any of the Early Iron Age village ruins that identifies the settlers by name. Taking into account Merneptah's Inscription, however, which places Israel on the scene in Palestine at the end of the thirteenth century, and also the biblical narratives that associate the Israelite tribes specifically with the central hill country, it makes sense to suppose that the Israelites and the Early Iron Age settlements were connected in some way.

It is not always a simple task to locate the archaeological ruins of particular cities and villages mentioned in the Bible, or, from the other direction, to identify archaeological sites in terms of their ancient names. Places like Jerusalem, which have been occupied continuously since ancient times, pose no problem. But for many abandoned sites whose ancient names have long since been forgotten, archaeologists must turn to the Bible and epigraphical sources for clues as to which ruins represent which ancient cities. The following are some of the cities that figure prominently in the biblical narratives and, in parentheses, the modern Arabic names of their respective ruins: Jericho (Tell es-Sultan), Ai (et-Tell), Gibeon (el-Jib), Samaria (Sebastiyeh), and Megiddo-Armageddon (Tell el-Mutesellim). When the ruins of biblical cities are excavated, naturally it is of interest to archaeologists and biblical scholars alike whether the archaeological findings corroborate the biblical record. In some cases, there seems to be a confirming fit. In other cases, there is obvious conflict. Often it is a matter of interpretation and debate. Research pertaining to the interface between biblical studies and archaeology sometimes is referred to as biblical archaeology.

Sociology

Historians necessarily work with conceptual models—hypothetical notions about how human society functions and what patterns of change tend to occur and under what circumstances. The Bible presents some very pronounced conceptual models and notions—for example, the idea that ethnic groups (Israelites, Moabites, Edomites, etc.) are extended families descended from individual male ancestors, that the direction of human history is guided by divine intervention, that Yahweh selected the Israelites as his special people and gave them the land of Canaan, and that the course of Israelite history was determined by Israel's fidelity or infidelity to Yahweh. These notions undergird the Genesis–2 Kings narrative, which in turn has provided the basic outline for postbiblical treatments of Israel's history throughout the centuries, all the way from Josephus to Bright.

As mentioned above, the Alt-Noth reconstruction of Israel's origins and early history relied heavily on the sociological theories of Max Weber. Specifically, Weber distinguished four basic social structures in ancient Palestine (nomadic bedouin, seminomadic herders, peasant farmers, and city dwellers) and three basic types of societal authority (legal, traditional, and charismatic). The conceptual models undergirding the Alt-Noth scenario have been seriously challenged in recent years. Several studies have suggested that seminomadic herding normally exists in symbiotic relationship with a village farming economy rather than in competition with it and that seminomadic herding is more likely to have derived from sedentary agriculture in ancient Palestine than to have intruded from the desert fringe.

The most aggressive challenge to Alt and Noth argued that the early Israelite tribes did not enter Palestine from elsewhere but emerged from a revolt within the indigenous Canaanite population. This would have been a peasant uprising against the oppressive Canaanite city-states that resulted in an egalitarian tribal society. This notion of a peasant revolt also is influenced by a sociological model, specifically Marxism. The peasant revolt model was very influential from the late 1960s through the 1970s but receives little attention now. But two aspects of this model remain influential—the idea that the early Israelite tribes emerged from the Canaanite population rather than entering the land from elsewhere and the recognition that any satisfactory explanation as to how this occurred must be well grounded in sociological research.

Recent Developments

Three major histories of Israel were published during the last decade, all of them appearing about the same time. H. Donner's *Geschichte des Volkes Israel und seiner Nachbarn in Grundzugen* (1984–1985) falls well within the Alt-Noth tradition. J. A. Soggin, in his *A History of Ancient Israel* (1984), finds the biblical presentation of Israel's history prior to the time of David as untrustworthy for the historian's purposes. Beginning with David, however, he places considerable confidence in the biblical narrative and follows it fairly closely. *A History of Ancient Israel and Judah* (1986) by J. M. Miller and J. H. Hayes also declines any attempt to reconstruct events prior to the establishment of the monarchy. Miller and Hayes are neither as reluctant as Soggin to speculate on the sociopolitical circumstances of the Israelite tribes from which the monarchy emerged nor as trusting of the biblical materials pertaining to monarchical times. Specifically, Miller and Hayes argue that

1. The clan was probably the basic sociopolitical unit among the early Israelite tribes, with the tribes themselves being essentially territorial groupings of clans whose sense of identity and mutual kinship developed in Palestine over a period of time.

2. The name "Israel" in premonarchical times probably referred specifically to the tribe of Ephraim and certain neighboring clans/tribes, such as Benjamin and Gilead, which Ephraim dominated.

3. This Ephraim-Israel tribal domain became the core of Saul's "kingdom," which itself remained essentially tribal in character.

4. Both Saul and David began their careers as military adventurers of a sort that may not have been typical of Ephraim-Israel but for which there was precedent nevertheless—that is, Saul and David followed in the tradition of Abimelech and Jephthah, who also had organized private armies with which they provided protection to their kinfolk in return for material support and engaged in raids on surrounding peoples.

5. David succeeded in carving out a territorial state that included as its core a southern grouping of tribes dominated by Judah, the city-state of Jerusalem, and the Ephraim-Israel tribes.

6. The biblical presentation of Solomon's "empire" is largely a literary fiction. Actually, his territorial domain probably was not any larger than David's, which did not even include some parts of Palestine (such as Philistia), much less all the lands between Egypt and the Euphrates.

7. Of the two kingdoms that resulted from the split at Solomon's death, the northern kingdom—which included the old Ephraim-Israel tribal domain and took the name Israel—emerged as the more powerful. Under the Omride dynasty, in fact, Israel achieved a level of commercial strength and international prestige superior to that achieved by either David or Solomon.

8. Beginning with the Omride period, moreover, and until Israel's defeat and annexation by the Assyrians, Judah often was little more than an Israelite vassal.

In yet more recent discussions about Israel's history the following positions have emerged. Some conservative biblical scholars continue to correlate an essentially literal reading of the biblical account of the Israelite conquest of Canaan with the available epigraphical and archaeological evidence. However, Albright's solution, which called for a thirteenth-century conquest, has been largely abandoned in favor of a conquest at the end of the fifteenth century. An opposite perspective is represented by scholars who regard the biblical materials as products almost entirely of exilic and postexilic Judaism and thus irrelevant for reconstructing the history of earlier periods. This means that we can know little about the history of earlier Israel beyond whatever information can be derived from epigraphy and archaeology and that, for all practical purposes, therefore, the history of Israel begins in the ninth century B.C.E.

Certain archaeologists have raised hopes that data from recent archaeological surveys and excavations will clarify such questions as whether the Israelites entered Palestine from elsewhere or emerged from the indigenous population, whether they were agriculturalists or pastoralists when they first settled in the hill country, and by what stages they spread throughout the land. Obviously, these new data are extremely important, but they are still inconclusive. For one thing, these archaeologists treat all of the Early Iron Age hill country settlements as Israelite and thus beg the question of what would have been meant by "Israelite" during premonarchical times and why the biblical narratives pertaining to this period distinguish between Israelite and non-Israelite villages in the hill country (cf. Judg. 19:12). Also, the chief proponents of this approach have not yet reached agreement on their interpretation of the new data with respect to Israel's origins.

Yet other scholars are calling for a highly multidisciplinary approach to ancient Israelite history, involving close attention to the geographical features of Palestine, its various ecological zones, long-range settlement patterns as indicated by archaeological surveys, agricultural techniques and potentials, international trade patterns, and so on. Informed by the most up-to-date anthropological and sociological theories and models, archaeologists utilize all of these various data to explain the process by which Israel came into being and gradually was transformed from tribal society into monarchy. One can only affirm the theoretical appropriateness of this approach; certainly all of the factors that these studies bring into consideration are relevant for understanding the history of ancient Israel. Perhaps their main contribution to this point, however, is that they raise new kinds of questions and warn against oversimplified answers. Thus far, in other words, it can hardly be said that this multidisciplinary approach has produced any notable breakthroughs or compelling clarifications—at least none that does not depend as much on the researcher's methodological presuppositions and working models as upon the various data compiled. An unfortunate characteristic of these studies is that they tend to use very jargonistic language—sometimes, it seems, belaboring the obvious. Also, they discuss such a wide range of factors at such an abstract and theoretical level that it is often difficult to understand what it all means with respect to the specific people and events of ancient Israel. The proponents of this approach tend to be deterministic in their social philosophy—that is, history unfolds in predictable fashion as determined largely by environmental circumstances; individual initiative plays a minor role in the course of human affairs, and specific events are incidental items in the broad sweep of social change.

Finally, the charge is being heard from several quarters that biblical studies in general, including historical-critical methodologies and treatments of ancient Israelite history, are biased to the core and should be approached from totally different perspectives. This bias begins, so the argument goes, with the ancient written sources, which tend to be male and elitist—that is, written records normally were produced by and for the powerful in ancient times (kings, priests, etc.). Even archaeology tends to present an elitist picture, since the substantial structures of the politically powerful naturally survive in greater proportion than the humble dwellings of the lower classes. This bias in the ancient sources has only been exacerbated by religious leaders in the Judeo-Christian tradition, it is charged, who usually have been men. Moreover, contemporary biblical scholarship in Western universities is decidedly Eurocentric—that is, culturally biased—in approach.

An increasing number of studies are appearing that attempt to redress the situation. Some attempt to do this by uncovering and correcting the old biases.

Others, apparently liberated by the recognition of modern historians that complete objectivity is an unattainable goal anyhow, put aside even any effort in that direction and write essays on historical topics that unabashedly replace the old biases and ideologies with new ones.

Notes

1. English edition, *The History of Israel*, 3rd ed. (London: Longans, Green & Co., 1871–1876).

2. English edition, *Prolegomena to the History of Ancient Israel* (Gloucester, Mass.: Peter Smith, 1973).

3. English edition, *History of Israel*, trans. Peter Ackroyd (New York: Harper & Row, 1960).

4. The Deuteronomistic History is a term for the books of Deuteronomy, Joshua, Judges, 1–2 Samuel, and 1–2 Kings, which scholars generally regard as originally a single work.

For Further Reading

Avi-Yonah, M. *The Holy Land, from the Persian to the Arab Conquests (536 B.C. to A.D. 640): A Historical Geography.* Rev. ed. Grand Rapids: Baker, 1977. A well-documented summary of the political chronology and geographical boundaries of Samaria and Judea under the Persians, Greeks, and Romans.

Bartlett, J. R. *Jews in the Hellenistic World.* Cambridge Commentaries on Writings of the Jewish and Christian World 200 B.C. to A.D. 200, vol. 1, part 1. Cambridge: Cambridge University Press, 1985. An introductory discussion of Josephus and other selected Jewish sources from the Roman period.

Bimson, J. *Redating the Exodus and Conquest.* Sheffield: Journal for the Study of the Old Testament, 1978. Taking the biblical account of Israel's exodus from Egypt and conquest of Canaan essentially at face value, Bimson seeks to demonstrate that this account is corroborated by archaeology. Read this as a balance to Van Seters's *In Search of History.*

Bowersock, G. W. *Roman Arabia.* Cambridge: Harvard University Press, 1983. Although it focuses on the Transjordan, this book is especially helpful for understanding the political context of Palestine during the Roman period.

Clements, R. E., ed. *The World of Ancient Israel: Sociological, Anthropological, and Political Perspectives.* Cambridge: Cambridge University Press, 1989. A very useful collection of essays that explores the influence of sociology and anthropology on biblical studies in general and on the study of ancient Israelite history in particular.

Edelman, D. *The Fabric of History: Text, Artifact, and Israel's Past.* Sheffield: Journal for the Study of the Old Testament, 1991. Essays on historiography and archaeology as related to the study of ancient Israelite history by six contemporary scholars.

Finkelstein, I. *The Archaeology of the Israelite Settlement.* Jerusalem: Israel Exploration Society, 1988. Provides a wealth of archaeological information about the Early Iron Age settlements in the central Palestinian hill country. However, readers should be cautious of the author's underlying assumption, reflected in the title of his book, that all of these Early Iron Age settlements were Israelite.

Hayes, J. H., and Miller, J. M., eds. *Israelite and Judean History.* Philadelphia: Westminster, 1977. Reprinted London/Philadelphia: SCM/Trinity Press International, 1990. Essays by an international group of scholars that signaled a move away from the Albright-Bright and Alt-Noth approaches to Israelite history. Especially useful is the opening chapter by Hayes, which surveys approaches and trends in the study of Israelite history from ancient to modern times.

Knight, D. A., and Tucker, G. M., eds. *The Hebrew Bible and Its Modern Interpreters.* Philadelphia/Chico, Calif.: Fortress/Scholars, 1985. A collection of essays that reviews scholarship pertaining to the Hebrew Bible since 1945. See especially the first three essays on "Israelite History" (J. M. Miller), "Syro-Palestinian and Biblical Archaeology" (W. G. Dever), and "The Ancient Near Eastern Environment" (J.J.M. Roberts).

Mazar, Amihai. *Archaeology of the Land of the Bible, 10,000–586 B.C.E.* The Anchor Bible Reference Library. Garden City, N.Y.: Doubleday, 1990. An up-to-date introduction to Palestinian archaeology (with coverage from prehistoric times through most of the Iron Age), with close attention to possible connections between Palestinian archaeology and Israelite history.

Meyers, C. *Discovering Eve.* New York: Oxford University Press, 1988. Seeks to give more adequate attention than do standard histories to the role and circumstances of women in ancient Israel. See also in this regard the collection of essays edited by P. L. Day, *Gender and Difference in Ancient Israel* (Minneapolis: Fortress, 1989).

Miller J. M. *The Old Testament and the Historian.* Guides to Biblical Scholarship. Philadelphia: Fortress, 1976. Discusses more fully several of the issues raised in this chapter.

Miller, J. M., and Hayes, J. H. *A History of Ancient Israel and Judah.* London/Philadelphia: SCM/Westminster, 1986. A recent attempt to reconstruct the history of ancient Israel, which is concerned also to inform readers about the issues and uncertainties involved.

Pritchard, J. B., ed. *Ancient Near Eastern Texts Relating to the Old Testament.* Princeton: Princeton University Press, 1955. See also the companion volume, *The Ancient Near East in Pictures Relating to the Old Testament* (Princeton: Princeton University Press, 1954), and the supplement to both, *The*

Ancient Near East Supplement Relating to the Old Testament (Princeton: Princeton University Press, 1969). Still the most widely available and easily accessible collection of translated epigraphical texts relating to the Hebrew Bible.

Rogerson, J. *Atlas of the Bible.* New York: Facts on File, 1985. Useful for getting a grasp of the physical setting in which the history of ancient Israel and Judah unfolded and from which the Bible emerged. Another good atlas, written from a more conservative perspective, is B. J. Beitzel, *The Moody Atlas of Bible Lands* (Chicago: Moody, 1985).

Van Seters, J. *In Search of History: Historiography in the Ancient World and the Origins of Biblical History.* New Haven, Conn.: Yale University Press, 1983. An analysis of the biblical materials in comparison with other similar literature from the ancient world leading to a very skeptical view regarding its trustworthiness as a source for historical information. Read this as a balance to Bimson's *Redating the Exodus and Conquest.*

2
SOURCE
CRITICISM

Pauline A. Viviano

T HE historical-critical approach to interpretation has had a profound effect on the search for meaning in the biblical text. The new and often radical views of this century concerning the history of the biblical period and the formation of the Bible have been the direct result of the application of historical criticism to the Bible. This approach is not limited to one way of analyzing the text but employs many methods, which try to answer such questions as, Who wrote it? When and where was it written? Why was it written and to whom? Each method has its own distinct concerns. But just as these questions are interrelated, so the concerns of the different methods overlap. The often complex answers given to these questions lead in turn to other questions dealing with multiple authorship, the variety of forms, numerous and conflicting purposes, and so on. One of the methods at the foundation of this process of questioning the text is source criticism.

Definition of Source Criticism

The historical approach presupposes that a literary work carries the imprint of the historical age in which it was produced and that the interpretation of a work is best served by situating it within its historical context and determining the intent of its author. A major difficulty in the application of the historical-critical method to the biblical text, however, is that neither authorship nor date, both essential for the method, can be ascertained readily. Indeed, complicating the issue is the fact that many books of the Bible give evidence of an extremely complex history of development, making questions of authorship and date virtually impossible to answer. Source criticism analyzes the biblical text in order to determine what sources were used in its formation. Once sources are isolated, the source critic considers issues of authorship, date, style, setting, and intent of each source. The primary focus of source criticism is the determination of written sources. Although the determination of oral sources can theoretically be included in source criticism, it has become the provenance of form criticism and tradition criticism and will not be considered here.

When source criticism emerged in the eighteenth century it was called "literary criticism," and well into the twentieth century the terms have been and continue to be used interchangeably.[1] Nevertheless, it is common today to draw a distinction between "source criticism" and "literary criticism." While both pay close attention to the literary features of a text, noting stylistic characteristics, vocabulary usage, repetitions, contradictions or inconsistencies, and other literary traits, their respective goals are different. Source criticism tries to discover the sources behind the text by examining its literary features. More recent literary criticism grounds meaning in the literary or surface structure of a text; it focuses on the text as it is, not on the text as it came to be. To avoid ambiguity, we will use the designation "source criticism" for the method known to eighteenth- and nineteenth-century scholars as "literary criticism."

The search for sources begins with a close examination of the biblical text itself. It is clear that in certain instances sources were used in the compilation of various parts of the Bible—for these sources are explicitly mentioned, such as the Book of the Wars of Yahweh (Num. 21:14) and the Book of Jashar (Josh. 10:13; 2 Sam. 1:18).[2] Apart from the title[s] of these sources, nothing about them is known directly. But it is possible to draw conclusions about their nature by studying the quotations taken from them or the material in which those quotations are embedded. For example, the Book of the Wars of Yahweh may have been just that, a collection of stories of holy war, and the Book of Jashar may have been a collection of poems, for the Old Testament quotes two poems from it (Josh. 10:12b–13a; 2 Sam. 1:19–27). The "chronicles" used in 1–2 Kings and 1–2 Chronicles (see n. 2) most likely were court records containing details of the reigns of the kings of Israel and Judah.[3]

Although the study of explicitly mentioned sources is of some interest to source critics, their primary concern is to detect and study sources that are not directly mentioned in the Bible. It is assumed that the biblical authors did not make up the stories they tell but that these stories were already in circulation in their communities in oral or written form. While we should not underestimate the creative genius of these ancient authors, source critics assume that they incorporated, rewrote, and reinterpreted traditional material—whether they explicitly say so or not—to produce their versions of Israel's past. Source critics also maintain that these versions were then taken up by later authors or redactors who also incorporated, rewrote, and reinterpreted Israel's past for their own audiences, and that this process continued until the text received its present form.

Source critics seek to retrace this process by isolating each redactional layer, thus revealing the sources that have come together to form the text as we now have it. In order to do this, source critics rely upon certain criteria that, when applied to the final form of the text, enable them to separate out its sources. Based on the assumption that authors exercise a certain consistency in the way they write, in the terminology they use, and in their perspective, source critics view marked differences in any of these areas as an indication that sources have been incorporated into a text. Likewise, it is assumed that single authors do not include contradictory material in their work and that such contradictions reveal multiple hands at work in the production of a text. Intrusions into a text—breaks in the sequence of events or interruptions in the progression of thought—are seen as evidence that works by various authors have been combined by later redactors. Multiple versions of the same basic story, as well as repetitions within a story, are taken as further proof that more than one author's work lies behind the present form of a text. These, then, are the criteria used by source critics to determine the presence of written sources behind the text: variations in style, vocabulary, and perspective; contradictions and inconsistencies in a passage or between passages; abrupt interruptions that break the continuity of a passage; and various kinds of duplications or repetitions.

Historical Background

As indicated above, source criticism is part of the historical-critical approach to biblical interpretation that emerged in the eighteenth century. The approach was already being used by classicists to deal with problems in interpretation of the Homeric epics. It was "borrowed" by biblical scholars who wanted to delve beneath the surface of the text to uncover information regarding authorship, date provenance, and intent.

The area that received most attention in the application of source criticism to the Bible was the formation of the Pentateuch. Early source critics searched for the sources used by Moses in writing the Pentateuch, but eventually that search called Mosaic authorship itself into question. Challenges to Mosaic authorship of the Pentateuch had been raised prior to the eighteenth century,[4] but these challenges remained isolated until critics were able to offer a viable alternative to Mosaic authorship. That alternative was found in the Newer Documentary Hypothesis, articulated and defended most ably by Julius Wellhausen. Wellhausen's work was the culmination of a process whose origin can be traced to the work of Jean Astruc,[5] a French physician. In his *Conjectures on the Reminiscences Which Moses Appears to Have Used in Composing the Book of Genesis,*[6] Astruc sought to determine the sources used by Moses. Astruc himself did not deny Mosaic authorship, but his search for sources led inevitably in that direction. By dividing the text on the basis of the names for God found in the book of Genesis, Astruc posited two sources for this book, each using a different name for the deity. Source A used *"Elohim,"* translated "God" in English; Source B used "Yahweh,"[7] the personal name of Israel's God, often translated "LORD" in contemporary Bibles. Astruc's work was carried forward by J. G. Eichhorn in his *Introduction to the Old Testament.*[8] Eichhorn carefully analyzed the style and content of Astruc's two sources and set up additional criteria for the determination of sources, including repetitions or duplications, distinctive stylistic features, and characteristic terminology. Once the idea of more than one source or document in the Pentateuch was accepted, it remained to subsequent scholarship to determine the number and extent of the sources, their dates, and their interrelationship. In the process, the Newer Documentary Hypothesis emerged, but not before two alternate theories about the formation of the Pentateuch were developed: the Fragmentary Hypothesis and the Supplementary Hypothesis.

While the Documentary Hypothesis draws its strongest evidence from Genesis and the beginning of Exodus, the Fragmentary Hypothesis is based on evidence provided by the various law codes in the Pentateuch. A. Geddes,[9] credited with the origin of the Fragmentary Hypothesis, argued that fragments of varying lengths, rather than sources or documents, lay behind these law codes. He further argued that these fragments were put side by side without much consideration given to connecting links. The Pentateuch itself, like the law codes, was formed over a long period of time by the same process of combining fragments of varying lengths. According to J. S. Vater,[10] who accepted Geddes's position, the process of formation began with a collection of laws, now found in the book of Deuteronomy, dating from the time of David and Solomon but rediscovered during the reign of Josiah (621 B.C.E.).

Although the Fragmentary Hypothesis offered another way to account for the diversity in the Pentateuch, it did not account satisfactorily for the structural consistency of the Pentateuch, especially in terms of its chronology. While the Pentateuch has many diverse elements, it seems too unified to have been formed by the piecing together of fragments. The attempt to account for the extensive unity of the Pentateuch grew into the Supplementary Hypothesis, whose origin is attributed to H. Ewald.[11] Ewald maintained that the core of the Pentateuch was an "Elohistic" work that a compiler supplemented by drawing material from other sources. This Elohistic work was one connected strand, thus accounting for the Pentateuch's unity of theme and structure; the fragments, worked into this core, account for the diversity of style, vocabulary, and perspective.

Neither the Fragmentary Hypothesis nor the Supplementary Hypothesis found much support among scholars. Instead, the Documentary Hypothesis was revised and came virtually to control the field of source criticism in its formulation as the Newer Documentary Hypothesis. This process began with

H. Hupfeld's *The Sources of Genesis and the Nature of Their Combination*.[12] Before Hupfeld, it was assumed that the Elohistic narrative, called the Foundation Document, was the oldest and most comprehensive of the Pentateuchal sources. Hupfeld showed that the Foundation Document was actually comprised of two sources, both of which used the name *Elohim* for God. Thus the Elohistic work was divided in two, an early and a late Elohist. The third source was the Yahwistic source (J),[13] which used the name Yahweh for God. In the later development of the Newer Documentary Hypothesis, Hupfeld's early Elohistic source would be identified as the Priestly source (P).

The claim that the Deuteronomic Code (Deuteronomy 12–26) is not a compilation of the sources found in Genesis-Numbers (J, E, P) was advanced by W.M.L. de Wette.[14] De Wette maintained that this code was the law book discovered in the Temple during King Josiah's reform (2 Kings 22–23). De Wette dated the Deuteronomic Code shortly before 621 B.C.E., the date when it was discovered in the Temple and thus provided a fixed date around which to group the other sources. The dating of sources had been a major problem for source critics because the texts themselves give little evidence upon which to make a determination with respect to dates. Once the date of Deuteronomy was established, however, progress was made in dating the other sources. In *The Historical Books of the Old Testament*[15] H. Graf convincingly argued a suggestion made by his teacher, Eduard Reuss—that P was the latest of the sources. Graf maintained that the ceremonial and ritual laws found in the Pentateuch could not reflect Israel's early period but emerged only after the exile, after the prophets. In the books of Deuteronomy, Joshua, Judges, 1–2 Samuel, and 1–2 Kings, the ritual laws of Exodus, Leviticus, and Numbers are not presupposed and so must be later than Deuteronomy–2 Kings.

W. Vatke showed in his *The Religion of the Old Testament*[16] that ritualization is found at the end of a long process of religious development, not at its beginning. He maintained that J, E, 1–2 Samuel, and 1–2 Kings reflect the primitive period in Israel's religious development, which was replaced by one of ethical consciousness, emerging with the prophets and found in Deuteronomy. The latest stage of Israel's religious development was characterized by a more ceremonial religion that emphasized external rituals and is found in priestly law.[17] Vatke's position was based on Hegelian historical and philosophical assumptions, not on literary-critical grounds. Nevertheless, the conclusions drawn by Graf and Vatke revolutionized future scholarship and its understanding of the development of Israelite religion. By understanding Mosaic law as the latest development in the history of Israelite religion, they forced subsequent scholars to abandon a simplistic understanding of Israel's religious development. Now the history of Israel could be approached rationally and comprehensibly.[18]

It remained for Wellhausen to combine source analysis with the arguments of his predecessors. Wellhausen's *History of Israel*[19] is noted not so much for its originality as for the way in which he organized and built upon the work that had preceded him. In fact, the dominance of Wellhausen's view in all subsequent discussion of Pentateuchal sources is a testimony to his ability to synthesize and articulate the work of his predecessors. He showed the importance of the history of Israel's religious development as described by Graf and Vatke for dating the individual sources of the Pentateuch. Wellhausen also strengthened the foundation for the view that Mosaic legislation was postexilic. He made common property the view that there was a progressive development in Israel's religion from a spontaneous natural observance of religion to the reforms of the prophets, which were subsequently superseded by the ceremonial and ritual laws of the priests. Thus it was the prophets, according to Wellhausen, who established a truly ethical faith in Israel. Wellhausen's work became a standard in biblical criticism, not simply for the next generation but for generations to come.

The Newer Documentary Hypothesis as promulgated by Wellhausen maintains that four sources or documents were edited together to form the Pentateuch. The oldest of these is the Yahwistic source (J). It is linked to the period of intellectual growth and national consciousness under David and Solomon (ca. 950 B.C.E.). Its author, the Yahwist, used the name Yahweh for God from the beginning of its narrative (Gen. 2:4b). He tells vivid stories in a folkloric style and reflects a southern provenance (i.e., from the kingdom of Judah). The Yahwist provides the basic story line for Genesis and Exodus, beginning with creation in Gen. 2:4b; J material is also found in Numbers.

The work of the Elohist (E), a more or less fragmentary source, originated in the Northern Kingdom during the height of its power (ca. 850 B.C.E.). It is not found in the primeval history (Genesis 1–11) but begins with the Abraham story in Genesis 15.

The Deuteronomic source (D), generally believed to be confined to Deuteronomy 12–26, is a law code with a sermonic style characterized by stereotyped phrases. It is marked throughout by a sustained exhortation to obedience to the law. D is presumed to be of northern provenance and is dated prior to its discovery in the Temple during Josiah's reform (621 B.C.E.). The Deuteronomic source is thought either to have been written prior to the fall of the Northern Kingdom and brought south by refugees fleeing at the time of the fall (721 B.C.E.) or to have been written by northern refugees after they fled south and deposited in the Temple, where it was forgotten until Josiah's reform.

The latest of the sources is the Priestly work (P). This source provides the chronological framework of the Pentateuch and, as the name suggests, was primarily concerned with priestly matters: ritual laws, the origin of shrines and rituals, and genealogies. P has a formal, rigid, repetitive style. It is said to have emerged from priestly circles in Jerusalem during the period of the exile (ca.

550 B.C.E.,). It begins in Gen. 1:1 and is juxtaposed to J and E, or intertwined with J and E throughout Genesis, Exodus, and Numbers. Leviticus is regarded as the work of P exclusively.

In Wellhausen's view, these four documents—J, E, D, and P—were combined to form the Pentateuch as we now have it. First, the Yahwistic source was supplemented by the Elohist, most likely after the fall of the Northern Kingdom. To this the Deuteronomic Code was added some time after 621 B.C.E. After the exile, the Priestly work was joined to the other sources. Since the final redaction bears the stamp of the Priestly author and carries the chronology of this source, it is supposed that the Priestly author himself or someone from the same priestly circles was the final redactor.

The generations following Wellhausen saw the emergence of a scholarly consensus regarding the Newer Documentary Hypothesis. Once this consensus was reached, source criticism in the Pentateuch turned to the task of examining the four documents and defining them more precisely. The only major change in the hypothesis was to view the documents as having undergone a long process of growth and therefore as being less unified than was once assumed. Attempts to trace the sources beyond the Pentateuch into Joshua-Kings have met with little success.[20] Successors of Wellhausen claimed to have discovered other sources beyond J, E, P, and D, but none of these additional sources has gained wide acceptance.

Despite refinements, the general contours of Wellhausen's view have remained dominant. Nearly every historical-critical scholar of the twentieth century, either explicitly or implicitly, has affirmed the Newer Documentary Hypothesis. Every critical introduction to the Old Testament written in this century has given prominence to the Newer Documentary Hypothesis, which has been considered an assured answer to the complex question of the formation of the Pentateuch and a firm basis for reconstructing the history of religious development in ancient Israel.

As early as 1924, it was suggested that source criticism had gone as far as it could and that it had no further problems to solve.[21] G. Von Rad, a little over a decade later, agreed: "So far as the analysis of source documents is concerned, there are signs that the road has come to a dead end."[22] Other questions began to call for the attention of biblical scholars, and other methods, notably form criticism and tradition-historical criticism, were developing to address these new questions. Source criticism, it was felt, had done its job and had given such assured results that no change in the understanding of the formation of the Pentateuch was envisioned. The following statement by E. Kraeling is typical of the confidence concerning the achievements of source criticism.

> Universally it is conceded that Old Testament scholarship has
> given us a new, realistic and dependable picture of the way in

which the literary materials of the Old Testament arose and of what they mean historically. While the future may bring many corrections, nothing that could be adduced along critical lines could change the situation very much in principle.[23]

The extent to which the Newer Documentary Hypothesis continues to dominate the field even today is evident in the spate of books and articles on the individual sources themselves.[24] This level of acceptance makes it hard for its critics to be taken seriously. Nevertheless, dissatisfaction with the Newer Documentary Hypothesis has persisted and in the last few decades has been growing in intensity. Criticism is directed not only against the Newer Documentary Hypothesis but also against source criticism itself, as we will see in the final section of this chapter.

Illustration of the Method

For purposes of illustration we will apply the source-critical method to Genesis 1–11.[25] This section of Genesis has the advantage of being manageable in size and a part of the Pentateuch about which there is some consensus regarding the presence and nature of its sources. We will begin with an application of the criteria used by source critics to discover sources behind a text: differences in style, vocabulary, and perspective; contradictions and inconsistencies; interruptions or abrupt changes; and duplications or repetitions.

Style

The most obvious stylistic characteristic of the opening chapter of Genesis is its repetition, which is a result of the framework surrounding each of the eight acts of creation: "And God said. . . . Let there be. . . . And it was so. . . . And God saw that it was good. . . . And there was evening and there was morning, x day." While not all elements of the framework are found each time, enough are present to characterize the style as formal and repetitive. This repetition gives a solemn, hymnic tone to the entire account. The repetitive style abruptly changes in Gen. 2:4b, which begins the first of several stories containing the usual elements of a narrative: characters and plot. In contrast to Gen. 1:1–2:4a, we find in Gen. 2:4b–4:26 a deity actively involved in shaping, breathing, and planting. There is interaction between creator and creature in a vividly told story filled with suspense and drama. Creation unfolds, not as the result of a series of commands but as an action taken by the deity with a kind of experimental flair. It is unclear what will happen once the man and the woman, the animals and the garden, have been created. Will God's will prevail, or will humans transgress the one command they were given? A new and unusual character, the serpent, is introduced, and the tension builds as the story moves from temptation to sin to punishment and on into Genesis 4. These narratives in Genesis 2–4 have all the elements of good story-telling: plot, characterization, action, dialogue, and suspense. The stories use an evocative vocabulary with poetic words like "mists" and "deep sleep." They employ word plays: *ʾādām* (humanity)/ *ʾădāmāh* (ground), *ʾiššāh* (woman)/ *ʾîš* (man), *ʿărûmmîm* (naked)/ *ʿārûm* (cunning), *qānāh* (gotten)/Cain. Such clever word plays hold the interest of the hearer or reader. Even in the genealogy of 4:17–26, where one would expect to find repetition, there are short narrative-like sections (4:17b, 19–24). In the genealogy of Genesis 5, a style that is repetitious as a result of a recurring framework, as in Gen. 1:1–2:4a, resumes. This repetitive framework is as follows: "When x had lived y years he became the father of z. x lived yy years and had other sons and daughters." Both Gen. 4:17–26 and Genesis 5 are genealogies, but their respective styles are very different. In Genesis 6–9 and 11:1–9 we find the same kind of vividly told stories that characterize Gen. 2:4b–4:26. There are characters and action as well as word plays: *šēm* (name)/ *šām* (there), *bālal* (confused)/Babel. In Genesis 10 and 11:9–32, repetition again comes to the fore, as in Genesis 1 and 5. Thus Gen. 1:1—2:4a; 5; 10; and 11:9–32 are consistent in style but different from the style of Gen. 2:4b–26; 6–9; and 11:1–9. Genesis 6–9, though similar in style to Gen. 2:4b–26 and 11:1–9, presents a special case, as will be clear when we examine its vocabulary, duplications, and inconsistencies.

Vocabulary

In comparing vocabulary, we will focus on different terms that have the same referent. For example, it is clear that *"Elohim"* and "Yahweh" are different terms for the deity. The same applies to terms like "image and likeness"/ "living being," "male and female"/"man and woman," and "create"/"form." The terminological distinctions in these early chapters of Genesis are illustrated in Table 2.1.

Table 2.1

Genesis 1:1—2:4a	*Genesis 2:4b–5*	*Genesis 5*
Elohim	Yahweh or Yahweh *Elohim*	Elohim
These are the generations of		These are the generations of
Image and likeness	Living Being	Likeness of God
Male and female	Man and woman	Male and female
Create	Form	Create

It is important to note that the vocabulary patterns in the chart occur elsewhere in Genesis 1–11. The name *Elohim,* used in Genesis 1 and 5, is found again in Genesis 6–9. The phrase "these are the generations of" (2:4a) is found again in Gen. 6:9; 10:1, 27; and 11:10, 27, and a similar phrase, "according to their generations," occurs in 10:32. The following phrases also recur: "the deep" (1:2/7:11), "male and female" (1:27/6:19), "in his image" (1:26–27/9:6), "be fruitful and multiply" (1:28/9:1, 7). In addition to Gen. 2:4b–25, the name Yahweh is found again in Genesis 3–4; 6–9; and 11:1–9, but not in the other chapters of Genesis 1–11. Furthermore, in Gen. 7:2 "man and woman" (NRSV: "the male and its mate") is the same as in Gen. 2:23–24, and the notion of the "ground" being cursed because of humanity repeats the motif of 3:17.

The fact that both *Elohim* and Yahweh are found in Genesis 6–9 is significant and calls for a closer examination of this section. In Gen. 6:5 Yahweh observes the "wickedness" of "humanity," in contrast to 6:12 where *Elohim* sees that the "earth" is filled with "violence," "corrupted" by "all flesh." In Gen. 6:7 Yahweh decides to "blot out humanity" from the "ground," whereas in 6:13 *Elohim* will make an "end" of "all flesh" and also of the "earth." In Gen. 7:12 we find "rain" rather than "the great deep" of 7:11. "Yahweh said in his heart" (Gen. 8:21) stands in contrast to "*Elohim* blessed Noah" (Gen. 9:1). The promise that Yahweh will "never again curse the ground" (Gen. 8:21) is paralleled by "I will establish my covenant" (Gen. 9:9, 11). Table 2.2 illustrates these differences.

Just as there are different styles in Gen. 1:1–2:4a; 5; 10; and 11:10–32 on the one hand and Gen. 2:4b–4:26 and 11:1–9 on the other, so also 1:1–2:4a; 5; 10; and 11:10–32 have a distinctive and recurring vocabulary, different from that of 2:4b–4:26 and 11:1–9. There are different sets of vocabulary

Table 2.2

Genesis 6:5, 7; 7:12; 8:21	*Genesis 6:13, 22; 7:11; 9:1, 8, 11*
Yahweh	*Elohim*
Wickedness	Violence, corruption
Blot out	Make an end
Humanity	All flesh
Ground	Earth
Rain	Great deep
Said in his heart	Blessed Noah
Never again curse the ground	Will establish my covenant

throughout Genesis 6–9, indicating a blend in these chapters of the vocabulary from 1:1–2:4a; 5; 10; and 11:10–32 with that from 2:4b–4:26 and 11:1–9.

Perspective

In addition to stylistic and vocabulary differences, there are differences in perspective throughout Genesis 1–11. In Gen. 1:1–2:4a, God is presented as a majestic, transcendent being. The world is created by the mere power of God's word. In 2:4b–25, a different picture of the deity emerges. God is depicted in anthropomorphic terms. Here, God is involved in creation, "getting his hands dirty," so to speak, as the deity forms clay like a potter and breathes life into that clay. This God is not distant but is as close as humanity's next breath. Far from the organized God of Genesis 1, this God seems to decide what to create in the very process of creating, and sometimes gets it wrong, as when the animals are formed as partners for the man before God discovers that they are not at all suitable. In Genesis 4, the deity interacts in a humanlike fashion with Cain. God is also described in human terms in Gen. 6:5–8: Yahweh is grieved by humanity's evil; Yahweh is sorry that humanity was ever created. Yahweh even shuts the door of the ark! But the transcendent, majestic figure of God resurfaces in the decree issued in 6:13–14 and the commands God gives Noah (6:3–22). The more human picture of God appears again in 8:20, where Yahweh smells the sacrifice; the more majestic God issues further decrees and establishes a covenant (Gen. 9:1–17). With Gen. 11:1–9 we return to the anthropomorphic presentation of the deity found in Gen. 2:4b–25. God is alarmed at the potential of humanity and has to "come down" to earth to find out what humanity is doing. We are forced to conclude that there are two very different images of God in Genesis 1–11: a majestic, transcendent God in 1:1–2:4b and a down-to-earth, humanlike God in 2–4; 6–9 and 11:1–9. The God of 1:1–2:4b emerges again in Gen. 6:13–22 and 9:1–17.

Humanity is also viewed in very different ways in Genesis 1–11. In Genesis 1 humanity is created in the very image of God, suggesting an exalted view of what it is to be human and setting humans apart from animals. In Gen. 2:7 humanity is made from the dust of the ground and will be dependent upon the ground for food. Humans live because God breathes in them, and so humanity is dependent upon God for life. This dependent creature is much frailer and more vulnerable than humanity in Genesis 1. Humans and animals are both "living beings" (Gen. 2:7, 19); the only distinction given to humans is God's interest in them. Apart from the characterization of humanity as intent on evil, little can be said about how humanity is presented in the flood story. But in Gen. 9:6 it is affirmed that humanity is created in the image of God, and God gives the same command to humanity (9:1) as in Gen. 1:28: "Be fruitful and multiply." Thus in addition to two distinct styles and sets of vocabulary, Gen.

1:1–2:4a and parts of Genesis 6–9 differ in theological perspective from Gen. 2:4b–4:26, parts of Genesis 6–9, and 11:1–9.

Contradictions/Inconsistencies

Careful analysis of Genesis 1–11 reveals several contradictions and inconsistencies between Genesis 1 and 2 and within Genesis 6–9. In Gen. 1:1–2:4a, animals are created before humans (1:24–25 and 1:26–27), but in Gen. 2:7 the human is created before the animals (2:19). In Gen. 1:2, water (the deep) is present and must be restrained by the creation of the firmament and the earth. But in Gen. 2:4b–5, the earth is a desert, and water must be brought to it in order to facilitate creation. In Gen. 6:19–20 and 7:15–16, one pair of every kind of animal is brought into the ark, yet 7:2 says that seven pairs of clean and one pair of unclean animals are to be brought into the ark. The flood is caused by rain in Gen. 7:4, 12, and 8:2b, but 7:11 and 8:2a speak of the fountains of the deep that burst forth, causing a reversion to the primeval chaos (the deep) of Genesis 1. In Gen. 7:4, 12, the rain lasts 40 days, and it takes 21 days for the waters to recede (7:10; 8:8–12). But according to 7:24 and 8:2a, 3b the flooding of the earth takes 150 days, and by the time the waters recede (8:13), a year and ten days have passed. In Gen. 8:5, the mountains have appeared, but in 8:9 the earth is still covered by water. The contradictions and inconsistencies between Genesis 1 and 2 and in Genesis 6–9, taken in conjunction with the differences in style, vocabulary, and perspective we have already noted, indicate separate stories of creation that have been juxtaposed and perhaps two separate flood stories that have been merged.

Interruptions

The first abrupt change that confronts the reader of Genesis 1–11 is that Gen. 2:4b begins again what has supposedly been concluded in 2:4a; in 2:4b God begins again to create. The story line of Gen. 2:4b–23 continues into chapters 3 and 4. Even the genealogy of Gen. 4:17–26, which introduces a shift in literary form from narrative to genealogy, is not as abrupt as the shift to the genealogy of Genesis 5 and 10. The genealogy of Genesis 4 is worked into the narrative, but in Genesis 5 it begins with a formal introduction that echoes Gen. 2:4a. The story of the flood is interrupted to give genealogical information (Gen. 6:9–10) and begins again in 6:11. The genealogy of chapter 10 is interrupted by the narrative of Gen. 11:1–9 and resumes in 11:10. These interruptions occur at the very points where changes in style, vocabulary, and perspective begin.

Repetitions/Duplications

Lastly, we draw evidence from the repetitions and duplications found in Genesis 1–11. Most repetitions are found in the Genesis flood story. God observes the malice of humanity in 6:5 and 6:12 and resolves to destroy humanity in 6:7 and 6:13. The flood is announced twice: 6:13, 17 and 7:4. Noah is ordered to enter the ark twice: 6:18–20 and 7:1–3. Noah obeys God's commands in both 6:22 and 7:5 and enters the ark twice: 7:7 and 7:13. Twice, the waters increase and raise the ark (7:17 and 7:18ff.). All living creatures die in 7:21 and again in 7:22. The waters recede in 8:1 and again in 8:3b. God promises never again to destroy the earth by flood in both 8:21–22 and 9:8–17. Apart from these duplications, one notes that we have two accounts of creation (Gen. 1:1–2:4a; Gen. 2:4b–26), and the genealogy of Gen. 4:17–32 is repeated in a different order and with some variations in spelling in the genealogy of Genesis 5.[26] These repetitions and duplications support the view that two different stories of the flood have been merged, and, together with our other evidence, they indicate that Gen. 1:1–2:4a; 5; 10; and 11:10–32 can be attributed to one source and Gen. 2:4b–4:26 and 11:1–9 to another. In Genesis 6–9 both sources have been merged.

Conclusions

On the strength of the differences in style, vocabulary, and perspective in Genesis 1–11, together with the abrupt shifts, contradictions, and repetitions/ duplications in the same material, we may suggest that Genesis 1–11 is comprised of two separate sources. Furthermore, each source can be identified on the basis of what we have discovered. Gen. 1:1–2:4a; 5; 10; and 11:10–32, taken apart from 2:4b–4:26 and 11:1–9, has a consistency of style, vocabulary, and perspective. When the two strands are separated from each other, duplications and contradictions are eliminated. Genesis 1:1—2:4a; 5; 10; and 11:10–32 have been attributed to the Priestly author, and Gen. 2:4b—4:26 and 11:1–9 to the Yahwist. It is more difficult to separate the stories intertwined in Genesis 6–9, but this can be accomplished by the same application of criteria. A consistency of style, vocabulary, and perspective, without contradictions or repetitions, is found in Gen. 6:1–8; 7:1–5, 7–8, 10, 12, 16b–17, 22–23; and 8:2b–3a, 6–12, 13b, 20–22 (J), on the one hand, and in Gen. 6:9–22; 7:6, 9, 11, 13–16a, 18–21, 24; 8:1–2a, 3b–5, 7, 13a, 14–19; and 9:1–17 (P), on the other.[27] Beyond Genesis 11 the same criteria can be applied. Although it is impossible to assign every verse or part of a verse with absolute certainty, J and P appear to continue throughout the Pentateuch, with E being introduced in Genesis 15 and D in Deuteronomy 12–26.

Critique of the Method

Now that we have seen the method in operation, it remains to consider the weaknesses of source criticism and its most prominent theory, the Newer Documentary Hypothesis. While the focus of our attention will be on that hypothesis, the issues raised below apply to any area of biblical study where source criticism has played a dominant role.

From the time when source criticism emerged as a critical method, there were questions about its validity. The Fragmentary and Supplementary Hypotheses, as we have seen, offered alterative ways to account for the evidence cited by proponents of the Documentary Hypothesis. Other scholars have continued to argue for the unity of the Pentateuch by explaining the stylistic peculiarities that led source critics to posit multiple sources as the result of oriental modes of thought[28] or by providing theological or stylistic justification for incongruities in the text.[29] But by and large these scholars have not been taken seriously, as scholars have generally regarded the evidence for multiple sources as compelling. If anything, the evidence suggests an even more complex process of formation than conceived of by the Newer Documentary Hypothesis. Although an overall unity may underlie the Pentateuch, its component parts are too disparate to assume the activity of a single author.

A more serious challenge was presented beginning early in this century by scholars who accepted the Newer Documentary Hypothesis but used other methods of inquiry. H. Gunkel,[30] a pioneer in form criticism, began to focus on smaller narrative units and their origin in oral tradition, separating them from their literary context. He sought to move behind the written text and emphasized the importance of the oral prehistory for the formation of the Pentateuch. Gunkel saw J and E less as authors than as inheritors of an oral tradition that was already formed. A. Alt[31] used a similar approach to demonstrate that even the oldest law was preceded by oral tradition. The effect of the approach taken by Gunkel and Alt was to cut loose both narrative and law from the chronological scheme of Wellhausen, thus giving a broader picture of Israel's religious development than source criticism had allowed. G. von Rad[32] moved beyond what he saw as the impasse created by source criticism when he used form criticism to understand the Hexateuch as a genre. By focusing on larger complexes of tradition and the process of their transmission, rather than on "documents," von Rad led attention away from individual sources. His work, coupled with that of M. Noth,[33] prepared the way for a tradition-historical approach that stands in tension with source criticism. R. Rendtorff,[34] a successor to von Rad and Noth, has now moved completely away from the Newer Documentary Hypothesis, providing an alternate description of the formation of the Pentateuch based on tradition-historical criticism. He maintains that individual traditions underwent a long process of development wherein smaller units grew into larger ones. These were combined into single continuous accounts, which in turn were combined into larger and larger continuous accounts, until the Pentateuch as we have it was formed. This process would have taken centuries, so that the formation of the Pentateuch as such is dated late. Thus Rendtorff explains the formation of the Pentateuch not on the basis of the Newer Documentary Hypothesis but in opposition to it.

Scandinavian scholars since the middle of this century have also tended to emphasize the oral background of the text, objecting that the "book mentality" at the basis of the Newer Documentary Hypothesis—the notion that ancient authors "cut and pasted" from various documents—is more appropriate to modern culture than to that of the ancient world, which was primarily oral. In the background of the text, they hold, was an oral tradition that continued into the period of the exile and beyond. I. Engnell[35] maintained that there never were parallel continuous documents such as J and E. Variations in style, vocabulary, and perspective arose from the oral basis of the text, not from the splicing of documents. According to Engnell, contradictions and repetitions are to be expected given the cultural background of the Old Testament and the long period of time during which the text was in formation and passed on orally. During major crises, when there was a breakdown of normal communication, the need to commit traditions to writing arose. Then the tradition's oral form was replaced by a fixed written form.

In view of the ever-increasing knowledge of ancient Near Eastern culture, we are cautioned by these scholars against the application of modern literary categories to ancient literature. Nevertheless, the assumption that oral tradition dominated to the exclusion of written material is equally untenable. The many ancient texts uncovered as a result of archaeological excavation testify to a rich literary heritage dating back, not just centuries, but millennia before the biblical text. Biblical scholars need to be aware not only of the oral and written traditions of the ancient Near Eastern world but also of the interplay between oral and written forms in the development of a work like the Pentateuch.

The Newer Documentary Hypothesis has been significantly undermined by scholars who accept source criticism but dissent from the details of the hypothesis. For example, the fact that in most instances E cannot be extricated from J,[36] and that even when separated it does not yield a continuous narrative, has led some to challenge the existence of E as a continuous source.[37] In spite of recent attempts to save E,[38] it remains a fragmentary source and a problem for Pentateuchal analysis. Other scholars, however, have tried to divide J, E, D, or P even further on the basis of the same criteria that led to their initial identification. These critics see J, E, D, and P not as unified documents but as products of a "school" that generated more than one document and that shaped and reshaped these documents by further additions.[39] Still others have been led by further analysis of the Pentateuch to posit the existence of other sources: a "Lay" source (L), centered on matters of concern to laity as opposed to priests;[40] a "nomadic" source (N), which contains a negative evaluation of civilized life;[41] a "Kenite" source (K), which deals with the life of Moses;[42] and a Southern or Seir source (S),[43] limited to Genesis. Finally, Noth[44] posited a "foundational source" or *Grundlage* (G), from which both J and E independently drew their content. In this way, Noth accounted for the similarity of J and E, finding the major themes of the Pentateuch already present in G.

The arguments for these various subdivisions and additional sources have not gained acceptance by many scholars beyond the recognition that the identification and formation of source documents are far more complicated than was once assumed. The multiplication of sources and the fragmentation of the original four sources into other documents have undermined the Newer Documentary Hypothesis itself. The more "sources" one finds, the more tenuous the evidence for the existence of continuous documents becomes, and the less likely it is that four unified documents ever existed. Even for those able to avoid skepticism and confusion in the face of the ever-increasing number of sources, the only logical recourse seems to be to move away from the Newer Documentary Hypothesis toward a position closer to the Fragmentary Hypothesis.

Another serious threat to the Newer Documentary Hypothesis is posed by problems of dating. Wellhausen based his dating of sources on the Hegelian view that progress in history occurs in an evolutionary manner from thesis to antithesis to synthesis. This Hegelian outlook contributed to the acceptance and popularity of the Newer Documentary Hypothesis, but critics were quick to show that it was unsatisfactory.[45] In fact, the generations of scholars following Wellhausen have abandoned the evolutionary scheme underlining the Newer Documentary Hypothesis as inappropriate to their philosophical frame of reference. Moreover, the scientific study of religious development in this century has produced no evidence to support Wellhausen's view that religions evolved from a primitive, spontaneous, personal stage to a rigid, formalistic, and ritualistic stage. The process of religious development is far more complex and uneven than Wellhausen imagined. Without his evolutionary assumptions, his dating of sources can no longer be accepted, and contrary views cannot be ignored. Several scholars over the past century have disagreed with Wellhausen's dates, especially for D and P.[46]

While the early date assigned to J has remained relatively unchallenged until recent years, J. Van Seters[47] has now dated J to the exile because of the similarity of its vocabulary to that of the Deuteronomistic History and Deutero–Isaiah. Likewise, H. H. Schmid[48] has critiqued the Solomonic date of J, maintaining that parts of the J narrative reveal the influence of later forms and theological development and so must be pushed to the exilic period. According to Schmid, the kind of reflection found in J only occurs when national history is at an end and can be reflected upon. Though Schmid accepts the existence of the sources, J, E, D, and P, his late dating makes the provenance, date, and form of these sources very different from what they are held to be by most source critics.

While source criticism has always had its detractors, the past few decades have witnessed an escalation in the level of dissatisfaction with the method in general, and in particular with its best-known representative, the Newer Documentary Hypothesis. The most sustained and vehement attack on the Hypothesis is found in R. N. Whybray's *The Making of the Pentateuch: A Methodological Study.*[49] Whybray draws together the arguments of his predecessors, highlighting the inadequacies of the Newer Documentary Hypothesis, its presuppositions, and the criteria upon which it is based. But he goes further in calling for an abandonment of the Documentary Hypothesis, and for its replacement with the view that a single ancient historian wrote about the origins of the world and the people of Israel, possibly as a preface to the Deuteronomistic History. According to Whybray, this historian used sources, but they were of recent origin and were reworked with substantial creative additions of the historian's own, according to the canons of historiography of his day. No attempt was made to eliminate inconsistencies, contradictions, and unevenness. Although most source critics are reluctant to discard the Newer Documentary Hypothesis as readily as Whybray, future source-critical analysis of the Pentateuch must take his work into account, while reevaluating its presuppositions in light of the ever-increasing knowledge of ancient literature and its formation.

The Pentateuch is a large and complex work, and the evidence it supplies is vast and conflicting. So it is not surprising that there are alternate explanations of its formation, none of which is completely satisfactory. Many more complex questions are involved in the determination of sources than was once thought. While it cannot be denied that the biblical authors used sources, serious questions have been raised about the possibility of recovering them. The criteria source critics use are inadequate for identifying sources. For instance, stylistic variation does not always indicate different sources, and variations in vocabulary could be necessitated by a change of topic. Inconsistencies and contradictions may simply result from the presuppositions of ancient authors who do not share our notion of "contradiction."

Source criticism and the Newer Documentary Hypothesis should not be discarded. Rather, both need to be reevaluated and reconceived. We are rightly admonished to exercise caution[50] in our reevaluation of the Newer Documentary Hypothesis, but a wholesale acceptance of the hypothesis, which ignores its weaknesses, is not advisable either. Certainly we can no longer use the hypothesis as a basis for reconstruction of the history of the religious development of Israel, nor even as a basis for Old Testament theology. Still, it has made a lasting contribution to our understanding of the Bible, moving scholarship away from a naive approach to the biblical text and opening up new possibilities of meaning. It has disabused us of "the notion that the Bible is through and through literal history."[51] For these reasons alone, if for no others, source criticism and the Newer Documentary Hypothesis merit our appreciation.

Notes

1. See, for example, Norman Habel, *Literary Criticism of the Old Testament* (Philadelphia: Fortress, 1971), which is on source criticism.

2. The narrator of 1–2 Kings refers to the Book of the Acts of Solomon (1 Kings 11:41), the Book of the Chronicles of the Kings of Israel (1 Kings 14:19; 15:31; 16:5, 14, 20, 27; 22:39; 2 Kings 1:18; 10:34; 13:8, 12; 14:15, 28; 15:11, 15, 21, 26, 31), and the Book of the Chronicles of the Kings of Judah (1 Kings 14:29; 15:7, 23; 22:45; 2 Kings 8:23; 12:19; 14:18; 15:6, 36; 16:19; 20:20; 21:25; 23:28; 24:5). First and Second Chronicles likewise makes reference to the Book of the Kings of Israel (1 Chron. 9:1; 2 Chron. 20:34), the Book of the Kings of Israel and Judah (2 Chron. 27:7; 35:27; 36:8), the Book of the Kings of Judah and Israel (2 Chron. 16:11; 25:26; 28:26; 32:32), the Commentary on the Book of the Kings (2 Chron. 24:27), and a book called Chronicles (Neh. 12:23).

3. The verbal similarity between 1–2 Chronicles and 1–2 Samuel and 1–2 Kings suggests that the author of 1–2 Chronicles used 1–2 Samuel and 1–2 Kings as a source in addition to other "chronicles."

4. Already in the twelfth century, Abraham Ibn Ezra, a Jewish commentator, in discussing Gen. 12:6, had problems with the phrase "When the Canaanites were in the land," noting that it must come from a time after Moses when the Canaanites were no longer in the land. Carlstadt, in *De canonicis scripturis libellis* (Wittenberg: Ioannes Viridi Montanus, 1520), pointed out that the Pentateuch contains Moses' death and burial (Deuteronomy 34) and that it is unlikely that he wrote of these events. Both T. Hobbes, *Leviathan* (London: Andrew Crooke, 1651) and B. Spinoza, *Tractatus theologico-politicus* (Hamburg: Henricus Künraht, 1670) raised questions about Mosaic authorship in the seventeenth century. Richard Simon, a French priest, likewise questioned Mosaic authorship in *Histoire critique du Vieux Testament* (Amsterdam: D. Elzevier, 1678) and was immediately censured by the Church.

5. H. B. Witter in *Jura Israelitiarum in Palaestinam* (Hildesiae: L. Schröderi, 1711) had come to similar conclusions based on the divine name, but his work remained unknown until discovered by A. Lods in *Jean Astruc et la critique biblique au XVIIIe siecle* (Strasbourg: Librairie Istra, 1924); and "Un précurseur allemand de Jean Astruc: Henning Bernhard Witter," *Zeitschrift für die alttestamentliche Wissenschaft* (1925):134–35.

6. *Conjectures sur les mémoires originaux dont il paroit que Moyse s'est servi, pour composer le livre de la Genèse* (Bruxelles: Fricx, 1753).

7. Astruc used the term "Jehovah," an archaic form of the name Yahweh. "Jehovah" resulted from reading the vowels of *ʾădōnāy* ("Lord") with the consonants of "Yahweh." It was used often in the seventeenth and eighteenth centuries but has since been replaced by Yahweh.

8. *Einleitung in das Alte Testament* (Leipzig: Weidmanns, 1780–1783).

9. *The Holy Bible,* vol. 1 (London: J. Davis, 1792); *Critical Remarks on the Hebrew Scriptures,* vol. 1 (London, 1800).

10. *Commentar über den Pentateuch* (Halle: Waisenhaus, 1802–1805).

11. This is found in Ewald's review of J. J. Stähelin's *Critical Investigation of Genesis* (*Kritische Untersuchungen über die Genesis* [Basel: J. G. Neukirch, 1830]), in *Theologische Studien und Kritiken* 4 (1831):595–606.

12. *Die Quellen der Genesis und die Art ihrer Zusammensetzung* (Berlin: Wiegandt und Grieben, 1853).

13. J is the standard abbreviation for the Yahwist. It derives from the German spelling of Yahweh, which uses a "J" in place of the English "Y."

14. *Dissertatio critico-exegetica, qua Deuteronomium a prioribus Pentateuchi libris diversum, alius suiusdam recentioris auctoris opus esse monstratur* (1805).

15. *Die geschichtlichen Bücher des Alten Testaments* (Leipzig: T. O. Weigel, 1866).

16. *Die Religion des Alten Testaments* (Berlin: G. Bethge, 1835).

17. B. Duhm (*Die Theologie der Propheten als Grundlage für die innerer Entwicklungsgeschichte der israelitischen Religion* [Bonn: A. Marcus, 1875]) supported this view, demonstrating that the prophets do not presuppose P or D; rather, D depends on the prophetic movement, and P follows D.

18. The first to attempt a description of Israel's religious development that conformed to the chronology of Graf and Vatke was A. Kuenen, *The Religion of Israel* (*De Godsdienst van Israël* [Haarlem: A. C. Kruseman, 1869–1870]).

19. *Geschichte Israels* (Berlin: G. Reimer, 1878). With the publication of the second edition (1883) the title became *Prolegomena zur Geschichte Israels;* in English it is known as the *Prolegomena to the History of Ancient Israel* (Edinburgh: A. & C. Black, 1885).

20. Attempts were made by K. Budde (*Die Bücher Richter und Samuel, ihre Quellen und ihr Aufbau* [Giessen: J. Ricker, 1890]) to carry the search for the four sources of the Pentateuch into the books of Judges and Samuel. See also R. Smend, "JE in den geschichtlichen Büchern des Alten Testaments," *Zeitschrift für die alttestamentliche Wissenschaft* 39 (1921):181–217; I. Benzinger, *Jahvist und Elohist in Den Königsbüchern* (Berlin: W. Kohlhammer, 1921); O. Eissfeldt, *Die Quellen des Richterbuches* (Leipzig: J. C. Hinrich, 1925) and *Die Komposition der Samuelisbücher* (Leipzig: J. C. Hinrich, 1931).

21. Cf. H. Gressmann, "Die Aufgaben der alttestamentlichen Forschung," *Zeitschrift für die alttestamentliche Wissenschaft* 42 (1924):8.

22. "The Form-Critical Problem of the Hexateuch," *The Problem of the Hexateuch and Other Essays* (Edinburgh/London: Oliver & Boyd, 1966), p. 1.

23. *The Old Testament since the Reformation* (New York: Schocken, 1969), p. 7.

24. On J see P. F. Ellis, *The Yahwist: The Bible's First Theologian* (Notre Dame: Fides, 1968); H. Bloom, *The Book of J* (New York: Grove Weidenfeld, 1990). On E and P, see A. W. Jenks, *The Elohist and North Israelite Traditions,* Society of Biblical Literature Monograph Series 22 (Missoula, Mont.: Scholars, 1977); R. B. Coote, *In Defense of*

Revolution: The Elohist History (Philadelphia: Fortress, 1991); J. G. Vink, "The Priestly Code," *Oudtestamentische Studiën* 15 (Leiden: E. J. Brill, 1969), to mention but a few. R. E. Friedman's *Who Wrote the Bible?* (New York: Harper & Row, 1987) is remarkable in the utter confidence with which the author expounds on the documentary hypothesis, and indeed, on the authorship of nearly every other book in the Old Testament.

25. For a fuller treatment of Genesis see Habel, *Literary Criticism of the Old Testament*.

26. The similarities between the genealogies can be seen in the following list. The numbers indicate the order in which the names appear; the first name in each unit is from Gen. 4:17–26, the second is from Gen. 5: 1. Adam/1. Adam; 8. Seth/2. Seth; 9. Enosh/3. Enosh; 2. Cain/4. Kenan; 5. Mehujael/5. Mahalalel; 4. Irad/6. Jared; 3. Enoch/7. Enoch; 6. Methusael/8. Methuselah; 7. Lamech/9. Lamech; 10. Noah/10. Noah.

27. Some slight variations may be found in the assignment of verses to J or P by different scholars, but there is agreement on those verses wherein the main contours of the story are found.

28. B. Jacob, *Das erste Buch der Tora: Genesis übersetzt und erklärt* (Berlin: Schocken, 1934).

29. U. Cassuto, *La Questione della Genesi* (Florence: F. le Monnier, 1934); *The Documentary Hypothesis and the Composition of the Pentateuch*, trans. Israel Abrahams (Jerusalem: Magnes, 1961). Other scholars who have argued for the literary unity of the Pentateuch include Y. Kaufmann, *The Religion of Israel*, trans. M. Greenberg (London: Allen & Unwin, 1960); W. Möller, *Die Einheit und Echtheit der fünf Bücher Mosis* (Solzuflen, 1931); J. Dahse, "Naht ein Umschwung?" *Neue Kirchliche Zeitschrift* 23 (1912):748–56. More recently, the unity of the Pentateuch has been defended on other grounds; cf. Y. Radday and H. Shore, *Genesis: An Authorship Study in Computer-Assisted Statistical Linguistics* (Rome: Biblical Institute, 1985). But see also an evaluation of statistical data that leads to the opposite conclusion, by S. Portnoy and D. L. Petersen, "Statistical Differences among Documentary Sources: Comments on 'Genesis: An Authorship Study,' " *Journal for the Study of the Old Testament* 50 (1991):3–14.

30. *Genesis* (Göttingen: Vandenhoeck & Ruprecht, 1901). The introduction of this book was published in English as *The Legends of Genesis*, trans. W. H. Carruth (Chicago: Open Court, 1901).

31. "The Origins of Israelite Law," *Essays on Old Testament History and Religion*, trans. R. A. Wilson (New York: Doubleday, 1968), pp. 101–71.

32. "Form-Critical Problem of the Hexateuch."

33. *A History of Pentateuchal Traditions*, trans. B. W. Anderson (Englewood Cliffs, N.J.: Prentice-Hall, 1972).

34. *The Problem of the Process of Transmission in the Pentateuch*, trans. J. J. Scullion, Journal for the Study of the Old Testament Supplements 89 (Sheffield: Journal for the Study of the Old Testament, 1990).

35. *Gamla Testamentet. En traditionshistorisk inledning* (Stockholm, 1945).

36. This was noted by J. Pedersen in *Israel: Its Life and Culture* (London: Oxford, 1926).

37. For S. Mowinckel ("Der Ursprung der Bil'amsage," *Zeitschrift für die alttestamentliche Wissenschaft* 48 [1930]:233–71), E is reduced to a series of corrective additions to J. P. Volz (*Der Elohist als Erzähler. Ein Irrweg der Pentateuch-kritik?* Beihefte zur Zeitschrift für die alttestamentliche Wissenschaft 63 [Giessen: A. Töpelmann, 1933]) and later W. Rudolph (*Der "Elohist" von Exodus bis Joshua,* Beihefte zur Zeitschrift für die alttestamentliche Wissenschaft 68 [Berlin: A. Töpelmann, 1938]) adopted a kind of "supplementary hypothesis" in which E ceases to exist as a continuous document and, at best, designates a series of additions to a single document that took place over a long period of time. More recently, J. Van Seters (*Abraham in History and Tradition* [New Haven, Conn.: Yale University Press, 1975]) has expressed doubt about the existence of E, preferring to speak about stages in the development of J, which he dates to the exile.

38. Cf. A. W. Jenks, *The Elohist and North Israelite Traditions,* and R. B. Coote, *In Defense of Revolution: The Elohist History* (both cited in n. 24).

39. For example, R. Smend (*Die Erzählung des Hexateuch auf ihre Quellen untersucht* [Berlin: G. Reimer, 1912]) posited two separate strata of writing from the J "school," J^1 and J^2, and von Rad (*Die Priesterschrift im Hexateuch* [Stuttgart-Berlin: W. Kohlhammer, 1934]) argued that the structure and theology of P shows it to be the combination of two sources, P^A and P^B, the latter being more complex and more priestly in perspective than the former.

40. O. Eissfeldt, *Hexateuch-Synopse* (Leipzig: J. C. Hinrich, 1922). Eissfeldt actually divided J into two sources, calling the earlier one L and the later one J.

41. G. Fohrer, *Introduction to the Old Testament,* trans. David E. Green (Nashville: Abingdon, 1968). Fohrer's N was akin to Eissfeldt's L. Despite its "nomadic" nature, N's theology was as highly developed as J's, in Fohrer's view.

42. J. Morgenstern, "The Oldest Document of the Hexateuch," *Hebrew Union College Annual* 4 (1927):1–138. Morgenstern dated his K source to the reign of King Asa, believing it was produced to support Asa's religious reform.

43. R. H. Pfeiffer, "A Non-Israelite Source of the Book of Genesis," *Zeitschrift für die alttestamentliche Wissenschaft* 48 (1930):66–73; *Introduction to the Old Testament* (New York: Harper & Brothers, 1941). Pfeiffer dated S to the time of Solomon but believed that it had originated in Edom.

44. *A History of Pentateuchal Traditions,* trans. B. W. Anderson (Englewood Cliffs, N.J.: Prentice-Hall, 1972).

45. For example, B. P. Eerdmans (*Alttestamentliche Studien,* 4 vols. [Giessen: A. Töpelmann, 1908–1912]), rejecting the evolutionary model adopted by Wellhausen, sought to show that Israel's religion was not primitive in its early stage. Eerdmans was not alone in attacking Wellhausen's Hegelianism; see also J. Pedersen, "Die Auffassung vom Alten Testament," *Zeitschrift für die alttestamentliche Wissenschaft* 49 (1931):161–81.

46. A. Welch (*The Code of Deuteronomy: A New Theory of Its Origin* [London: J.

Clarke, 1924] and "On the Present Position of Old Testament Criticism," *Expositor* 25 [1923]:364–65) recognized archaic elements in D and argued that most of the P legislation was preexilic. E. Sellin (*Einleitung in das Alte Testament,* 5th ed. [Leipzig: Quelle & Meyer, 1929]) maintained that the narrative portions of P were as old as J, and E. Y. Kaufmann ("Probleme der israelitisch-jüdischen Religionsgeschichte," *Zeitschrift für die alttestamentliche Wissenschaft* 48 [1930]:23–32; 51 [1933]:35–47) held that P was entirely preexilic. G. Hölscher ("Komposition und Ursprung des Deuteronomiums," *Zeitchrift für die alttestamentliche Wissenschaft* 40 [1922]:161–255) went in the opposite direction, abandoning a preexilic date for D.

47. *Abraham in History and Tradition* (New Haven, Conn.: Yale University Press, 1975). See also his *Prologue to History: The Yahwist as Historian in Genesis* (Louisville, Ky.: Westminster/John Knox, 1992).

48. *Der sogenannte Jahwist* (Zürich: Theologischer Verlag, 1976).

49. Journal for the Study of the Old Testament Supplements 53 (Sheffield: Journal for the Study of the Old Testament, 1987).

50. E. W. Nicholson, "The Pentateuch in Recent Research: A Time for Caution," in *Congress Volume Leuven,* 1989, ed. J. A. Emerton, Supplements to Vetus Testamentum 43 (Leiden: E. J. Brill, 1991).

51. D. McCarthy, "Twenty-Five Years of Pentateuchal Study," in *The Biblical Heritage,* ed. J. J. Collins and J. D. Crossan (Wilmington: Michael Glazier, 1986), p. 39.

For Further Reading

History, Description, and Application of Source Criticism

Barton, John. *Reading the Old Testament: Method in Biblical Study.* Philadelphia: Westminster, 1984.

Clements, Ronald E. *One Hundred Years of Old Testament Interpretation.* Philadelphia: Westminster, 1976.

Eissfeldt, Otto. *The Old Testament: An Introduction.* Trans. P. R. Ackroyd. New York: Harper & Row, 1965.

Habel, Norman. *Literary Criticism of the Old Testament.* Philadelphia: Fortress, 1971.

Hahn, Herbert F. *The Old Testament in Modern Research.* Philadelphia: Fortress, 1966.

Noth, Martin. *A History of Pentateuchal Traditions.* Trans. B. W. Anderson. Englewood Cliffs, N.J.: Prentice-Hall, 1972.

Wellhausen, Julius. *Prolegomena to the History of Ancient Israel.* New York: Meridian, 1957.

Critique of Source Criticism

Blenkinsopp, Joseph. "The Documentary Hypothesis in Trouble," *Bible Review* (Winter, 1985).

Nicholson, E. W. "The Pentateuch in Recent Research: A Time for Caution." In *Congress Volume Leuven*, 1989, ed. J. A. Emerton. Supplements to Vetus Testamentum 43. Leiden: E. J. Brill, 1991.

Rendtorff, Rolf. *The Problem of the Process of Transmission in the Pentateuch.* Trans. J. J. Scullion. Journal for the Study of the Old Testament Supplement Series 89. Sheffield: Journal for the Study of the Old Testament, 1990.

Van Seters, John. *Abraham in History and Tradition.* New Haven, Conn.: Yale University Press, 1975.

Whybray, R. N. *The Making of the Pentateuch: A Methodological Study.* Journal for the Study of the Old Testament Supplement Series 53. Sheffield: Journal for the Study of the Old Testament, 1987.

3
TRADITION-HISTORICAL CRITICISM

Robert A. Di Vito

What Is Tradition-Historical Criticism?

To think of tradition-historical criticism in the Bible as a "method" may be misleading. To begin with, the word "method" itself evokes thoughts of a commonly agreed-upon procedure for reading the text that will yield to every reader objective results, that is, "correct" interpretations of the text. On this understanding, the method controls the reading of the text and guarantees the validity of the results obtained, chiefly by eliminating those subjective intuitions and prejudices of the reader that are thought to falsify understanding. Obviously, the ideal here is that of the natural sciences, with their goal of producing results that are always and everywhere valid for anyone who follows the same procedure. Yet it is not at all clear that such an ideal is appropriate for humanistic disciplines such as biblical criticism. The successful act of reading is precisely the one that engages a reader, in the way a great work of art does, in an interpretive enterprise that knows no end and is in principle new on each act of reading.[1]

In this sense, tradition criticism is no less "methodical" than any other form of biblical criticism. But there is another sense in which the application of the word "method" to tradition criticism can be a source of confusion. The traditional methods of textual criticism, source criticism, and form criticism present a more or less systematic body of specific procedures for analyzing a text according to certain guidelines. But tradition criticism lacks any generally accepted techniques or evaluative criteria of its own. Indeed, it cannot be viewed simply as one method among other methods of biblical criticism. Tradition criticism is at once less and more than other types of criticism. It is less because it is entirely dependent upon their procedures; but it is also more because it represents an approach to the biblical text that formulates investigative goals for synthesizing the manifold conclusions arrived at through "other"

53

methods. Put simply, it formulates the use of results obtained from the operation of several distinct methodologies, but above all from source- and form-
critical studies.[2]

Although the word "tradition" can be so broad in its meaning as to embrace
the entire ongoing life, customs, and practices of a group or community over
successive generations, it is used here in a narrower sense to refer specifically
to verbal tradition, that is, to words and texts transmitted from one generation
to the next orally and/or by means of writing.[3] Examples include proverbs,
riddles, songs, poems, epics, and various kinds of folk narratives. While theoretically originating with "someone," such traditions are essentially "anonymous" in character, being developed and shaped over the course of their
transmission by the group or groups who have a direct interest in their preser-
vation and for whom they play a vital role. In that sense, whatever their origin,
traditions become the "common property" of a community or a group, alive
only as long as they are functional in meeting the evolving "needs" of the
group. Necessarily, then, traditions must change, or develop, over the course
of their transmission if they are to continue to be viable. They can enjoy only a
relative degree of stability over time.

The degree to which traditions change over the course of their transmission
is variable for another reason. One must reckon with such factors as, for example, whether the transmitted material is memorized *verbatim* (which is the
exception) or handed down in a freer form (the normal mode of transmission),
and whether written versions exist that can act, in some fashion, as "standards" for the material's accurate transmission.[4] As a living process engaging
the interests and concerns of traditionists (those who hand on a tradition), the
only rule the transmission of tradition knows is change. Even the wording of a
memorized speech (e.g., a prayer or a song) varies over the course of time, as
does the degree of fixity that a written tradition can achieve. For that, among
other things, depends on the degree and kind of authority a written tradition
possesses.

Put simply, then, tradition-historical criticism seeks to reconstruct the history of the transmission of the various individual traditions and tradition complexes that are to be found in the Old Testament. Beginning with a
recognition of the historicality of the Bible and its contents, it views the Old
Testament, and its various component parts, as a body of largely "traditional"
literature. This means that unlike the free creation of an individual author (in
the modern sense of the word), the Bible is the product of a long process of
composition and transmission. Moreover, it is a process that quite often did not
begin simply with the writing of those texts that eventually comprised the
books of the Bible or even the earlier written sources utilized in them. The
process that tradition-historical criticism envisions and, in fact, is most concerned with extends back beyond the written stage of the Bible's formation to

embrace stages that can be discerned in the preliterary history of a textual unit. For many tradition historians it is really this *oral stage* of a tradition's composition and transmission that is of utmost importance for understanding its particular characteristics.

Tradition-historical criticism, in other words, deals with the entire sweep of history that a tradition passes through, from its earliest beginning as an independent tradition unit to its final elaboration and expression within the Bible. It embraces both the oral phase of a tradition's composition and transmission as well as its "recomposition" in writing and final literary redaction. For the Old Testament this can, of course, mean a history extending over the course of a thousand years. Nevertheless, the goal is to reconstruct within that long history the various stages a particular tradition, or tradition unit, passed through in its growth and development. Indeed, it may even include a tradition's "postliterary" history—that is, how it finally fits within broad intellectual currents that characterized the life of ancient Israel (e.g., the wisdom movement or the Deuteronomic movement).

To achieve such a comprehensive view of a tradition's history, tradition-historical criticism necessarily presupposes and utilizes the results of textual criticism, source criticism, form criticism, and redaction criticism. This is not difficult, because, for all their differences, each method is always directly concerned with the course of the Bible's composition. So textual criticism seeks to recover as far as possible the earliest stages of a text's actual wording on the basis of extant Hebrew manuscripts and ancient versions. For its part, source criticism investigates the literary plan or structure of a text, its themes and language, with a view to determining its integrity (that it stems from a single author) or the degree of its compositeness. If the text turns out to be composite, source criticism attempts to discern the relationship of the compositional elements to each other (older/primary versus younger/secondary) and the nature of those elements (i.e., are they derived from other, perhaps larger written documents, as fragments, or are they redactional supplements to the text, such as introductions, conclusions, or explanatory glosses?).[5] Such an analysis of the written development of a textual unit might further be complemented by redaction criticism, with its particular emphasis on describing how these various compositional elements eventually came together to produce the text in its present form and what intentions or concerns guided those responsible for it. Nevertheless, the key role in tradition history is played by form criticism.

Form criticism represents the indispensable means of tradition history. For form criticism investigates precisely the crucial preliterary history of a text thought to contain ancient tradition, as well as traditional formulas that occur within it. Indeed, it is largely only through form-critical work that the tradition historian is able to identify a textual unit as a piece of tradition as opposed to the free creation of an author. This it characteristically accomplishes by recognizing that a given unit, whether prose or poetry, is an instance of an originally oral genre (e.g., historical tale, proverb, psalm, prophetic saying), with a characteristic content and the product of a particular kind of recurrent situation or situations (e.g., instruction, worship, etc.), which specifically shaped its intentions or goals. While a recognition of the genre to which a unit belongs does not in itself guarantee the antiquity of a particular unit, it goes a long way toward showing the possibility. And historically, form criticism has expended much effort in determining not only the genre to which a text belongs but also the earliest form, or forms, of the unit that might be recognizable over the course of its literary and especially preliterary (oral) transmission. Along with a determination of a unit's original setting-in-life (*Sitz im Leben*), this provides tradition history with the analysis and material necessary to reconstruct the history of a particular tradition or tradition complex. Such reconstruction is the comprehensive goal of tradition history.

Up to this point, we have restricted our discussion of tradition-historical criticism to one of the two facets of verbal tradition, namely, that of the viewpoint of the material handed down (*traditum*). But, as mention of a unit's *Sitz im Leben* suggests, tradition-historical criticism is also concerned with the process (*traditio*) by which this material is passed down from generation to generation.[6] Clearly, without an exploration of the forces and influences that exerted themselves on a tradition in the process of its transmission, little headway will be made in reconstructing the individual stages a particular unit of tradition went through. Under this rubric, tradition-historical criticism moves in several different directions,[7] among which three lines of research are particularly prominent.

First, form criticism's determination of the setting(s)-in-life of a particular tradition provides what is in many cases the only point of departure for ascertaining the group or the community responsible for the development and transmission of a tradition, the so-called traditionists. Quite simply, the more we know about such traditionists and their institutional commitments—the more we know about the social, political, and religious forces that operated through them and on them—the more we can understand the real meaning of a tradition and the vital role it played in the life of ancient Israel. Examples of such groups in ancient Israel are the priests at the local shrines or the Temple in Jerusalem, the bands of disciples of the great prophets, and the so-called "wise."

Second, the geographical area or location with which a tradition is associated is a topic of interest to tradition history. For it is through the localization of a tradition (e.g., the association of early exodus traditions with the north or messianic traditions with Judah) that its interpretation acquires the kind of specificity and concreteness that allows us to appreciate a tradition's historical significance and function within the life of ancient Israel. The localization of tradition allows one to bring to bear on its interpretation whatever knowledge we possess of the various historical, geographical, economic, and cultural-political forces affecting a locale and its population. Such forces comprise the matrix that nourishes the growth of a tradition and shapes its ongoing formation.

A third line of research important to tradition-historical criticism is the study of the processes by which the creation and transmission of tradition take place. This means an investigation not only of "authorial" and scribal practices in the ancient Near East and the extent and nature of written communication but also (and especially) of the nature and dynamics of oral composition and oral transmission. For the latter, contemporary folklore studies, based on present-day oral cultures, have become absolutely indispensable, since the only access we have to oral tradition in the ancient world is filtered through written materials. Given how little we know about ancient society, a host of questions arises. For example, what kind of stability and longevity can be expected of oral tradition? Who is responsible for a society's oral memory? What techniques are used in the composition and transmission of oral literature? Are different kinds of materials handled in different ways? What are the role and extent of memorization and improvisation in the transmission of tradition? What is the relation between written and oral communication? What precipitates the writing down of an oral tradition, and what changes does it undergo in the process? Such questions and many others have been hotly debated within tradition-historical research and will continue to be in the foreseeable future.[8]

As previously noted, there is little consensus today concerning the focus and methods of tradition-historical criticism. Some will argue that it already possesses, or must still develop, methods distinctly its own, or that the scope of tradition-historical criticism must be strictly limited to the preliterary, oral stages of a tradition's transmission.[9] The particular view presented here, however, is congruent with the history of the discipline's practice, and it would be helpful at this point to consider briefly some of the factors behind its emergence. By looking at the work of a few of its early practitioners, one achieves a better understanding of not only what tradition-historical criticism has been but also, and as important, what issues and problems will shape its development in the future.

The Emergence of Tradition-Historical Study

The origin of the discipline may be found in an impasse that had been reached as a result of source-critical studies in the Pentateuch, culminating in Julius Wellhausen's classic formulation of the Documentary Hypothesis at the end of the nineteenth century. In Wellhausen's view, the four sources that comprised the Pentateuch were substantially the product of the creative efforts of their authors, who worked much the same way as modern authors. To be sure, legends about early times were at their disposal, but these were unconnected to one another and were of only limited value as historical sources. The older they were, the more likely they were to be simply the product of popular fancy.[10] As a result, the original sources behind the present form of the Pentateuch provided the historian with little or no access to the period before they were actually written, certainly not to a period much before the time of David. Consequently, historical knowledge of the patriarchs was impossible, and very little could be known even of the Age of Moses.[11]

By directly challenging Wellhausen's view of the role of the Pentateuch's "authors," however, Hermann Gunkel was able to show a way behind the written text of the Bible to earlier sources of Israel's history. In Gunkel's view, the writers of the Pentateuch were not so much authors as they were collectors ("redactors") of the traditions of their people, adding little of their own to what they had received. And what they received was merely the latest stage of a long process of these traditions' formation, in which they had been passed down faithfully over many generations by word of mouth. Over time, with each new telling, the originally independent short "sagas" or legends (which, for example, comprise the narrative cycles of Genesis) changed and developed according to the needs of their hearers. As they did so, however, they continued to bear with them authentic traces of their origins as well as of their subsequent history. In this way, Gunkel believed, a whole history of the religious, ethical, and aesthetic ideas of ancient Israel can be derived from Genesis.[12]

Had Gunkel merely challenged Wellhausen's conception of the Pentateuch's sources as written documents, his influence would probably not have been so great. But Gunkel also developed a method congruent with the nature of the Pentateuch's sources as "traditional" literature. That method was form criticism, and by means of it, Gunkel found a way to explore beyond the limitations of the written text, not only in Genesis but throughout the Bible. Indeed, his goal was to recover by means of form-critical analysis the earliest form of a tradition or a tradition unit. The tradition itself pointed the way, its variants, its inconsistencies, and its blind motifs betraying earlier stages of a long development. In this way, one could hypothetically describe a tradition's entire history on the basis of the tradition itself, its "inner history," as Gunkel called it.[13] And for this realization, he is justly recognized as the chief pioneer of tradition-historical criticism.[14]

While Gunkel himself did not regard the products of oral tradition as appropriate material for specifically historical reconstruction,[15] a number of scholars who followed in his wake took note of his insistence on the antiquity of oral traditions behind the biblical narratives and on the fidelity of oral transmission.

Confident of their ability to separate history from legend, they sought to reconstruct the earliest periods of Israel's history and religion. For example, on the basis of the sagas of Genesis, Albrecht Alt offered a description of the distinctive nature of patriarchal religion before the rise of Yahwism at the time of Moses.[16] In turn, his research had a particularly strong influence on two scholars whose names are more closely associated with tradition-historical criticism than even that of Gunkel himself—Gerhard von Rad and Martin Noth.

Gunkel had focused his form-critical attention on the smallest units of tradition, an emphasis that left largely unaddressed the question of the origin of the Pentateuch's/Hexateuch's larger thematic structures.[17] In texts such as Deut. 26:5–9; Deut. 6:20–24; and Josh. 24:1–18, von Rad found preserved what he considered to be nearly identical old summaries of Israelite belief, or "creeds," originating in Israel's worship at an ancient shrine (Gilgal).[18] As he saw it, these creeds formed the basis of the structure of the present Hexateuch, with whose outline they were essentially identical. Thus rather than being something that has grown up on its own accidentally, "a casual recollection of historical events," the thematic structure of the Hexateuch itself rests on ancient tradition, a "canonical pattern . . . long since fixed as to its details."[19] Only the Sinai tradition of covenant making (Exodus 19–Numbers 10) was lacking in the old "creeds." However, von Rad concluded that it too derived from old tradition, having originated in a covenant renewal feast at Shechem. It was inserted by the Yahwist into the framework established by the old creeds, and this, along with the prefixing of the primeval history in Genesis 1–11, led to the creation of the present Hexateuch.

Although Noth states explicitly that the task of his history of Pentateuchal traditions is the investigation of its whole growth and formation from beginning to end, the critical period as far as he is concerned is the preliterary, which for him, even more than for von Rad, gave the Pentateuch its essential shape.[20] Moreover, Noth goes beyond von Rad in positing behind the earliest written sources of the Pentateuch, J and E, a common base from which both had been independently derived and that *already* contained in a unified form what he identifies as the five major themes of the Pentateuch: the exodus, the guidance into the land, the promise to the patriarchs, the guidance in the wilderness, and the revelation at Sinai.[21] The last is noteworthy, for it was this tradition complex that von Rad had seen as an addition by the Yahwist. Consequently, aside from the primeval history, Noth is able to push the entire thematic structure of the Pentateuch back to the period of the Judges and the worship of the twelve-tribe confederacy.

Since each Pentateuchal theme is composed of its own block of individual traditions with its own history of development, however, still another stage of tradition formation must be imagined. During this stage, the individual themes and their associated traditions developed separately, only gradually growing together around the theme of the exodus from Egypt—the "kernel of the whole subsequent Pentateuchal tradition" and a "primary confession of Israel." With it, Noth believed he had reached "the bedrock of an historical occurrence."[22] In fact, for Noth, this attainment of the unique historical events giving rise to the Pentateuch's themes defined the real goal of his tradition-historical studies.[23] And to that end, in the course of detailed analyses of individual traditions that filled out the framework of the Pentateuch, he articulated various principles for separating out earlier traditions from later ones (e.g., the attachment of early traditions to specific places, the priority of cultic traditions over secular traditions, anonymity and typicality, etc.), which subsequently became major topics of tradition-historical discussions.[24] Though they have been severely criticized, they nonetheless highlight the kind of explicit criteria that will have to be found if tradition-historical criticism is going to succeed in its goal of reconstructing the history of tradition's transmission.

It is impossible here to consider further the lines of research opened up by von Rad and Noth or by the numerous other scholars, particularly in Scandinavia, who have taken up tradition-historical research. They sought to apply its guiding insights to other parts of the Bible, such as the prophetic corpus or the wisdom books, as well as to investigate in a more systematic fashion the process of oral tradition itself.[25]

Problems and Issues
in Tradition-Historical Criticism Today

Today widespread disagreement remains concerning the specific object of tradition-historical research—whether it is restricted only to the phase of oral tradition or is all-inclusive—and concerning its methods of investigation, particularly as these relate to other forms of biblical criticism. Despite the best efforts of many scholars, this situation is likely to continue for some time into the foreseeable future, given the scope of the challenge tradition-historical criticism has posed for itself. Whether through naïveté or simple overconfidence, the magnitude of this challenge has not always been sufficiently recognized. We have only the written texts at our disposal; nevertheless, tradition-historical criticism has set itself the job of studying, if not actually recovering, nothing less than the entire prewritten phase of their composition!

It must be acknowledged that until the last fifteen years or so, much of the enthusiasm for tradition-historical studies came from their promise of breaking the methodological impasse created by Wellhausen's restriction of historical knowledge to the time in which the Bible's sources were actually written. This can be seen in Noth's tradition-historical work on the Pentateuch, which laid the groundwork for his efforts to reconstruct the history of ancient Israel.[26]

Despite the rigor of many studies, numerous others failed to distinguish clearly between the history of a tradition and the question of its historicity. What was irreducible in a tradition was taken as historical; what was secondary, either as historically untrustworthy or as having an independent historical foundation.[27] But can "originality" itself settle the question of the historicity of these traditions? And what of the criteria used to decide primary and secondary elements of tradition? Noth, for example, had argued that the earliest traditions are formulated in small units in a concise style, and that cultic traditions are earlier than comparable secular traditions.[28] Yet both criteria have been roundly rejected.[29]

In addition to skepticism regarding various criteria for judging the relative age of traditions, another issue key to penetrating the remote periods of Israel's history is the question of the very stability of tradition. While acknowledging that changes in the form and the content of traditions inevitably occurred in the course of transmission, Gunkel and those who followed him also insisted on the "fidelity" of the transmission process even over long stretches of time. But what exactly constitutes faithful transmission? Surely, early studies exaggerated the role of memorization in the process of oral tradition, ignoring its restriction to a limited number of situations and forms; moreover, recent field studies in folklore emphasize that the transmission of oral tradition occurs largely through a process of recomposition, or re-creation, so that a text (even in poetry) never remains unchanged, even on the lips of the same person.[30] Thus the "fixity" of tradition over time can no longer be assumed but must be determined on the basis of tradition-historical investigations.

Perhaps more seriously, questions now are raised about our ability to reconstruct preliterary stages of a tradition on the basis of written documents.[31] After all, how does written Hebrew actually relate to spoken Hebrew? Although most scholars acknowledge differences between oral communication and written communication in general, what constitutes these differences is not always easy to determine. If, for example, one points to repetition as characteristic of spoken versus written communication, what is to be made of the unmistakable repetitive rhetorical style of Deuteronomy and the Deuteronomist? May not written language sometimes imitate spoken language? In fact, the issue of the "orality" of written texts is more pressing than it might at first appear, for it calls into question the very ability to discriminate between texts rooted authentically in oral tradition and those that are purely literary inventions.

Perhaps this discussion is sufficient to indicate some of the central issues facing tradition-historical research today. Of course, these concerns necessarily relate to the current practice of source criticism and form criticism. Tradition-historical criticism remains dependent on progress in these methods even as it will continue to reflect their limitations.

An Illustration of the Approach

A brief illustration of the applicability of tradition-historical criticism to a specific biblical text will draw together the various points made here and show concretely both the prospects and the limitations of its approach. The text to be considered is Gen. 32:22–32 (Hebrew 32:23–33).

Anyone who has thoughtfully investigated the story of Jacob's encounter with the mysterious "man" in Genesis 32 can attest to the many obscurities with which it confronts the discerning reader. Yet if we follow the form-critical lead suggested by Gunkel for tracing the history of a tradition,[32] these obscurities are clear indications of the antiquity of the story and the long history of its transmission. Along with the presence of possible variant traditions, these indications provide the concrete means by which one may reconstruct the history of the tradition in question.

Such indications within the text of Genesis 32 include apparent vestiges of "primitive" religious conceptions, the narrative's lack of connection to the immediate context, the unevenness of the present form of the story, and its multiple etiologies and conclusions. Also, a variant form of the tradition in Genesis 32 occurs in Hos. 12:3b–4a (Hebrew 12:4b–5a), where the prophet indicts Israel for following in the footsteps of her eponymous ancestor:

> In his manly vigor he [Jacob] wrestled with a "god";
> He [Jacob] wrestled a "god" and prevailed.
> (The god) wept and besought his favor.[33]

On the basis of these two lines of evidence at least four stages in the growth of the tradition may be discerned.

Analysis proceeds by working "back" from the present narrative, beginning with the results obtained from source-critical study. Such study generally affirms the literary integrity of Gen. 32:22–32 and attributes the text to the work of the Yahwist.[34] The only exception concerns v. 32, along with its referent in v. 25b ("and Jacob's hip was put out of joint"). Verse 32 contains a strange dietary abstention on the part of Israelites (unknown elsewhere) and is the second of two successive etiologies, neither of which belongs to the essential story. Although older scholarship tended to regard the mere presence of an etiology as a sign of the etiological intention of an entire narrative, current scholarship recognizes that etiologies are often secondary additions, or redactional elements.[35] Consequently, a number of scholars have taken at least v. 32, along with v. 25b, as a late, postexilic, "midrashic" accretion to the text.[36] As the text stands, v. 25b is certainly puzzling in view of the man's cry in v. 26 (" . . . Let me go . . . "), and its loss would only help smooth out the story.

At this last stage of the tradition, Gen. 32:22–32 has become an element in the composite created by the Priestly (P) redaction of earlier Pentateuchal sources. Although P probably introduced no changes into the tradition itself or into its position within the larger Jacob cycle, the new broader literary setting fabricated by P broadened and deepened the theological horizon. Genesis 32:22–32 now represents an episode under the auspices of the eternal covenant God established with Abraham to be the God of his descendants (chapter 17). As such, it falls within the third and penultimate historical age, according to the Priestly scheme of "salvation history."

The third stage of the tradition's development occurred with its inclusion in the Yahwist source. At this stage, a number of significant developments took place in the tradition, as perhaps it was reduced to writing for the first time. To begin with, the Yahwist is most likely responsible for the present "artful" position of Gen. 32:22–32 in the Jacob cycle, with which it has otherwise little in common. In the cycle, Jacob generally makes his way by trickery and cunning; here it seems to be a question of his strength. By inserting this text directly into the middle of the story of Jacob's perilous reunion with Esau (note the lack of an entirely consistent transition from 32:21 to 32:22), the story now forms a perfect counterpart to the theophany at Bethel (28:10–22). Thus Jacob's flight from Esau and his perilous return are both marked by special revelations of divine providence. The two incidents frame Jacob's "exile," otherwise lacking in religious color, and show it to have been under God's protection.

In addition, the Yahwist is probably responsible for the identification of Jacob's mysterious opponent with God. This is accomplished by the concluding etiology of the place name "Penuel" in v. 30, which puns on the meaning of the name ("For I have seen God face to face"). And it is probably indicated by the change of Jacob's name in v. 28, with the explanation given there of the name "Israel." In fact, it is likely that in the story inherited by the Yahwist, v. 29b ("and he blessed him") followed directly upon Jacob's demand in v. 26 (compare Hos. 12:4b–5a above) as the boon won by the hero's victory. In other words, the Yahwist is responsible for introducing the entire motif of the change of Jacob's name to Israel, vv. 27–29a, and with it, the effort to articulate the meaning of "Israel." (In Hos. 12:4a, there is a Hebrew pun on the name Israel, but no expansion of this into a change in the patriarch's name.) This becomes the center of attention, and to some extent, it moves an identification of the text's genre, which continues to puzzle commentators, in the direction of an etiology of the name,[37] if not of the existence of Israel.[38] For the Yahwist, the struggle of the eponymous hero Jacob typifies Israel's spiritual struggles with God, a struggle that, as he sees it, constitutes her destiny and deepest identity.

Identification of a second stage in the development of the tradition is perhaps warranted by the variant tradition appearing in Hosea. Were the Hosea tradition a true variant to Gen. 32:22–32 from the form-critical point of view rather than simply an allusion to a story, a reconstruction of the earliest form of the tradition could proceed on other than speculative grounds. Nonetheless, the tradition Hosea employs suggests a prior stage in the tradition of Jacob's struggle, less developed than the Genesis tradition. First, at this stage Jacob is not yet the eponymous hero of a united Israel, but only of the Northern Kingdom.[39] Second, Jacob's opponent is only identified as an "ʾĕlōhîm," an identification which of itself need only indicate a supernatural, or superhuman, being (compare the usage in 1 Sam. 28:13, where it refers to the ghost of Samuel; see n. 33). Third, although the Hebrew in Hos. 12:5a contains a pun on the name of "Israel" (*yiśar ʾēl*, "he wrestled God/a god"),[40] the pun is not developed into an etiology for the change of Jacob's name. If this is the case, at this stage of the tradition's transmission, the narrative as a whole lacks any strong etiological thrust, further suggesting an identification of the unit's original genre as that of folktale. And fourth, in the tradition the prophet utilizes (albeit, negatively, as an example of the eponymous hero's brazen daring), the depiction of Jacob's extraordinary feat of strength is clearly cast in a "heroic" mode. Jacob successfully wrestled with this superhuman being and won from it some kind of blessing or boon. There is little hint of the later "spiritualization" of the incident, which earlier had clearly been a source of popular pride. Most likely the tale circulated as merely one of a number of such folktales about the eponymous hero of the Northern Kingdom, perhaps part of the "stock in trade" of professional storytellers who roamed the countryside entertaining the populace wherever a crowd might be likely to gather.

Although it is merely speculation, one can conjecture a still earlier stage of the tradition's development. Perhaps to this stage belong originally those elements of the story such as the motif of the "magic touch" (v. 25a) or of the demonlike creature whose power is restricted to the night and who seeks to block the hero's passage. Given the ubiquity of such stories in folklore (compare, too, Exod. 4:24–26), there is no reason to think the story in this original form even concerned the eponymous hero Jacob or had its present localization. Surely, the delightful pun on the name "Israel," in evidence at the second stage of the tale's transmission, is in no way essential to the action of the basic story. It probably was introduced later, as part of the "Israelitizing" of the tale when it became associated with the figure of Jacob. So, too, perhaps came the introduction of the river's name "Jabbok," which in Hebrew puns on the name Jacob, as well as on the word for "wrestle."

Enough has been said to indicate the lines of the tradition's possible transmission and development, up to and including its final redaction in Genesis. By seeking to uncover the richness of this intriguing text's long and complicated history, tradition-historical criticism reveals something of the riches of biblical narrative, which could take a popular tale about a hero and transform it into a profound statement of the vocation and destiny of Israel. At the same time, we also learn something about the historical development of Israel's religious beliefs and of her own spiritual sojourn, as she walks in the footsteps of her ancestor Jacob. Like Jacob, she too only discovers along the way that the Mysterious Presence with whom she has had to struggle continually in her history bore the name of her God.

Notes

1. For a penetrating examination of this question, see H.-G. Gadamer, *Truth and Method* (New York: Seabury, 1975).

2. So G. M. Tucker, *Form Criticism of the Old Testament*, Guides to Biblical Scholarship (Philadelphia: Fortress, 1971); J. Barton, *Reading the Old Testament* (Philadelphia: Westminster, 1984), p. 10; K. Jeppesen and B. Otzen, "Status Quaestionis," *The Productions of Time: Tradition History in Old Testament Scholarship* (ed. K. Jeppesen and B. Otzen [Sheffield: Almond, 1984]), p. 129. K. Koch (*The Growth of the Biblical Tradition*, trans. S. M. Cupitt [New York: Charles Scribner's Sons, 1969], p. 53) regards tradition history as simply a branch of form-critical work. Of course, this is not the self-understanding of many who have been and are proponents of tradition history. See, for example, D. A. Knight, *Rediscovering the Traditions of Israel*, Society of Biblical Literature Dissertation Series 9 (Missoula, Mont.: Scholars, 1975), esp. pp. 193–94.

3. Knight, *Rediscovering the Traditions*, p. 1.

4. R. C. Culley "An Approach to the Problem of Oral Tradition," *Vetus Testamentum* 13 (1963):115–17.

5. R. Knierim, "Criticism of Literary Features, Form, Tradition, and Redaction," in *The Hebrew Bible and Its Modern Interpreters*, ed. D. A. Knight and G. M. Tucker (Philadelphia: Fortress, 1985), pp. 130–34.

6. For the distinction, cf. Knight, *Rediscovering the Traditions*, pp. 5–20.

7. Ibid., pp. 5–10.

8. For a valuable discussion of the problem in relation to Old Testament studies, see, in addition to Culley ("An Approach to the Problem of Oral Tradition," pp. 113–25), mentioned above, B. O. Long, "Recent Field Studies in Oral Literature and Their Bearing on OT Criticism," *Vetus Testamentum* 26 (1976):187–98.

9. For example, O. H. Steck, "Theological Streams of Tradition," *Tradition and Theology in the Old Testament*, ed. D. A. Knight (Philadelphia: Fortress, 1977), esp. pp. 183–85; see also the review of methodological positions in Knierim, "Criticism of Literary Features," pp. 146–48.

10. J. Wellhausen, *Prolegomena to the History of Ancient Israel* (Gloucester: Peter Smith, 1973), pp. 296, 326. Wellhausen's work was first published in German in 1878, with a second edition in 1883.

11. Ibid., pp. 318–19.

12. H. Gunkel, *The Legends of Genesis* (New York: Schocken, 1964), p. 99.

13. Ibid., pp. 100–102.

14. Knight, *Rediscovering the Traditions*, p. 72

15. Gunkel, *The Legends of Genesis*, pp. 1–12.

16. A. Alt, "The God of the Fathers," *Essays in Old Testament History and Religion* (New York: Anchor, 1968), pp. 3–100.

17. J. Van Seters, *Abraham in History and Tradition* (New Haven, Conn.: Yale University Press, 1975), p. 142.

18. G. von Rad, "The Form-Critical Problem of the Hexateuch," *The Problem of the Hexateuch and Other Essays* (London: SCM, 1984), pp. 1–78.

19. Ibid., pp. 2, 8.

20. M. Noth, *A History of Pentateuchal Traditions* (Englewood Cliffs, N.J.: Prentice-Hall, 1972), p. 1.

21. Ibid. pp. 38–41.

22. Ibid. pp. 49–50.

23. B. W. Anderson, "Introduction: Martin Noth's Tradition-Historical Approach in the Context of Twentieth-Century Biblical Research," in *A History of Pentateuchal Traditions*, pp. xviii–xxi.

24. See Anderson's (ibid., pp. xxiii–xxviii) formulation of these principles.

25. For the contribution of the so-called Scandinavian School to tradition-historical criticism, as well as for examples of other studies, see the excellent survey of Knight, *Rediscovering the Traditions*, pp. 177–92, 217–399.

26. M. Noth, *The History of Israel* (New York: Harper & Row, 1958).

27. T. L. Thompson, "The Joseph-Moses Traditions and Pentateuchal Criticism," in *Israelite and Judaean History*, ed. J. H. Hayes and J. M. Miller (Philadelphia: Westminster, 1977), pp. 170–71.

28. Anderson, "Introduction," pp. xxiii–xxiv.

29. R. Polzin, "Martin Noth's *A History of Pentateuchal Traditions*," *Bulletin of the American Society of Oriental Research* 221 (1976):113–20, esp. 115–16.

30. R. C. Culley, "Oral Tradition," pp. 119–50.

31. R. Lapointe, "Tradition and Language: The Import of Oral Expression," in *Tradition and Theology in the Old Testament*, pp. 125–42, esp. 131–34.

32. Gunkel, *The Legends of Genesis*, pp. 99–100.

33. The scripture translations in this chapter are the author's own. The reconstruction of the Hebrew text for the first colon of v. 4 follows the one proposed by S. L. McKenzie ("The Jacob Tradition in Hosea XII 4–5," *Vetus Testamentum* 36 [1986]:312–14). I depart in taking the subject of the second colon to be Jacob's opponent, which I understand as an unspecified type of supernatural being. Compare the use of the word "god" (ʾelohim) for the shade of Samuel in 1 Sam. 28:13.

34. C. Westermann, *Genesis 12–36: A Commentary* (Minneapolis: Augsburg, 1985), p. 515.

35. See B. Childs, "A Study of the Formula 'Until This Day,' " *Journal of Biblical Literature* 82 (1963):179–92.

36. So Westermann, *Genesis 12–36*, p. 520.

37. G. W. Coats, *Genesis*, Forms of Old Testament Literature 1 (Grand Rapids: Eerdmans, 1983), p. 230.
38. Tucker, *Form Criticism*, p. 49.
39. W. D. Whitt, "The Jacob Traditions in Hosea and Their Relation to Genesis," *Zeitschrift für die alttestamentliche Wissenschaft* 103 (1991):22–24.
40. McKenzie, "The Jacob Tradition," pp. 313–14.

For Further Reading

Cross, Frank M. "The Epic Traditions of Early Israel: Epic Narrative and the Reconstruction of Early Israelite Institutions." In *The Poet and the Historian: Essays in Literary and Historical Biblical Criticism*, ed. Richard E. Friedman. Harvard Semitic Studies 26. Chico, Calif.: Scholars, 1983.
Culley, Robert C. "An Approach to the Problem of Oral Tradition." *Vetus Testamentum* 13 (1963):113–25.
Gunkel, Hermann. *The Legends of Genesis: The Biblical Saga and History*. New York: Schocken, 1964.
Knight, Douglas A. *Rediscovering the Traditions of Israel*. Society of Biblical Literature Dissertation Series 9. Missoula, Mont.: Scholars, 1975.
Koch, Klaus. *The Growth of the Biblical Tradition*. New York: Charles Scribner's Sons, 1969.
Long, Burke O. "Recent Field Studies in Oral Literature and Their Bearing on OT Criticism." *Vetus Testamentum* 26 (1976):187–98.
Noth, Martin. *A History of Pentateuchal Traditions*. Trans. with an introduction by Bernhard W. Anderson. Englewood Cliffs, N.J.: Prentice-Hall, 1972.
Rast, Walter E. *Tradition History and the Old Testament*. Guides to Biblical Scholarship. Philadelphia: Fortress, 1972.
Van Seters, John. *Abraham in History and Tradition*. New Haven, Conn.: Yale University Press, 1975.
Von Rad, Gerhard. "The Form-Critical Problem of the Hexateuch," *The Problem of the Hexateuch and Other Essays*. Trans. E. W. Trueman Dicken. London: SCM, 1984.

4

FORM
CRITICISM

Martin J. Buss

Introduction

ACCORDING to the psychologist Jean Piaget, who systematically studied the development of thinking both in individuals and in cultures, young people living in the present century pass from a "concrete" way of thinking to a "formal" one. Formal thinking deals not so much with specific objects or events as with the way in which they are related to each other within complex patterns. Piaget believed that this transition represents an intrinsic development of the mind, proceeding with an inner logic. That thesis is questionable, but within Western culture there has indeed been a movement proceeding beyond an inclination to accept tradition, first to a concrete ("objective" or "historical") way of thought and then, during the last one hundred years, to a "formal" one, which is more abstract and relational. School education largely reflects this path of cultural development, in which earlier insights are not necessarily rejected but may be incorporated into newer and, if all goes well, richer perspectives.

One problem confronting students of biblical literature is that this subject is often not taught at educational levels below college. Thus youths are not trained step by step to apply reflective ways of thinking to it. Another problem lies in the fact that the professional study of the Bible has itself experienced difficulty in making the transition, as we will see.

The readers of the present chapter are, then, challenged both to think formally—not just concretely—in relation to the Bible and to take into account the fact that the discipline of biblical study includes significant divergences. To simplify the situation, we will consider only somewhat briefly several approaches that call themselves "form-critical." In more detail, we will sketch a line that is fully relational.

Form as Pattern

"Form criticism"—to give a definition with which perhaps everyone will agree—can be described as "integrative pattern analysis." The word "integrative" in this definition indicates that form criticism gives attention to all aspects of a text, including its language, content, and contextual function. The word "pattern" highlights the fact that the concern of form criticism is not merely with phenomena that appear once but with features that are shared or can be shared by other texts, past or present; texts possessing common features are regularly grouped into types, or "genres."

These two sides of form criticism—integration and a recognition of general patterns—go together. That is, a view that emphasizes connections between different aspects of a text is also one holding that textual features are at least potentially shared by other texts. It opposes an outlook that thinks of reality as consisting of separate, basically unrelated, items.

To clarify this issue, it is necessary to consider the different opinions about the nature of a pattern that have been held in Western thought. In fact, biblical form criticism, as it has been carried out during the twentieth century and earlier, can be well understood only against this background.

According to one traditional philosophy, a pattern or "form" is a nontemporal structure of which the observable world is an impure reflection. (A circle drawn on a board is an imperfect reflection of a real circle.) This position was argued by Plato in some of his writings.

Another view, held by Aristotle, regards form as the essential structure of an object that it shares with objects of the same kind. For instance, a table or a human being is considered to have a basic structure, an "essence," that it shares with members of the same category; other features of these beings are thought to be superficial. According to this outlook, the most appropriate way to classify objects is to place them into groups whose members have their basic structure, their essence, in common.

A third position is that a pattern is only a convenient verbal or conceptual tool by which to refer to several similar objects together. This philosophy—which was anticipated in ancient Greece by Democritus and Epicurus, sharply formulated in the fourteenth century by William of Ockham, and then accepted increasingly until the nineteenth century—can be called "particularist." Those holding this position believe that only particular, individual objects belong to the primary level of reality. According to this outlook, objects can legitimately be classified in different ways, depending on one's purpose.

A fourth view regards a pattern as a system of relations that are an intrinsic part of reality. An important feature of relations is that they include both particularity and generality, for the objects related to one another are particular, but a relation itself is general. For instance, the relation of sisterhood or of one person being taller than another applies to more than one set of beings, although these each have distinct identities. A perspective that regards relations as a part of fundamental reality thus assumes that particularity and generality are equally ultimate, neither having been secondarily derived from the other. (In a theological formulation, one can say that they are both aspects of God.)

This "relationism" maintains that associations between objects or phenomena are not merely a matter of accident (as particularism holds) but that they have intrinsic reasons that can be stated in general, including logical, terms. Yet it also does not hold that connections are altogether necessary or inevitable, for without the semi-independence of objects there is nothing to be related. Rather, it regards as basic to existence a duality of partial connectivity and partial separateness.

One of the relations in which an object stands is with an observer. Thus according to relationism (at least in a thoroughgoing form of it), a pattern is perspectival; that is, it is relative to the standpoint from which a perspective is taken and represents that aspect of the object to which one gives attention. Such a view accepts a variety of possible classifications, but it differs from particularism in that a pattern exists for it not only in the observer's mind or speech but also in the object, or—perhaps more precisely—in the relation between the object and the observer, neither of which is believed to have characteristics in isolation.

A way of thinking that emphasizes relations was implicit in early Jewish and Christian thought, as well as in other traditions (e.g., African and Asian). In Western philosophy, a distant approximation of it was presented by the Stoic Zeno, partly on the basis of a Near Eastern (perhaps Jewish) background. A more systematic relational view was developed from the end of the nineteenth century on by the American philosopher C. S. Peirce and others. It has come to permeate much of the procedure of the natural sciences and, to some extent, of the humanities; it is accepted by this writer as the best outlook available at the present time.

A fifth perspective has a certain similarity with the one just described in that neither particularity nor generality is seen as being by itself absolute. Instead of affirming both, however, it casts doubt on both and opts for skepticism. Skepticism has been especially strong during periods of cultural and social dissolution, specifically in the late phase of Greek civilization and during the transition from the medieval to the modern order in Western Europe. A strong opposition to the possibility of truth was formulated by Friedrich Nietzsche at the end of the nineteenth century, after particularism reached its height and came to be questioned both intellectually and morally. Since that time, skepticism has been widespread in various versions; it may mark the end of individualistic culture and perhaps of a long-standing patriarchy. By itself, a skeptical attitude is only negative; it has a value, however, in pointing to the limitation of all human thought.

These five views have different sociopolitical implications. Plato's perspective was aristocratic or elitist; it implied that ordinary people should be guided by persons in possession of high truth. The Aristotelian vision was partially democratic. Particularist traditions have lent themselves either to libertarian politics (each person has a right for self-assertion, with no special regard for those who are weak)[1] or to authoritarianism (the one on top has the right to rule for the sake of the collective good).[2] In contrast, relationism is associated with populist and communitarian political involvements, which are concerned with general social welfare while supporting differences between human beings[3]—a commitment shared by the present writer; the approach has at least indirect connections with feminism. Skepticism can justify a noninvolvement in politics; when it moves toward "nihilism," a (paradoxically) positive denial of truth, it supports the naked assertion of power, as happened, to a large extent, in Nazism.

This overview indicates that if one is intellectually consistent, the kind of criticism one chooses reflects a larger worldview, which is also expressed in one's attitude toward society. The application of a method is not just a mechanical process but implies a basic intellectual and moral orientation in life. Specifically, form criticism involves a definite social concern, over against pure individualism.

Biblical Form Criticism: Some Varieties in History

Form criticism of biblical literature began within the Bible itself, although it was carried out there only implicitly, without systematic reflection. Especially striking is the fact that the books of the Bible were, by and large, internally organized and externally arranged by groups in such a way that similar kinds of material stand next to one another. An arrangement in this manner was true for the several known orderings of the Jewish scriptures as well as for the New Testament. In fact, biblical books and groups of them each present specimens of a unique literary type, such as laws or proverbs. Since a kind of speech represents an aspect of existence, different aspects of life are thus covered in the Bible.

Interpretation during the subsequent centuries applied rhetorical and literary principles that were associated with then-reigning philosophical views. Within the Roman Empire, a favored way of apprehending the text was Platonic, with the admixture of a Stoic orientation. Aristotelian exegesis became dominant in the High Middle Ages (as in Maimonides and Thomas Aquinas). Particularist approaches arose gradually thereafter and came to play a major role in nineteenth-century historical criticism. Toward the end of that century, when many voices were raised against unbridled individualism, an interest in general literary types reemerged in biblical studies. A pivotal figure in that pursuit was Hermann Gunkel, who had a strong social orientation (in politics and otherwise) together with a concern for individuality.

Reacting against a purely particularist way of looking at the texts, Gunkel provided a careful characterization of genres or types of speech. Genres, in his view, each have a characteristic content, a definite linguistic form, and a "seat [normal location] in life" (*Sitz im Leben*)—a connection with a repeating social occasion. This formulation was useful for stimulating research, but it was also misleading since the correlation of content, linguistic form, and "seat in life" was asserted too strongly. It is clear that in literature these three aspects do not strictly cohere with one another; a certain idea can be expressed in more than one linguistic form and under different external conditions. Gunkel knew that such variation was true for written products, but he imagined that in oral life a given content would regularly be expressed in a characteristic manner on one kind of occasion. That notion, however, was not based on any empirical observation and was, on the whole, simply mistaken.

Gunkel's rigid characterization resembled the Aristotelian concept of species, according to which each type exhibits a peculiar essence or well-defined structure. In fact, he believed that there is a single correct or "natural" classification for literary texts. Other scholars have followed him in this. They discuss such questions as whether a given piece of biblical literature is truly a psalm of lament or truly a biography (e.g., of Jesus); they ask what is "the" genre of a text or to which genre a text "belongs," as though a clear classification, and only one, is appropriate for it. Such an essentialist outlook is quite widespread in current biblical scholarship, although it often stands in an illogical combination with a particularist view of genres, according to which they are regarded only as conventions.

In fact, Gunkel's mistaken belief in the regularity of genres on an oral level gave his approach a special historical twist. He, and even more, some of his followers, thought it possible to reconstruct oral antecedents for the written texts present in the Bible on the assumption that such antecedents exhibited the features of a single genre "purely" or "simply." Accordingly, for some interpreters—especially in New Testament studies—"form criticism" became identified with a reconstruction of oral forms of expressions lying behind the text. Pursued in this way, form criticism became a tool for historical criticism, instead of being considered worthy in its own right as a quest for patterns in human expression and life. Thus it was subsumed under an older, historical approach.

Over a period of several decades, however, it became apparent that form criticism is not well suited for the task of answering historical questions such as those that concern oral antecedents. Especially when belief in the simplicity of oral forms was rejected, little basis remained for speculative reconstructions. Thus the attempt to use the method as a tool for reconstructing early forms has now largely been abandoned.

Following a rather different line, a number of exegetes renewed an interest in forms as normative models. An orientation of this kind had been implicit in the structure of the biblical canon (in which each portion serves as a model for an aspect of life) as well as in a more general religious concern with archetypes, or transtemporal models; Plato had produced for this orientation a philosophical version.

A major advantage in an analysis of biblical structures as model patterns is that it avoids treating the Bible as though each individual item speaks separately. The interrelationship of biblical data was important for early and medieval exegesis, which gave attention to the function of literary genres (prayers, exhortations, laws, narratives, etc.) and to the structure of faith that forms the basis of spiritual and practical interpretations. When, through modern criticism, the details of the Bible were rendered questionable both historically and morally, an approach seeking dynamic wholes—such as structures of a covenant or promise and of expressions of joy—became attractive to those who maintained an attitude of respect toward that literature. Not specific items of history or of law but the patterns of which they are a part are regarded as having a claim on belief or action. Such an outlook is now widespread for biblical interpreters—including persons who believe in verbal inspiration of the Bible but who hold that God made use of different genres (see L. Ryken).

A potential problem with this outlook is that it gives no ground other than authority or tradition for treating biblical forms as models to be followed. Why should precisely these patterns and not some others be normative? An authoritarian answer to that question refers to the mystery of divine revelation, with the implication that there is no reason. An answer relying on tradition is purely relativist ("this is the belief of our community, which need not be that of another") and ends in self-defeating skepticism. Both of these answers implicitly rely on force, whether divine or human; either God or the community is thought to have the power and therefore the right to impose regulations and prescribe beliefs. With these two answers, a problem arises in regard to change. The validity of change must be denied—God's will is eternal or tradition is to stay firm—as long as the models are accepted strictly.

Although Gunkel's reach toward forms took place in the context of a general cultural turn toward a relational perspective, several of the paths taken by twentieth-century form criticism thus have continued previous ways of interpretation, singly or in combination: essentialist, particularist (historical), or archetypal. It is now appropriate to turn to a kind of form criticism that goes more clearly beyond the older orientations, while accepting useful insights that have been reached by work within them.

Relational Form Criticism

Gunkel's simultaneous attention to content, linguistic form, and context and his interest in generality are still important for form criticism. Yet a number of his specific views need to be modified to bring them in line with further insights and with a more adequate philosophical position.

First of all, his already-discussed belief that oral genres are firmly fixed while written forms are variable must be rejected as unfounded. Both oral and written forms are probabilistic structures—neither rigid nor freely variable. The notion of probability, in fact, is an integral part of a relational philosophy; it points to the fact that there is not only a connection but also a partial independence between phenomena if they are to stand in a relation.

Second, it should be recognized that classifications emerge, properly, from an interaction between the text and the interpreter, not from either one alone. The interpreter brings to the literature some interests and a knowledge of other texts and, therefore, certain questions and expectations. It is helpful to be aware of one's prior mindset—not in order to impose it on a text (as easily happens when one is unaware of it!), but to sharpen or enrich a prior understanding. There is, in fact, little advantage in approaching a text ignorantly. Rather, the apprehension is usually deeper if the observer also knows other texts and is familiar with a variety of angles of vision, such as the psychological, sociological, philosophical, and aesthetic.

The classificational distinctions employed can be based on a number of different criteria as they represent the interests of the interpreter. For instance, it is possible to deal with poetry in contrast to other kinds of literature. Or, the focus can be on differences between prophetic and priestly speech, regardless of whether it is poetic or not. An alternative project is to look at all positive expressions (hymns of praise, blessings, prophecies of weal, descriptions of the wise, etc.) in distinction from the negative ones. Divisions made according to these different criteria cut across one another so that they constitute a multidimensional array. Such a system of organization stands in contrast to a hierarchical one, according to which literature is, say, first divided into priestly, prophetic, and other kinds, with each then subdivided into poetic, narrative, and other forms and these, as a next step, are broken down into positive and negative versions, etc. A hierarchical organization (which may reflect a classifier's hierarchical view of society) assumes, unnecessarily, that some distinctions are primary in relation to others. An advantage for a multidimensional view is that it can conveniently handle characterizations that apply only by degrees; for example, a text might be heavily priestly, largely poetic, partially negative, etc.

Since an analysis needs to be related to one's questions, it is appropriate to reflect on what are basic goals in studying a text. An elementary formulation is that the goal is to understand what is expressed. The word "understand," however, has at least two meanings. According to one, it means to recognize someone else's thought. (This is the major aim of a so-called idealist, thought-centered historiography.) For instance, if someone says, "the window is open," the idea conveyed is that the window is set in such a way that air can pass through it. A second meaning of "understand" answers a "why" question. It involves the grasping of relationships, including those of purpose and cause. Thus in this sense of the word, we "understand" someone's saying the above-quoted sentence when we know its purpose (perhaps to get another person to close the window) and its cause (presumably including the natural desire to maintain a moderate temperature). To reach toward this kind of understanding is possible for relational form criticism.

Specifically, such form criticism asks in what ways content, linguistic form, and the human context are related to one another. Are observable correlations accidental, or are there intrinsic connections? Particularism, which denies any intrinsic relations, regards all associations within speech as being due to arbitrary conventions. There is partial truth in this view, for language is indeed to a large extent a matter of convention. Yet ordinary language is not without a reason for its forms; it observes well-established principles for effective coding and is adapted to the human body as well as, to some extent, to the reality spoken about. More important, correlations between content (thought and mood) and life are usually not fortuitous. For instance, in view of common human forms of relationship, it is understandable that grief is expressed at a funeral, either because genuine sorrow is felt at a loss of a loved one or because the mourner wants to pretend attachment and respect.

In order to engage in the different levels of analysis, several steps need to be taken. An elementary one—the only one possible within a particularist view—is descriptive; it gives an account of the patterns of expression current in a given society. This process is useful for furnishing a knowledge of conventions, which is necessary for a first level of "understanding." For example, it is helpful to know that "dear," followed by a name, frequently opens a letter without any necessary indication of affection.

A second step probes further and asks for reasons that account for the patterns of expression that are used. Thus it is possible to recognize that an opening "dear" reflects the important rhetorical principle that speech or writing should begin with the establishment of a bond, as, in fact, most of Paul's letters in the New Testament do. This principle is not merely a matter of convention but a part of communicative pragmatics that can be analyzed in terms of universal or near-universal rules.[4] Amateur psychology and sociology are enough to provide reasons for why it is useful to begin a communication with a friendly word. It is, after all, a matter of common experience that a friendly approach tends to elicit a cordial response and that communication is usually more effective and more pleasurable if the partners involved have a friendly disposition toward each other.

Probing still further, it is possible to develop a theoretical framework for such considerations. Theories of that sort fall into the domains of professional psychology, sociology, and anthropology. A reflective form criticism thus needs to interact with these fields. It can do so by drawing on established theories, but it can also modify these or create new ones so that insights move in both directions. In fact, at the heart of the sciences—including the humanities— lies a constant checking of existing theories and the creation of new ones on the basis of the data being examined. A past barrier to an interaction between biblical and other fields has been a belief that the Bible is special to such an extent that its processes of operation are not shared with those of other human expressions; yet if the Bible can shed no light on human life, it represents only a curiosity.

Gunkel himself did not hold to an isolationist view of the biblical material; on the contrary, he frequently compared it with texts in many parts of the world, including those that are far distant from Israel. He did not deny the peculiarity of major aspects of the Bible, but even specialness can be recognized only through comparison. He was interested in the psychological and sociological dimensions of texts. A similar breadth of perspective characterized Sigmund Mowinckel and other major figures who have dealt with the forms of biblical literature (see the bibliography).

An important concept for Gunkel, indeed, was the connection of a genre with "life." For such an association, it is true, he made the ungrounded assumption that forms of expression originate in concretely describable settings, such as those of a temple ritual or of a legal process; this assumption can no longer be supported. Verbal expressions are, however, closely linked with basic human processes, which include a search for healing (which need not occur at a temple) and an attempt to resolve a conflict (which may not involve an assembled court). It is primarily upon these general human processes that light can be shed through an examination of texts.

We have come to a fundamental assumption of form criticism: a pattern is general in the sense that it is shared or shareable; it thus has a relevance to present existence. This assumption stands in contrast to the fact that if objects are purely particular, they belong only to their own time. The general applicability of the pattern of a text can hold even if this text is the only one that actually exhibits that structure. A form of organization does not need to be actually shared by more than one entity in order to be treated as a pattern; it need only be potentially so (we can thus speak of a clothes pattern, even if no one copies it).

A major interest of historical criticism in postmedieval times has been to emphasize particularity and thus differences and to show, through differences, that the structures of the past, such as those of the Bible, do not need to be taken as a blueprint for one's current way of life—in a deliberate rejection of an earlier view that regarded ideal patterns as unchanging. This antitraditional emphasis was important for the development of "modern" (including capitalist) society. In contrast, a relational approach, going beyond a merely particularist historical one, combines differences with sameness. In applying older texts, it uses the principle of analogy: Two different complexes are analogous if elements within one bear the same relation to one another as corresponding elements do in the other. For instance, a biblical critique of bribes can find a partial analogy in a current provision for legal aid, in that both of them move toward providing equality in the legal process.

An appropriate transformation of a structure, which serves some of its former ends under new conditions, is possible only through an understanding of its rationale. This is a major reason why one should "understand" texts in the second, deeper sense—grasping the nature of relationships. Insight of this sort means that the use of ancient texts need not be simply authoritarian. If one sees their grounds and purposes, one can, rather, find in them stimuli for one's own life and will have a basis for an at least partial acceptance or rejection of them.

Relations to Other Approaches

"Formal analysis," in general, can be defined in line with a typically twentieth-century understanding of form as the study of a system of relationships. Form criticism is a comprehensive version of it. A number of other approaches, which are similarly formal, focus more specifically on one aspect of texts. Structuralism, as normally conceived, deals largely with logical relations between elements of a pattern; poststructuralism has a similar focus but includes special attention to inconsistencies. Social-scientific and reader-response criticisms highlight dynamic relations of texts with either actual or potential contexts. Rhetorical criticism (which varies greatly according to its philosophical orientation) either deals with general persuasive characteristics (when following a classical outlook) or concentrates on style (so, in the particularist tradition). Narrative criticism examines the characteristics of one manner of expression. When different textual relations—including content, style, and role—are integrated and comparison is made between a number of texts so that it is possible to see they are not merely accidental, an observer has an insightful grasp of a pattern, which is the object of form criticism.

Formal analysis stands as one of a trio of approaches to literature, of which the other two are the historical (factual) and the evaluative (expressing one's faith or overall orientation toward life). These three perspectives can be distinguished theoretically. In practice, however, the different considerations can never be treated entirely in isolation from one another; in fact, they influence each other.

To begin with, formal analysis contributes to historical study. For instance, the application of form-critical analysis to a particular task in its own setting is a historical task. Since one's understanding of the meaning of a text and one's assessment of its likely factuality are affected by this, indirect light is shed also on the extraliterary historical matters for which the text serves as evidence. Furthermore, the tracing of the development of a literary form is a historical enterprise.

Conversely, historical study contributes to form criticism. It does so primarily by furnishing large-scale background information concerning the cultural and physical context of literature studied. For instance, a knowledge that Genesis employs the Hebrew language and presupposes locations both west and east of the Jordan River is important for perceiving a meaning in the book. Nevertheless, it should be noted that a grasp of the dynamic structure of the book (its "form") is affected only to a limited extent by its precise circumstances.

The looseness of form criticism in regard to historical details is fortunate, for otherwise the understanding gained by it would be limited to professional scholars, who alone can handle a detailed history. True, the form-critical approach is a demanding one. However, a relevant knowledge of psychology, sociology, anthropology, and the history of religion—all of which are extremely important for form criticism—is often available to those who are not biblical specialists even when less important technical information is not. Since the end of the nineteenth century, in fact, the study of literary patterns has been a favored way of introducing the Bible to the general reader. Furthermore, since little commitment to controversial historical hypotheses is required, form criticism is a procedure in which religious liberals and conservatives can cooperate.

Formal analysis also interacts reciprocally with faith, that is, with one's overall orientation toward life. In fact, form-critical analyses commonly exhibit a deeply emotional tone because of their proximity to basic human issues. As has already been seen, conceptions of the nature of a form are connected with overall (including social and political) commitments. To give another example of this association: A person who believes that humanity is an integral part of nature should not object to a continuity between the humanities and the natural sciences and to a use by form criticism of the behavioral sciences, which share features of both of these fields of knowledge. Finally, the specific patterns to which attention is given will reflect vital concerns.

In a reverse movement, the apprehension of a form contributes to an investigator's sense of existence. Life commitment, it is true, involves an intuitive orientation that goes beyond what can be understood, for all understanding is limited. Yet a recognition of forms enters into a faith that is not blind. Form criticism, by giving insight into relations between phenomena, allows human beings to have reasons for their intellectual and practical decisions, so that these are neither externally imposed nor arbitrarily chosen.

Illustration: Genesis 1 and 2

Even a quick look at Genesis 1 and 2 reveals that these two chapters are narrative in character. In fact, there seem to be two stories here, the second one beginning in the middle of the fourth verse of chapter 2.

The first story deals with how the different parts of the world were "generated" (2:4a), that is, came to be. Its organization involves six creative days and a day of rest for God. The second one describes how relations of human beings with each other (male and female) and with God, animals, and so forth, were established.

In terms of content—which Gunkel regularly listed first among the characteristics of a genre—the narratives are, clearly, origin stories. Origin stories represent a genre that is extremely common in religious traditions. In fact, the notion of origin is one of a small number of basic religious categories. In these two chapters, the origin of much of what lies in one's normal field of vision (animals, celestial objects, etc.) is accounted for. Other parts of the Bible deal with the origin of social organizations (including that of the people of Israel) and, especially in the New Testament, with the basis of salvation, including love (where does love come from?). Sometimes, origin narratives are called "myths"; this is confusing, however, for there is no agreed-upon meaning for that term. It is much clearer to use the term "sacred stories."

When one reflects on the notion of origin, it becomes apparent that this category deals not so much with temporal objects or events as with the question of where they come from, that is, with the relation of such limited realities to what is infinite or ultimate. The transtemporal nature of the concept of origin has long been recognized in philosophy and theology. It is also implicit in the way in which originating events—including the Exodus, a critical part of the origin of Israel, and Jesus' death, viewed as a basis of salvation—are presented again and again, with disregard to temporal distance, in ritual. According to Gen. 2:3, rest after creation is to be repeated in the ritual of the sabbath.

Why are religions concerned with origins? One reason surely is that human beings have a perspective that extends beyond the limit of their own lives (they may be the only beings who know that they are born and will die). Given such a large perspective, human beings must see specific, concrete problems in its light. It is true, individuals are usually engrossed in little problems without asking the larger questions, but values expressed in a culture cannot be maintained, it seems, without providing a frame for them.

Questions of origin are, then, not just idle ones. One important issue they address is the question of what is good and legitimate. (Bronislaw Malinowski has described origin stories as "charters," that is, as authorizations for life.) The biblical creation account makes explicit that the physical world is "good," to be valued and accepted. It authorizes, and even commands, sexual propagation. In later parts of the Bible, the origin of Israel is presented in conjunction with extensive legal and ethical implications stated in the laws on Mount Sinai.

Another question that origin stories seek to answer is how what is good (or what is evil) has been brought about. In social psychology, that is known as the question of "attribution": To whom, or to what, should one attribute the cause of an event? Most religious stories, certainly those of the Bible, give credit to Deity especially for that which is good. Such an acknowledgment has a number of practical implications. In relation to the past, it involves gratitude, which many persons express ritually by giving thanks at mealtime. Gratitude counteracts a vaunting pride and, insofar as it is genuine, leads to a readiness to give care to others who are also objects of divine concern. In relation to the future, a belief that true life comes from God leads to an attitude of receptivity toward divine action or support.

A biblical symbol for divine action is that of speech by God. Although a symbol contains elements of arbitrariness, its meaning is based largely on a correspondence between the symbol and that which is symbolized. Divine speech stands for a process in relation to which one is receptive—as one normally is in relation to another's speech—and which, like all speech, has "personal" (both intellectual and emotional) qualities. To allude to a current idiom, something "speaks to" one. Thus in Genesis 1, God creates by giving a command, "Let there be. . . . " An expected and encouraged human response is to allow oneself and the world to be created. There is not an emphasis here, however, purely on receptivity, for human beings are also asked, as "images of God," to participate in God's rule. Both receptivity and activity, in fact, are extremely important in human life. Research has shown, for instance, that they play a role together in creativity and in a sense of well-being.

There are social advantages (as well as disadvantages, perhaps) in a focus on a divine action and will. By imaginatively adopting the orientation of a reality larger than themselves, human beings move out of a strictly self-centered mode of operation. Human society, in fact, relies for other-oriented ("altruistic") activity not so much on automatic reflexes as on the mental and emotional "de-centering" of individuals (i.e., on their finding a center of perspective outside of themselves). This cultural—partially voluntary—process allows for more flexibility than does a strictly biological one. Its openness supports adaptability and creativity. Of course, it also creates the possibility of deviations from social ideals. The topic of evil as a consequence of disobedience, in fact, comes next in the biblical narrative.

It is clear that the stories have a major symbolic and guiding function in human life. They have this not because they are connected with a specific occasion, such as being customarily or originally recited on the sabbath, but because they express a basic kind of human interaction and experience. That is, a text's external "setting" is not as important for form criticism as is its sociopsychological functioning, which is its logical and effective (more clearly "formal") connection with life.

If origin stories are concerned with the relation of the spatiotemporal world to something more encompassing, it follows that their details should not be understood as representing events within that world. In other words, historical accuracy is not an interest of this sort of literature. A recognition of their looseness in regard to history is not simply a recent Western one but has been reported from so-called "primitive" groups (which are not unsophisticated) and has been widespread in Christian theology since at least the third century, after appearing already in the thought of the first-century Jewish thinker Philo. Within this biblical text a disinterest in sequential detail is shown by the fact that two somewhat contradictory accounts are laid side by side. The editor and early readers of the accounts can hardly have failed to notice an apparent discrepancy in regard to the sequence of the creation of animals, but the divergence apparently was not a problem for them. Similarly, a person giving thanks before a meal is not worried about the exact manner by which God provided the food.

If origin is a somewhat abstract (not simply factual) category, why are creation accounts given in narrated form? A major reason appears to be that we commonly shape our life orientations in the form of stories. Narratives are vivid, picturing acting persons, which we can readily visualize. They contain at least some tension, resulting in a drive toward resolution that maintains interest. This practical literary reason—namely, that the form comes close to human life and thus captures attention—can also have a theoretical significance, for the employment of temporal imagery in an account of intimacy can imply that temporal processes are valued highly. It is necessary, to be sure, to exercise caution here, for literary form and thought do not always strictly cohere. Nonetheless, it appears to be significant for Israel's view of life that the biblical account projects Deity as dynamic, dealing with tensions and with the realization of possibilities. Humanity, which mirrors the divine, is accordingly expected to be active in time.

Most of the observations made so far apply to both Genesis 1 and 2. However, a single type of speech—in this case, that of creation narratives—can vary considerably in the form it takes. One difference between the two accounts is that the narrative style of Gen. 1:1—2:4a is more orderly and stately than that of the subsequent material. The orderly style fits the priestly orientation of the first story, which is reflected in its reference to the sabbath. A major task of priests is the execution and supervision of ritual, one of the characteristics of which is the maintenance and establishment of order (i.e., regularity). Orderliness appears not only in the style but also in the content of the first story; beings are described as classified and as systematically "ruled" (with the sun and the moon over day and night and humanity over animals).

The story beginning in Gen. 2:4b places, in comparison, more emphasis on exploration and surprise. It, too, arrives at a duality (and, perhaps, equality) of the sexes, but it does so as a result of a movement in which God appears genuinely in doubt about how to proceed and fails in an experiment. The actions of human beings in the chapter that follows lead to difficulty, which in turn provides a challenge for God. Certainly, human life, like all of existence, requires both order and disorder. Thus only a combination of both of these accounts provides a realistic image.

We have examined the contents, stylistic features, and sociopsychological roles of these texts in their relation to one another. We have dealt with generality (two creation stories in Genesis and other origin stories in the Bible and elsewhere) to shed light on the particular texts and, more importantly, to indicate that the questions addressed by them, as well as some of their answers, have a wide-ranging relevance. Such a process constitutes form criticism.[5]

Limitations

The analysis of Genesis 1 and 2 just presented makes virtually no contribution to the dating of the chapters or to answering other historical questions. On the contrary, its value for these issues may lie in raising the reader's level of caution in regard to them. For instance, dating the texts may be difficult precisely because they deal with important issues that must have been discussed many times in Israel's history.

Another limitation of this analysis is that it does not remove the need to make a decision about how one sees one's own origin—whether or to whom one is grateful and to what reality, if any, one owes allegiance. The investigation, it is true, can aid a person in making such a commitment in a more reflective manner than would otherwise be possible. It can draw attention to a significant dimension of existence—in this case, to that aspect of life in which a person is "spoken to," such as by the pain or joy of another or the presence of nature or sheer mystery. It cannot, however, do this actual speaking.

Notes

1. This includes much of nineteenth-century "liberalism" and the program of the current "Libertarian" party in the United States.
2. That includes positions emphasizing royal authority, as advocated by Jean Bodin

(sixteenth century) and Thomas Hobbes (seventeenth century), as well as Leninism and fascism.

3. Examples are "populism" and twentieth-century "liberalism" in the United States, European "social democracy," and most current "liberation" movements.

4. The social philosopher Jürgen Habermas treats such rules as central for social action and human morality. The present writer has indicated elsewhere that patterns of Chinese letter writing agree in major ways with those of the Bible. See M. Buss, "Principles for Morphological Criticism: With Special Reference to Letter Form," in *Orientation by Disorientation: Studies in Literary Criticism and Biblical Literary Criticism Presented in Honor of William A. Beardslee,* ed. R. A. Spencer (Pittsburgh: Pickwick, 1980), pp. 84–85.

5. It is true that within form-critical procedure there are possible variations that have not been chosen in this analysis. If the discussion had followed an essentialist line, it would have asked such questions as whether the stories are myths or not, assuming that there are clear-cut categories in existence. If it had adopted particularism, it would have emphasized external circumstances and would have treated all forms strictly as conventions, with the implication that the texts have no relevance for the present. (It is possible, of course, that God may have the same word for persons in the present as for the ancient Israelites, but such a congruence would be treated as a matter of accident.) If the analysis had thought of the stories as eternally normative archetypes, it would not have left the final decision about existence to the reader or hearer (see the section on limitations) and might not have made an effort to explain the role of the patterns, as is done now in order to aid such a decision. These alternative ways of proceeding can all be called "form-critical," but they do not follow the relational outlook here assumed, which accepts both commonality and a degree of nonrational divergence.

For Further Reading

Aune, David E. *The New Testament in Its Literary Environment.* Philadelphia: Westminster, 1987. A comprehensive view of genres, treated as conventions, with detailed bibliographies.

Brueggemann, Walter. *The Creative Word.* Philadelphia: Fortress, 1982. A form-critical treatment of the canon as a combination of divergent and perhaps complementary structures.

Coats, George W. *Genesis.* Grand Rapids: Eerdmans, 1983. A volume in the series The Forms of the Old Testament Literature, both more essentialist and more particularist in conception than the present essay but very helpful for detailed study.

Dibelius, Martin. *From Tradition to Gospel.* New York: Scribners, 1965. A classic work (originally published in German in 1919) seeking to recognize preliterary forms of the Gospels.

Fontaine, Carole R. *Traditional Sayings in the Old Testament.* Sheffield: Almond, 1982. In many ways a model study, strong in regard to the function and logical structure of quoted proverbs.

Gunkel, Hermann. *What Remains of the Old Testament and Other Essays.* London: Allen & Unwin, 1928. A collection of essays exhibiting Gunkel's involvement in literary theory and in the history of religion.

Hayes, John, ed. *Old Testament Form Criticism.* San Antonio: Trinity University, 1974. A comprehensive overview; the contribution by M. Buss is to appear enlarged and revised in a volume that will provide supporting evidence for the present essay.

Ryken, Leland. *How to Read the Bible as Literature.* Grand Rapids: Academic Books, 1984. An insightful survey, analyzing literary structures as they reveal and interpret human experience, with helpful bibliographies.

Theissen, Gerd. *The Miracle Stories of Early Christian Tradition.* Philadelphia: Fortress, 1983. A sociological and psychological analysis combining historical with transhistorical perspectives.

Via, Dan O., Jr. *The Parables: Their Literary and Existential Dimension.* Philadelphia: Fortress, 1967. An examination of literary patterns, largely according to content, in relation to experiential structures.

Westermann, Claus. *Praise and Lament in the Psalms.* Atlanta: John Knox, 1981. An analysis of patterns of expression, with reference to patterns of existence in faith.

5
REDACTION
CRITICISM

Gail Paterson Corrington

The Method and Its History

REDACTION criticism, a translation of the German *Redaktionsgeschichte* (history of redaction), is a rather cumbersome and unlovely technical term for what is arguably the most significant advance in Gospel scholarship of this century. Redaction criticism is a method of analysis that is primarily applied to the Synoptic Gospels. It fully acknowledges that the Gospel writers, albeit inheritors both of common and specific traditions, are also creative theologians and not mere transcribers or collectors. New Testament scholar David Barr has forcefully acknowledged the impact of this method of interpretation on biblical scholars: "The excitement many of us felt on our first exposure to redaction criticism is due to the ability of this method to take seriously the differences between the gospels, to explain the differences without explaining them away."[1]

The appeal and acceptance of the redaction-critical method has been such that few introductions to the New Testament fail to include a description of it, however cursory, in their surveys of modern biblical criticism. And their analysis of the Gospels in virtually every case relies upon the perspective of redaction criticism. In fact, other fields of New Testament studies that attempt to interpret the New Testament writers as theologians depend upon the basic insight offered by redaction criticism—that each evangelist is a uniquely creative theologian, as well as an inheritor of tradition. In the United States in particular, this has been true for methods of literary criticism. These literary-critical approaches (see Part 3 of this book), especially the more recent ones, include structuralist and post-structural analysis, rhetorical criticism, narrative criticism, and reader-response criticism. The latter two have tended to preoccupy American biblical scholars using the literary-critical approach.[2] As Norman Perrin, the foremost American exponent and practitioner of the redaction-critical method, has put it:

Once it was recognized that the final author was in fact an *author* and not merely a transmitter of tradition, it became natural and inevitable to inquire into his purpose and theology, not only into his redaction of previously existing tradition. In this connection redaction criticism shades over into general literary criticism, especially in redaction critical work carried on in America, where the influence of general literary criticism is strong on New Testament scholars.[3]

But even when it began to be utilized in German scholarship following World War I, redaction criticism was not regarded as an exclusive method, nor did it even have a name. It both depended upon and intersected with the insights of form and source criticism and belonged under the general category of the historical-critical method, which it advanced. As Perrin has it, the method was born out of research on the so-called "Marcan hypothesis."[4] David F. Strauss was the pioneer of "historical Jesus" research (*The Life of Jesus Critically Examined*, German, 1835–1836). His followers reasoned that Mark, which they noted was the briefest and most unadorned of the Gospels since it lacked what they termed "mythical elements," was the earliest Gospel and therefore the most "historical." Hermann Gunkel's work on form criticism as applied to the Hebrew Bible had taught that in the oral tradition from which the written works were assembled, units of that oral tradition (pericopes) could be isolated and analyzed, with a view to discovering the "life-setting" (*Sitz im Leben*) of the communities in which they arose.

Although it would be several years before these insights could be combined with those of redaction criticism by Martin Dibelius (*From Tradition to Gospel*, English translation [ET] 1935) and Rudolf Bultmann (*History of the Synoptic Tradition*, ET 1963), they were used, along with close attention to the literary structure of Mark, by Wilhelm Wrede in 1901 to produce his epochal work on Mark's theology, *The Messianic Secret in the Gospels* (*Die Messiahgeheimnis in den Evangelien*, ET 1971). Based on his close and careful analysis of Mark and a comparison with parallels in Matthew and Luke, Wrede noted in Mark especially the paradox of the simultaneous exposure and deliberate concealment by Jesus of his messianic nature, especially in connection with his performance of miracles (e.g., Mark 1:43–45). Reasoning from numerous examples, Wrede concluded, in contradiction to previous scholars, that while Mark may have been the earliest Gospel, it was no more historically accurate than the others, nor did it have fewer "mythical" elements. Indeed, the recurrent theme of the "messianic secret," uniquely emphasized by Mark, pointed to the existence of the evangelist's own "dogma."[5]

This idea of Mark as a theologian was later developed and delineated by Willi Marxsen in the post–World War II era in his redaction-critical study *Mark the Evangelist* (*Das Evangelist Markus*, 1956; ET 1969). It is probably thus fitting that Marxsen should have been the first New Testament scholar to use the technical term *"Redaktionsgeschichte"* (redaction or editorial history) to describe the method he and others were using.[6] Following the work of Dibelius and Bultmann, who combined form-critical with redaction-critical perspectives,[7] three significant treatments of the Synoptic evangelists appeared in postwar Germany: the previously mentioned work by Marxsen on Mark; Günther Bornkamm's study of Matthew, *Tradition and Interpretation in Matthew* (with G. Barth and H. J. Held, ET 1963); and Hans Conzelmann's influential study of Luke-Acts, *The Theology of St. Luke* (ET 1954).

Much of the work in redaction criticism, like that in form criticism on which it depends, was pioneered in Germany. But English-speaking redaction critics, though initially few in number, have also developed the discipline, often in ways significantly different from those of the German scholars. Both Perrin and Barr credit R. H. Lightfoot's Bampton Lectures of 1934 with "anticipating" the later work of Marxsen, Conzelmann, and Bornkamm; indeed, Perrin calls Lightfoot "the first redaction critic," although Marxsen coined the term.[8] In the United States, Norman Perrin has been the foremost redaction critic, using the insights of the method to write his own introduction to the New Testament (*The New Testament: An Introduction*, 1974). However, as has been previously noted, American scholarship has tended to focus upon various literary-critical methods, either in addition to, as a result of, or in reaction against the redaction-critical method. Nevertheless, according to Barr, a practitioner of narrative criticism, these same interpretive techniques are largely reliant upon the insights of redaction criticism and its "attempt to understand the gospels as unified stories."[9]

Distinctiveness and Current Applications of the Method

The insights into evangelistic creativity offered by the redaction-critical perspective also lend themselves readily to other, more recent methods of biblical criticism, including sociological and sociohistorical criticism. Although its application has mainly been to the Synoptic Gospels, the redaction-critical method has also been fruitfully applied to such noncanonical documents as the Gospel of Peter (John Dominic Crossan, *The Cross That Spoke*, 1988). Indeed, redaction criticism may be particularly valuable in connection with such noncanonical works. For they help to shed light not only on the various versions of Jesus' teaching and traditions about Jesus that were circulating in early Christianity, but also on the selection process involved in, and the interests that lay behind, the shaping of the present canon. Here the insights of redaction criticism intersect with those of canonical criticism. Indeed, based upon his use of form, source, redaction, and literary criticism, John Dominic Crossan has contended that the noncanonical Gospel of Peter may actually be the *earliest* of the Gospel passion narratives.[10] Such a contention revolutionizes the study of the canonical Gospels and brings us back almost to the point at which redaction criticism began: the question of which traditions are closest to the "historical Jesus," and in what ways those traditions have been altered. The idea of layers of tradition and contributions made to that tradition by authorial and community interests is also applicable to studies of the apocryphal Acts, using the canonical Acts as a means of comparison (e.g., Dennis R. MacDonald, *The Gospel and the Apostle,* 1982). Redaction-critical work on the book of Acts itself has been done by Conzelmann (*The Book of Acts,* ET 1963) and Ernst Haenchen (*Acts,* ET 1971). In fact, Luke-Acts has been the focus of many recent redaction-critical studies, including those by J. C. O'Neill (*The Theology of Acts,* 1961) and Leander Keck and J. Louis Martyn (*Studies in Luke/Acts,* 1966).

Finally, the redaction-critical method has either been readily presupposed as foundational (and therefore dismissed) or regarded as superseded and ultimately rejected by approaches that spurn the "intentional fallacy" (the idea that one can discover from the text itself the intention of its "author").[11] Nevertheless, redaction-critical studies continue to abound. The existence of the Redaction Criticism and the Two-Gospel Hypothesis Group as a program unit of the Society of Biblical Literature is one indication of the method's continuing viability for biblical studies, particularly of the Gospels. Another important contribution of the method to recent scholarship has been analysis of the "authenticity" of certain sayings of Jesus, a task first undertaken in the United States by Perrin, *Rediscovering the Teachings of Jesus* (1976). This study is in some sense a response to a redaction-critical introduction to the New Testament by J. Rohde, *Rediscovering the Teachings of the Evangelists* (ET 1969). Perrin's seminal work, which presents three criteria for isolating "authentic" Jesus material in the sayings (dissimilarity, coherence, multiple attestation), has had a profound influence on Gospel scholarship in the United States, including the work of the Jesus Seminar, a two hundred–member group of biblical scholars who have worked for six years to determine the relative authenticity of sayings attributed to Jesus in the canonical Gospels.

Other work to which redaction criticism has contributed includes studies of early Christian "titles" for Jesus and studies of early Christologies, such as H. E. Todt's *The Son of Man in the Synoptic Tradition* (ET 1965) and R. H. Fuller, *The Foundations of New Testament Christology* (1965). Redaction criticism has also been interwoven with feminist criticism by Elisabeth Schüssler Fiorenza in her feminist reconstruction of Christian origins, *In Memory of Her* (1983). Such undertakings are further evidence of the value of redaction criticism not merely in providing yet another chapter in historical Jesus research but also in investigating the scope and variety of early Christian beliefs about Jesus.[12]

Application of the Method in Practice: Luke 4:16–30
(Jesus' Sermon at Nazareth)

The best way to demonstrate the validity and richness of the redaction-critical approach to the study of the Gospels is to show it in an actual analysis of a pericope. When I was taught exegesis, our German-educated professors used a highly formulaic way of interpreting a selected passage. First, they isolated the passage, determining its logical beginning (introduction) and end. Next, they looked it up in Bultmann's *History of the Synoptic Tradition*, in order to classify its form and *Sitz im Leben* (life-setting). They then translated it from the original language (or compared English translations), noting certain "lead" or "key" words. They taught us to look these up in the *Theological Dictionary of the New Testament* (*TDNT*), aware that such "word studies" have limited value for the understanding of concepts. They then outlined the passage, seeing where it "fit" into the overall outline of the Gospel. (For this "outline," I have found Perrin's *The New Testament: An Introduction,* 1974, as helpful today as in the past.) Next, they compared the pericope with its versions in other Gospels, using Bruce Throckmorton's *Gospel Parallels* (1967).[13] As a final step, our professors taught us to compare evidence from at least three commentaries on the passage, especially with regard to "difficult" or puzzling language. This was necessary before we could come to any conclusions concerning what the evangelist inherited, how the evangelist transformed the tradition according to an individual theological purpose, and how that purpose differed from those of other early Christian "authors." This approach, while rather mechanical, essentially replicates the steps undertaken by redaction critics in reaching new insights on the theological perspectives of early Christian communities, although such a process may never contribute to the achievement of Perrin's overly optimistic hope for the writing of a complete "theological history" of early Christianity.[14]

Let us use as an example of the method the passage in Luke's Gospel where Jesus preaches his first sermon at Nazareth: Luke 4:16–30.* According to Perrin, this passage is the one in which the "purpose" of Jesus' ministry is "set out" by Luke.[15] It serves as an illustration of the theological concerns of Luke, who, in Perrin's opinion, usually remains "reasonably true, in our sense of the word, to his sources," unless he has "theological reasons," in which case he alters his received tradition considerably.[16] This passage should provide an excellent example of how analysis of a redactor/author's use of sources helps to reveal theological interests.

Luke 4:16–30 falls within the first half of the Gospel (i.e., prior to the decision to go up to Jerusalem in 9:51), at the beginning of Jesus' ministry.

---

*Scripture translations in this chapter are the author's own.

The introduction to the Gospel, 1:1–4, indicates Luke's consciousness of himself as a deliberate narrator. The Gospel reflects a sense of definite arrangement of "the things that have been accomplished among us" and has an identified audience, Theophilus, whose Greek name suggests that he is a representative of the Gentiles or "God-fearers," who probably were Luke's primary audience.[17] This introduction is followed by 1:5–4:13, a section that comprises the "pre-history" of Jesus' ministry, by anticipating even the birth of Jesus with that of the last of the prophets, John the Baptist, in whom the spirit of prophecy is revived (1:17). The activity of the Spirit is also evident in Jesus' birth (1:35) and the prophecies of Zechariah (1:68–79), Simeon (2:29–32), and Anna (2:36–38). The centerpiece of this section of spirit-filled activity, however, is the Song of Mary (1:46–55). It is linked in terms of language and theme to Hannah's song of rejoicing over the conception of Samuel (1 Sam. 2:1–10), and, by Luke's use of the term "female slave," to the theme of the outpouring of the spirit on "all flesh" prophesied by Joel. This prophecy is quoted by Peter at Pentecost in Acts 2:18: "And I will pour out my spirit in those days even upon your male and female slaves." Most important, however, the Song of Mary sets up the theme echoed throughout the Gospel of Luke: the reversals of status that occur through the hand of God (1:51–55). This "good news to the poor" is the theme also of Jesus' first sermon (4:18) and of his Sermon on the Plain, Luke's version of Matthew's Sermon on the Mount, which departs from the Q tradition in having not only blessings upon the poor but also woes upon the rich (Luke 6:20–49).[18] This preliminary section of Luke ends, after Jesus' receipt of the spirit in visible form at baptism (3:21–22) and the incarceration of John (3:20), with the departure of the devil (4:13) after the Temptation, until an "opportune time," which occurs with his entry into Judas in 22:3. The stage is thus set for the spirit-inaugurated ministry of Jesus to begin, and it is fitting that Jesus begins his first sermon with a reading from Isaiah about the "spirit of the Lord" resting upon him (Isa. 61:1–2).

Proceeding to the structure of the passage itself, we shall compare Matthew's and Mark's versions to that of Luke in order to reveal his unique concerns. Speaking form-critically, the Lucan passage is a narrative that serves as framework for two units defined as "aphorisms" by Crossan: "The Prophet's Own Country" (4:24), which appears in the Synoptic tradition, and "Physician, Heal Yourself" (4:23).[19] Also within the framework of the narrative is a "biographical apophthegm" on Jesus' family (4:22), adapted from Mark,[20] and a logion or "dominical saying" (defined by Bultmann as a pronouncement of Jesus as "lord of the church") on Jews and Gentiles (4:25–27), which is unique to Luke.[21] Also traditional is the introduction to the passage (4:16), which has parallels in Matt. 13:53–54a and Mark 6:1–2a, indicating that Luke probably derived it from Mark, whose general framework he follows. Yet, as we shall see, comparisons with similar passages in Mark 6:1–6 and Matt.

13:53–58 will show how Luke freely alters traditional material to suit his purposes. To summarize, the material inherited by Luke consists of v. 16, the introduction; v. 22 (a Lucan adaptation of Mark 6:2b–3); and vv. 23–24 (the two aphorisms on "the Physician" and "the Prophet"), combined only by Luke. Verses 17–21, the reading and interpretation of Isaiah, are unique to Luke, as are vv. 25–27, Jesus' teaching on Elijah and Elisha's ministry, and vv. 28–30, the violent reaction of the audience.

Let us begin with v. 16: "And he came to Nazareth, where he had been raised, and entered the synagogue according to his custom, on the day of the Sabbath, and he got up to read." Judging from the parallels in Mark 6:1–2a and Matt. 13:53–54a, Luke received from Mark the tradition of Jesus' going to the synagogue in his native country (Mark; Matthew) and on the sabbath. Luke adds "as was his custom," a characteristic Lucan emphasis of Jesus' fulfillment of Jewish custom, which he already has established in the birth narratives (2:21, 22–24, 27, 41–42). David Barr points out the further linkage to Jewish custom by Jesus' being "called up" to read from the scroll of the prophet.[22] The reading from the Isaiah scroll (Isa. 61:1–2; 58:6) and its subsequent interpretation (Luke 4:18–21), however, emphasize characteristically Lucan themes: Jesus is the Messiah, who is anointed (*echrisen*, v. 18) to "preach good news to the poor" and to announce the "acceptable (*dekton*) year of the Lord," which is in Luke's understanding the coming of the Kingdom of God in which reversals of the present situation will occur (cf. 1:46–55; 6:20–49).[23]

The reaction to this announcement of Jesus' understanding of his call—which, like that of Luke, is to announce the good news to the poor and the oppressed[24]—is astonishment. This astonishment echoes the reaction of the crowd in the synagogue in Mark 6:2b–3 and Matt. 13:54b–56, but in Luke it is a reaction to a *specific* pronouncement. It prepares the reader for the crowd's further reaction, extreme anger at Jesus' delineation of the purpose of God as including the excluded—the Gentiles particularly—whom God may even *prefer* (vv. 25–27). When the people of Nazareth hear Jesus' interpretation, they try to "locate" him: "Is this not the son of Joseph?" (v. 22). Whereas in the Marcan and Matthean versions Jesus' entire family is included in the question, Luke mentions only Joseph, as if to point out the irony of their question, having already in the Temple episode (2:49) established the fact that Jesus' true "father" is God. Further, the crowd at this point in Mark and Matthew "takes offense" at Jesus for presuming to teach them, providing the occasion for the saying on "the Prophet in his own country." Luke postpones their "taking offense" and Jesus' quotation of the saying on the Prophet in order to set up an opposition between Jesus' "own" and those "outside," an opposition that in Luke's scheme provokes the wrath of the audience because it inverts their expectations (vv. 28–30).

In Luke's version, the saying "Physician, heal yourself" (v. 23), one with no parallels in the Synoptic tradition, is the preface to an anticipated request: "The things which we have heard were done in Capernaum, do even here in your own native country." This "request" for miracles, not contained in Mark or Matthew, is perhaps Luke's explanation of Jesus' unwillingness to perform miracles, rather than his inability to do them because of the lack of faith of the people, as in Mark 6:4 and Matt. 13:57. The implied request is also the occasion for Jesus' saying in Luke about the Prophet's own country (v. 24): "Truly I tell you that no prophet is acceptable (*dektos*) in his own country." The fact that Luke alters the Marcan version of the saying that is followed by Matthew ("A prophet is without honor [*atimos*] in his own country") is perhaps intended as a play on words with the proclamation of "the acceptable (*dekton*) year of the Lord" (v. 19). Through this word play, Luke implies that neither the Prophet/Messiah nor his message is "acceptable."[25]

At this point in the Marcan and Matthean versions of the narrative, the audience has "taken offense" (*eskandalisen*) at Jesus because of what they perceive as his presumption, and he is unable, because of their lack of faith in him, to do any "mighty work" (Mark 6:56; Matt. 13:58). The lack of faith of the crowd is offered by Mark and Matthew as an occasion for the saying on the Prophet. Luke's version does not end at this point, nor with this saying. For Luke, the reaction of the crowd is not a mere (unspecified) "taking offense," nor is Jesus' reaction an inability to do miracles. The "offense" in Luke is deeper. In vv. 25–27, which follow thematically the saying on the Prophet, Jesus mentions two of the mightiest prophets in Israelite history—Elijah (whose miracle of resurrection, alluded to by the mention of the Sidonian widow, is replicated by Jesus' raising of the widow's son at Nain, Luke 7:11–17) and Elisha. Luke's choice of words here indicates not only that the prophets had dealings with non-Israelites (Elijah with a widow from Sidon, Elisha with the Syrian Naaman) and that the prophet's ministry is to the excluded and outcast (a widow, a leper) but also that God's *intention* is to send prophets to such persons. In this case, the excluded are pointedly Gentiles. The use of the passive voice indicates that these prophets, like Jesus, are the agents of God to the outcast: Elijah is "sent out"; Naaman "is cleansed."

The audience's reaction to this story, which Bultmann believes is an "independent" piece in the tradition, itself a "prophetic saying,"[26] appears to be out of proportion to the saying. But in the context of Luke's purpose, it is entirely appropriate. Not only is offense taken, but great offense indeed: All are "filled with anger," and they intend to throw Jesus off the brow of the hill at Nazareth (vv. 28–30). The startling reaction of the crowd is perhaps intended by Luke to make his readers question why the crowd was so angry with Jesus that they wanted to kill him. In Bultmann's view, the saying in vv. 25–27 "may well be a secondary community construction, introduced into the anti-Jewish polemic of the Gentile Christian Church."[27] The reaction of the crowd may also thus belong to the same construction, indicating Luke's community's understanding that Jesus was sent to the Gentiles (themselves) from the beginning, and not just after his rejection by Israel as in Matthew and Mark, where the rejection occurred *because* of his sending. Without adopting Bultmann's certainty as to the location of Luke within purely Gentile Christianity, we might point out that unlike Mark and Matthew, Luke has no saying of Jesus' in reply to the Gentile woman's importunity on taking the "children's" (Israel's) bread and throwing it to the "dogs" (Gentiles) (cf. Mark 7:24–30; Matt. 15:21–28). This is prefaced in Matthew with Jesus' saying that his mission is "only to the lost sheep of the house of Israel" (Matt. 15:24). Thus we see that even if Luke does not specifically reflect an anti-Jewish polemic in vv. 25–27, he does show not only that God had always intended the inclusion of the excluded but also that his activity is specifically directed to them.

What has our redaction-critical analysis of this particular passage shown us about the activity of Luke as a theologian? In the first place, Luke's setting of the passage as a "programmatic statement" of the purpose of Jesus' ministry shows us what Luke believed that ministry to be. Jesus' messiahship ("anointing," 4:18) through the "spirit of the Lord" is a prophetic mission of proclamation of God's "acceptable year," which includes "good news to the poor," "release to the captives," and "restoration of sight to the blind" (4:18). It includes more than just pronouncement, however: The anointed one is also "to send forth in liberty those who have been oppressed" (v. 18). Luke's Jesus thus understands his ministry as a prophetic call to inaugurate God's "acceptable year" by including those who have been excluded. For Luke, the Kingdom of God is located in this activity: It is "in the midst of you" (17:23). God's intention, fulfilled by Jesus and carried on by the disciples, is toward those for whom it is not expected, including the Gentiles. Mere inclusion of the Gentiles, moreover, is not the point: The Messiah is *sent* to the Gentiles *because* they belong to the "excluded." By this means Luke also explains the "problem" of Israel's rejection of Jesus as the Messiah by putting it in the framework of the unexpected, radical reversals that are the hallmark of God's activity: The rejection is part of God's plan and even hastens the inauguration of the Kingdom of God.

Limitations and Drawbacks of the Method

The foregoing redaction-critical analysis of a specific passage in Luke has offered a method for gaining insights into the unique theological contributions of Luke to early Christianity. This is not to say that the method does not have significant drawbacks, which current thinking in biblical scholarship recognizes. The primary drawback is that crediting the evangelists with individual perspectives is an example of what some literary critics, who maintain that an author's intentions cannot be known or are irrelevant, call the "intentional fallacy." That is to say that, when seeing the evangelist as an "author," the critic thereby assumes that the "author" is speaking from a definite "viewpoint," one that can be determined with some degree of accuracy from evidence in the text and that governs the text's meaning at later stages. Most redaction critics try to distinguish characteristic language and recurrent themes or "leading ideas" (*Leitmotifs*) and isolate certain passages in the Gospels themselves as the "key" to the author's "life-setting" and hence intention. Marxsen, for example, understands the "Little Apocalypse" of Mark 13 as the "key" to Mark's situation; indeed, it is in connection with this passage that Marxsen speaks of Mark's "intent."[28] Marxsen's analysis of Mark, Conzelmann's study of Luke-Acts, and Bornkamm's treatment of Matthew, three landmark redaction-critical studies of twentieth-century biblical scholarship, have tended to dominate subsequent views of the author's "intention." This intentional approach, unless used with extreme caution, may result in an "interested" or biased interpretation, which ignores its own presuppositions and thus takes the path of circular argumentation. The technique may therefore be incompatible with other modern forms of biblical criticism, such as poststructuralist (deconstructive) criticism, methods that do not assume one can know the "intention" or "purposes" of an author, or that it is central to the interpretation of the text.

Another drawback to redaction criticism is that it appears applicable only to the New Testament (but see Chapter 3, on tradition history), and until quite recently it has been applied only to the Synoptic Gospels. This limitation is understandable, since redaction criticism developed out of work on the "Synoptic problem" and because the Synoptic Gospels are associated with the name of an "author" and may be readily compared with one another form-critically. Thus layers of tradition, interpretation, and the redactor's (or author's) own contributions are most easily recognizable here. The method is less readily applied, therefore, when it is more difficult either to discern layers of tradition or to compare the author's work with that of another inheritor of the same tradition. Nevertheless, redaction criticism has been applied to the Gospel of John (J. Louis Martyn, *History and Theology in the Fourth Gospel,* 1968), often in combination with source criticism (Raymond Brown, *The Gospel According to John,* 1966; Robert Fortna, *The Gospel of Signs,* 1970). Nonetheless, although redaction criticism throws into high relief the idea of individual "authors," paradoxically it does not work as well with one of the known and most prolific authors of the New Testament, Paul. This may be because Paul, while at times giving a nod to the "things I received" (cf. 1 Cor. 15:3–8), was for the most part consciously battling any visible reliance upon "tradition," especially that coming from Jerusalem (cf. Gal. 1:14—2:11). Although it is conceivable that studies of Paul as a redactor of inherited traditions could be undertaken, a more fruitful approach might consider Paul's followers (the "authors" of the Deutero-Pauline and Pastoral epistles) as redactors of the tradition that *they* received from Paul and handed on to their own communities, with their own necessary alterations.

Despite its drawbacks, the redaction-critical method, as a part of the historical-critical paradigm, attempts not to straitjacket interpretation but to discern both layers of tradition in the Gospels and the distinct contributions of the evangelists as theologians within early Christian communities.

Notes

1. David Barr, *New Testament Story* (Belmont, Calif.: Wadsworth, 1987), p. 144.

2. Stephen D. Moore, *Literary Criticism and the Gospels: The Theoretical Challenge* (New Haven, Conn.: Yale University Press, 1989), pp. xx–xxi.

3. Norman R. Perrin and Dennis Duling, *The New Testament: An Introduction,* 2nd ed. (New York: Harcourt Brace Jovanovich, 1982), p. 236.

4. Perrin, *What Is Redaction Criticism?* Guides to Biblical Scholarship, New Testament Series (Philadelphia: Fortress, 1969), p. 3.

5. Wilhelm Wrede, *Das Messiahgeheimnis in den Evangelien* (Göttingen: Vandenhoeck & Ruprecht, 1901), p. 131; cited in Perrin, *What Is Redaction Criticism?* p. 3.

6. Perrin, *What Is Redaction Criticism?* p. 1.

7. Dibelius, however, referred to redaction criticism as "composition history," or "composition criticism" (*Kompositionsgeschichte*); cf. Perrin, *What Is Redaction Criticism?* p. 1.

8. Barr, *New Testament Story,* p. 144; Perrin, *What Is Redaction Criticism?* pp. 22–23.

9. Barr, *New Testament Story,* p. 145.

10. John Dominic Crossan, *The Cross That Spoke* (San Francisco: Harper & Row, 1988), pp. 21ff.

11. The "intentional fallacy" was defined as a fallacy in literary and aesthetic criticism by W. K. Wimsatt, Jr., and Monroe C. Beardsley in an article entitled "The Intentional Fallacy," *Sewanee Review* 54 (1946):468–88.

12. Cf. Helmut Koester, "The Structure and Criteria of Early Christian Beliefs," in *Trajectories in Early Christianity,* ed. James M. Robinson and Helmut Koester (Philadelphia: Fortress, 1972), pp. 205–31.

13. A newer version, one that is easier to use and that incorporates Gnostic, apocryphal, and patristic parallels, is Robert Funk's two-volume *New Gospel Parallels* (Philadelphia: Fortress, 1985). Other insights are offered by John Dominic Crossan's *Sayings Parallels* (1986) and John S. Kloppenborg's *Q Parallels* (Sonoma, Calif.: Polebridge, 1988).

14. Perrin, *What Is Redaction Criticism?* p. 39.

15. Ibid., p. 63.

16. Ibid., p. 28.

17. Cf. Barr, *New Testament Story*, pp. 207–8, for possible interpretations of the introduction and its audience.

18. "Q" is an abbreviation for the German word *Quelle* and is used by New Testament scholars to designate their reconstruction of a source document represented by the material common to Matthew and Luke but lacking in Mark.

19. This appears in the Thomas tradition (Gospel of Thomas 31; Papyrus Oxyrhyncus 1 31) and in Genesis Rabbah 15c, but not in Mark or Q, the two sources common to Matthew and Luke.

20. Rudolf Bultmann, *History of the Synoptic Tradition*, trans. John Marsh (New York: Harper & Row, 1963), p. 31.

21. Ibid., pp. 116, 127.

22. Barr, *New Testament Story*, pp. 212, 215.

23. Cf. Elisabeth Schüssler Fiorenza, *In Memory of Her* (New York: Crossroad, 1983), for Luke's theme of reversal.

24. Perrin, *Rediscovering the Teaching of Jesus* (New York: Harper & Row, 1967), p. 63.

25. Cf. Hans Conzelmann, *The Theology of St. Luke*, trans. Geoffrey Buswell (New York: Harper, 1961), pp. 36–37, for a different perspective on Jesus' nonperformance of miracles in this passage.

26. Bultmann, *History of the Synoptic Tradition*, p. 116.

27. Ibid., pp. 116, 127.

28. Willi Marxsen, *Mark the Evangelist*, trans. James Boyce et al. (Nashville: Abingdon, 1969), p. 167.

For Further Reading

Introductions and Overviews

Bultmann, Rudolf. *History of the Synoptic Tradition.* Trans. John Marsh. New York: Harper & Row, 1963.

Dibelius, Martin. *From Tradition to Gospel.* Trans. B. L. Woolf. New York: Scribner's, 1935.

Lightfoot, R. H. *History and Interpretation in the Gospels.* Bampton Lectures, 1934. New York: Harper & Row, 1935.

Perrin, Norman. *What Is Redaction Criticism?* Guides to Biblical Scholarship, New Testament Series. Philadelphia: Fortress, 1969.

Studies of Specific New Testament Books

Bornkamm, Gunther, Barth, G., and Held, H. J. *Tradition and Interpretation in Matthew.* Trans. Percy Scott. Philadelphia: Westminster, 1963.

Conzelmann, Hans. *The Theology of St. Luke.* Trans. Geoffrey Buswell. New York: Harper & Row, 1960.

Martyn, J. Louis. *History and Theology in the Fourth Gospel.* New York: Harper & Row, 1968.

Marxsen, Willi. *Mark the Evangelist: Studies on the Redaction History of the Gospel.* Trans. James Boyce et al. Nashville: Abingdon, 1969.

O'Neill, J. C. *The Theology of Acts in Its Historical Setting.* London: SPCK, 1961.

PART TWO
EXPANDING THE TRADITION

6

SOCIAL-SCIENTIFIC
CRITICISM

Dale B. Martin

No title given to this chapter will please every scholar whose work is discussed within it. Some scholars are content to define themselves as social historians, seeing their own work as a continuation of traditional historical criticism of the Bible except that they explore social aspects of biblical issues that have traditionally been analyzed from a theological point of view. Other scholars explicitly call their work "social-scientific," indicating that they self-consciously appropriate concepts and models from sociology and anthropology and attempt to explain ancient Israelite and early Christian developments by use of those models. Still others resist the labels of "sociologist" or "social historian" entirely and prefer to characterize their work as "cultural anthropology" or "ethnography of ancient Israel or early Christianity." All these approaches will be considered in this essay as attempts to interpret early Christian literature and history through categories borrowed from the social sciences, sociology and anthropology in particular.

Although social-scientific criticism as a subspecialty within biblical studies has a relatively brief history, beginning only about twenty years ago, it owns what may be called a long "prehistory" within historical criticism of the Bible. Indeed, as Elisabeth Schüssler Fiorenza insists, modern historical research has always had social interests: "I don't think there is a historical method without a social or sociological awareness and conceptualization. For example, historiography as a discipline has been conceptualized as one of national states and their identity, and that is a social or sociological concept."[1] In fact, in its inception the discipline of sociology owes something to nineteenth-century biblical scholarship, since Max Weber, one of the pioneers of sociology, was influenced by Rudolph Sohm's debates with Adolf von Harnack, as well as by Julius Wellhausen's analysis of the development of ancient Israel.[2] Around the turn of the century, Marxist scholarship took the lead in the social analysis of early Christianity. In 1894 Friederich Engels argued that early Christianity

103

was a social movement of the dispossessed with remarkable similarities to modern working-class movements, while in 1925 Karl Kautsky expanded the thesis to present an account of early Christianity from a (rather simplistic) Marxist point of view.[3] Such arguments affected even mainstream biblical scholarship of the time, as scholars such as Ernst Troeltsch and Adolf Deissmann tried to broaden the scope of traditional theological analysis to pose questions about the social significances of the New Testament.[4] Although the early Marxist account of incipient Christianity has generally been rejected by historians, including most Marxists, their interests in the social locations of early Christians and the social and political ramifications of Christian language live on in all contemporary social-scientific approaches to the New Testament.

Other movements of early twentieth-century scholarship—the history-of-religions school, form criticism, and the so-called Chicago School of social analysis—may also be seen as precursors to social-scientific criticism. The history-of-religions school refers to those scholars who made connections between New Testament concepts and practices and religious elements from the surrounding (primarily Greco-Roman) environment.[5] Early form critics, notably Martin Dibelius and Rudolph Bultmann, wanted to isolate sections of the New Testament text, reconstruct their *Sitz im Leben* or "setting-in-life," and show how those originally oral units functioned in early Christian contexts of preaching, worship, prayer, or other social activity.[6] "The Chicago School," represented mainly by Shailer Mathews and Shirley Jackson Case, also addressed social issues, such as why Christianity succeeded among Gentiles when it did not among Jews, and the social level of early Christians.[7]

Several contemporary scholars have pointed out, however, that none of these precursors of the current social-scientific approach had a direct influence on the rise of similar concerns in the 1960s and 1970s. As Wayne Meeks puts it, "The *religionsgeschichte Schule* [history-of-religions school] pursued a history of ideas and mythology, lacking any kind of sociological dimension. And the form critics, who talked about *Sitz im Leben,* did not use anything that resembles sociological method in order to define what the typical life settings were."[8] John Elliott says much the same thing about the Chicago School: "Nobody out of that school is responsible for stimulating any of us when we revived [the social-scientific approach] in the sixties and seventies. Though we can look back and see interesting insights in the Chicago School, the approach was quickly dropped."[9] Recent social-scientific criticism of the New Testament, in its multiple embodiments, thus dates from the 1960s and 1970s. From a variety of perspectives, scholars began to ask social questions about the New Testament. The discussion below sketches the beginnings of that recent history by mentioning the seminal works (though not necessarily the most recent or ultimately most important) of four scholars who led the way in social-scientific methods and the New Testament. Although the account offered here is necessarily selective and partial, it is nonetheless representative of the various ways in which New Testament scholars became interested in social-scientific criticism.

In 1967–1968 John Gager was teaching an introductory course on the study of religion at Haverford College, in which he had students read the works of Clifford Geertz, Evans Pritchard, Max Weber, Peter Berger, and Edmund Leach, among others. At that time, New Testament scholars generally made no use of such sociologists and anthropologists for their own work. The result of Gager's attempt to do so was the publication in 1975 of *Kingdom and Community,* in which he applied different social-scientific theories and methods to early Christian texts.[10] For example, Gager analyzes early Christianity as a "millenarian movement" that developed in ways similar to modern movements expecting an imminent end to the present world order. When the *parousia* failed to occur in the first century, early Christians experienced "cognitive dissonance," a psychological tension resulting from a discrepancy between two constructions of reality, in this case their expectation of Jesus' return and the nonoccurrence of that event. They reacted to that dissonance by renewed missionary activity, as have modern groups documented by sociologists of religion. Gager's work provoked great controversy and disagreement, a reaction that testifies to the seminal impact of *Kingdom and Community* on biblical studies.

In the mid-1960s John Elliott was involved in the Civil Rights movement, first in St. Louis and then in San Francisco. Later, through his participation in protests against the Vietnam War, his attention turned increasingly to the social and political ramifications of religious belief and action. Moreover, his political activity brought him into contact with others, like Old Testament critic Norman Gottwald, who were pursuing ways to combine social analysis with historical study of the Bible. For Elliott, the result was an analysis of 1 Peter, *A Home for the Homeless,* the manuscript of which was completed in 1978.[11] Originally, Elliott called his study a "sociological exegesis" of 1 Peter, but he has since decided that the term is inappropriate since it excludes reference to anthropology, which provides important theoretical scaffolding for his claims. Elliott appropriates Bryan Wilson's typology of sects to argue that the Christians reflected in the text of 1 Peter saw themselves—or the author saw them—as "resident aliens," living in but opposed to the dominant Greco-Roman culture.[12] Recognition of the sectarian nature of the community illuminates the possible social functions of elements of the letter, such as the household code of 1 Pet. 2:18–3:7. By reading 1 Peter with social-scientific concerns, Elliott suggested a possible historical reconstruction of one community of early Christianity.

Although the majority of social-scientific criticism has taken place in North America, few scholars anywhere have been as influential in this field as Gerd Theissen, a German. Influenced by sociological "functionalism," Theissen first analyzed the early "Jesus movement" by applying concepts derived for the most part from Max Weber and his later American disciple Talcott Parsons. Functionalism conceives of societies as something like organisms whose different elements (religious practices, belief structures, mechanisms for dealing with conflict, etc.) interact with one another to integrate different members and groups into the whole organism, diffusing conflict through repression and/or change. Conflict is often considered by functionalism a natural element in the development or evolution of a society, but it is usually seen as resolving itself within the modified but coherently "functioning" unity. In an important article first published in 1973, Theissen used the Gospel texts to reconstruct the prehistory of Palestinian Christianity, arguing that many Gospel sayings reflect a social role of the "Itinerant Radical" who, due to socioeconomic tensions and problems in first-century Palestine, abandoned normal social structures such as job and family to wander about preaching Jesus' message. Other early Christians in Palestine remained in their traditional social roles and provided support and communal structures for these "wandering charismatics." Theissen's ideas were later expanded in a book, *The Sociology of Early Palestinian Christianity,* and in several essays on Paul and the Corinthian church. Although Theissen's work has been repeatedly criticized, it continues to have enormous influence on all branches of social-scientific criticism of the New Testament.[13]

One of the disseminators of Theissen's work on this side of the Atlantic has been Wayne A. Meeks, who, like other pioneering practitioners of social-scientific methods, became interested in them through a combination of pedagogical and research concerns. Meeks began teaching at Indiana University in 1966. Becoming more and more disenchanted with exclusively theological categories for teaching New Testament studies to undergraduates, he searched other disciplines for (in his words) "some sense of reality" not provided by a traditional history-of-religions approach. Unimpressed by most psychological models and many sociological ones, Meeks eventually settled on what may be identified as a moderate Weberian functionalism, although his work also shows strong influences from the "sociology of knowledge" theories of Peter Berger and Thomas Luckmann and from the cultural anthropology of Clifford Geertz. Meeks's most important work to date is *The First Urban Christians,* an analysis of Pauline Christianity using various social-scientific models and typologies. But the early piece that launched Meeks's social-scientific voyage and influenced many other scholars was "The Man from Heaven in Johannine Sectarianism," an examination of Johannine Christianity using concepts of sectarianism borrowed from the sociology of knowledge.[14] According to Meeks, John's portrayal of Jesus as one rejected by his own people reflects the social rupture between the Johannine community and the synagogue: "One of the primary functions of the book, therefore, must have been to provide a reinforcement for the community's social identity, which appears to have been largely negative. It provided a symbolic universe which gave religious legitimacy, a theodicy, to the group's actual isolation from the larger society."[15]

In 1973 these diverse initiatives in the social analysis of the New Testament converged, at least in North America, with the establishment by the Society of Biblical Literature of a working group on "The Social World of Early Christianity," chaired by Wayne Meeks and Leander Keck. In the following years a split, reflected in the discussions of this working group, occurred among scholars interested in social analysis. At the risk of oversimplification, one may identify a break between those who are content to consider their work to be "social history" and others who more self-consciously practice a "social-scientific" method. The "social historians" (among whom one might include John Gager, Wayne Meeks, William Countryman, and Howard Kee) see themselves as using traditional historical-critical methods to explore the "social world" of early Christianity. The "social scientists" (John Elliott, Jerome Neyrey, Bruce Malina, Antoinette Wire, among others) argue, to the contrary, that the task of cross-cultural analysis necessitates a more self-conscious use of anthropological or sociological models, made explicit at the outset and tested thoroughly by application to the data mined from historical texts. The latter group has formed its own organs of dialogue and research, the most visible of which is the current Society of Biblical Literature Section called "Social Sciences and New Testament Interpretation."

It would be a mistake, however, to paint a picture of two distinct groups of scholars using opposing methods. Rather, in reading the numerous publications that use the term "social" somewhere in their self-descriptions and in talking to scholars engaged in such research, one senses a spectrum of opinion about what precisely a social-scientific method should be. Much of the debate, as is already obvious from the discussion thus far, centers on the use of "models" derived from the social sciences. Malina defines "models" as "an abstract, simplified representation of some real world object, event, or interaction constructed for the purpose of understanding, control, or prediction . . . a scheme or pattern that derives from the process of abstracting similarities from a range of instances in order to comprehend."[16] The problem with the term "model," however, is that it may refer to a classification system as abstract, rigid, and universalizing as Mary Douglas's "group-grid" construction, or to a conceptual construction as culturally specific, freely used, and content-oriented as patron-client systems or societal perceptions of honor and shame.[17] Few historical critics, if any, doubt the usefulness of knowledge about ancient patron-client structures for interpretation of early Christianity. Many scholars, on the other hand, have found the group-grid model to be too rigid or uninteresting, if not downright incomprehensible, when applied to New Testament texts.[18] Thus the debate over method becomes complicated by different uses of the term "model," which sometimes refers to an explicit appropriation of a carefully defined research practice or taxonomy, sometimes to a flexible appropriation of social-historical categories, and sometimes simply to the presuppositions of the exegete. The disagreement really centers around what particular models are used and how they are used.

Reflecting on social-scientific criticism of the New Testament, Wayne Meeks, for example, agrees that scholars need to be clearer about their methodological presuppositions but expresses reservations about some uses of models:

> Once one has a model, one is tempted to use it no longer as a pattern for sorting data or a heuristic model to look through, but as material to fill in gaps where we do not have evidence. One is tempted to reify things, not only models, but types, and treat them as real things in the world. I am not satisfied, however, that any of the models is comprehensive enough to account for all the historical material; some are too bound to a particular cultural setting, usually ours, and whether they fit the ancient setting is often very difficult to tell.[19]

John Elliott, on the other hand, has criticized scholars for not recognizing that their own presuppositions are actually "models":

> I think another word for "presupposition" is "model," if by that we think of how we imagine the structure, population, activities, and dynamics of the first-century world. That is a very large, abstract model. We have to be clear to ourselves what implicit models we are using, then indicate what they are to one another so we can more adequately communicate with one another, then finally get to the critical point where we can evaluate one another's work.[20]

As Meeks's comments imply, some scholars feel that models have too often been anachronistically employed, thus imposing modern sociological categories on ancient texts. William Countryman, for example, admits that "one should pay attention to social models in the hope that they will break up one's preconceptions." But he continues with more reticence: "I don't think models evolved to explain modern society will always explain ancient society. There is no society, in my opinion, that completely matches up with the ancient Mediterranean world, though there may be some that are more closely related than others."[21] Jerome Neyrey responds, however, that the very point of using self-conscious models is to avoid anachronism. "I take these models and test them. Do they apply to the first century? By and large I find that, yes, the honor and shame system described by anthropologists does apply to the ancient texts. This is not anachronistic, imposing a twentieth-century phenomenon. The same applies to patron-client models and structures."

Often, debate about the use of models is linked with concern over the "scientific" reliability or respectability of social approaches to the New Testament. In a recent survey, Bengt Holmberg raises the issue of the "scientific maturity" of the approach, criticizing, for example, the theory of "relative deprivation" used by Gager on the grounds that it is too "psychological," cannot be objectively verified, and resembles "metaphysical" speculation rather than "scientific precision."[22] Indeed, some scholars sound as if they believe that the use of social-scientific models that have been "tested" in the laboratory of anthropological research can deliver them from the dangers of ethnocentrism; they seem confident that the models will enable them to see things the way ancient Mediterraneans saw them.[23] Thus John Elliott, when asked whether he views his work as "scientific," answers, "Definitely yes. That is the reason I want to clarify the models, because if I can demonstrate that one abstract conception is more useful than another, I have been able to advance research. I don't want simply to say something interesting, but to advance the whole state of research in a particular area."[24]

Such a view, however, does not characterize all the scholars who use social-scientific methods. Susan Garrett describes her method not as "scientific" but as "hermeneutic." She explains:

> There is an insistence by some people that by formulating hypotheses and testing them one will be able to escape ethnocentric bias, and I think that is an illusion. One cannot escape it, and the very formulation of the hypothesis, of questions to apply to the data is already ethnocentrically biased. The data generated and collected is biased from the beginning, and there is simply no way out of that trap.[25]

Even John Gager, who is well known for his use of explicit models, resists the label "scientific":

> I am very much a humanist. I have no idea what the term "scientific" would mean in this context. The people who talk in terms of science sometimes also talk in terms of provability or demonstrability, and I am sufficiently a postmodern thinker that I do not believe that the notion of demonstrability or provability has any value at all in our field. It's just a red herring. If you talk to anthropologists these days, they don't put much weight on notions of demonstrability either but are more interested in aspects like the cogency, coherence, and persuasiveness of an account.[26]

As these diverse sentiments indicate, there is currently much debate over what constitutes a social-scientific method for biblical studies, and much of the debate centers around profound theoretical differences, particularly epistemological ones. Nonetheless, these various scholars share the belief that all language is ineluctably social, that religion is to be interpreted as woven into the complex fabric of social structures and symbolic matrices, and that sociology and anthropology can provide useful perspectives and methods for interpreting the function of religion in society.

Examples of Social-Scientific Criticism in Luke-Acts

Ready examples are at hand that illustrate these various social-scientific approaches in studies of Luke-Acts. Three such examples demonstrate how different scholars, with somewhat different theoretical presuppositions, use social-scientific methods for exegesis. The first is the analysis of "magic" from the cultural-anthropological perspective embodied in Susan R. Garrett's *Demise of the Devil: Magic and the Demonic in Luke's Writings*.[27] The second comes from Philip Francis Esler, author of *Community and Gospel in Luke-Acts: The Social and Political Motivations of Lucan Theology*, who uses a concept of "legitimation" derived from the sociology of knowledge practiced by Peter Berger and Thomas Luckmann. The third example is a recent article by Douglas E. Oakman, "The Countryside in Luke-Acts," which is the most explicit and rigorous in its use of a specific social-scientific model.

In *Demise of the Devil*, Garrett does not claim to employ any explicit model. Indeed, beginning with a discussion of anthropological studies of "magic," she criticizes an older model that differentiated "magic" from "religion" or "science" and that spoke of certain cultures as evidencing a "magical world view." Scholars who adopt this model consider magic to be "instrumental and goal-oriented" in its attempts to manipulate forces through ritualistic activities that practically guarantee results. Religion, on the other hand, is understood as a relationship among beings, communication rather than manipulation, and carries with it no assurance of "automatic efficacy."[28] According to this view, the anthropologist should be able to analyze how an activity is performed and decide whether the phenomenon falls under the category "magic" or "religion."

Garrett notes that such an approach is "etic," meaning that the activity is described from the anthropologist's rather than from the native's point of view, using categories of description and analysis that come from outside the cultural sphere being examined. Garrett characterizes her analysis, on the other hand, as balancing etic categories with "emic" ones. Instead of attempting to decide whether an action portrayed in the New Testament is "really" magical or religious, she tries to perceive the activity from the point of view of the "native," in this case, the writer and early readers of Luke-Acts. Borrowing language from cultural anthropologists like Clifford Geertz, Garrett states her working presupposition: "Like language, ritual acts are socially transmitted and contextually dependent. Hence, they have 'meaning' only as it is attributed to them by actors and observers (enemies and supporters), whose various interpretations are guided by their respective social locations and by the shape of their own cultural world."[29] This means that for Garrett's purposes, whether (for example) an action of Paul in Acts would have been considered magical or religious has little connection with what Paul actually did, but rather would have been decided by intricate social conventions of labeling and by the perceptions of the people who occupied Paul's own cultural, or subcultural, world. Garrett sees her role as something like an "interpretive ethnographer" of the "culture" of Luke-Acts, who, as a member of another culture, questions the text to ascertain "the symbolic forms—words, images, institutions, behaviors—in terms of which . . . people actually represented themselves to themselves and one another."[30] The fruitfulness of Garrett's approach is demonstrated by her exegesis of various passages in Acts, including the problematic text Acts 13:4–12. The crux of the problem is this: If Luke wants to contrast Christianity with magic, surely one of his goals, why does he portray Paul as "cursing" Bar Jesus—a deed that appears, at least to modern persons, just as "magical" as any action of Bar Jesus? What is the function of this conflict in Luke's narrative and worldview?

By comparing ancient Jewish and Christian works that speak of magic or cursing, Garrett demonstrates how references to magic function in Luke's overarching story as signals of the activity of Satan. Magic and religion cannot be differentiated on the basis of a phenomenological understanding of the activity itself. "In portraying Paul's curse of Bar Jesus, Luke reveals that he shared with ancient magicians . . . the presupposition that words backed up with sufficient authority could wreak terrible damage."[31] But in Luke's view, Paul's actions cannot be magic because magic is satanic, and Luke portrays Paul as "*conquering* magical-satanic powers." Of course, opponents of Christianity could easily construe the situation oppositely, seeing the healings and exorcisms of Luke-Acts as magic.

In her discussion of the Bar Jesus incident and others (including, for example, Acts 8:4–25 and 19:8–20), Garrett's interests are primarily exegetical: She is concerned with the inter- and intratextual connections in Luke-Acts and related documents. *Demise of the Devil,* therefore, is for the most part a traditional exegetical study in the historical-critical, philological tradition. Her use of social-scientific methods consists in her adoption of an ethnographic posture. In other words, she listens to the text of Luke-Acts and other ancient documents with the ears of an ethnographer; she attempts to trace unspoken connections, assumed meanings and references, underlying but unacknowledged myths. Other social-scientific critics, on the other hand, exhibit what might be called primarily historical interests: Although they are interested in exegesis, their ultimate concern is to reconstruct structures, conflicts, and developments of early Christian communities. Their concentration on the texts of early Christianity has as its goal more ascertaining the function of a particular document within the social history of early Christian groups than explicating literary problems internal to the documents themselves. An example of this latter approach is Philip Francis Esler's *Community and Gospel in Luke-Acts.*[32]

Esler begins by criticizing the view that Luke wrote his work to apply a previously developed theological position to social and political issues—that is, that Luke's theology came first and only derivatively had social or political significance. As Esler responds, "What if Luke did not sharply differentiate the theological realm from the social and political, but saw them, in fact, as closely inter-related? What if social and political exigencies played a vital role in the formation of Luke's theology, rather than merely constituting the areas in which it was applied?"[33] Of course, one traditional interpretation maintains that Luke-Acts is directly concerned with political questions, namely, that it is an apology for Christianity directed to a non-Christian Greco-Roman audience—or, alternatively, for the Roman Empire and the dominant Greco-Roman culture directed toward Christians. Esler rejects such readings of Luke-Acts, insisting that its function is not apology but "legitimation." Luke wanted to legitimate Christianity to his contemporary fellow Christians, both Jews and Gentiles, including some Romans, who "needed strong assurance that their decision to convert and to adopt a different life-style had been the correct one."[34]

Taking his model of legitimation from Peter Berger and Thomas Luckmann's writings, Esler defines "legitimation" as "a process which is carried out after a social institution has originated in the first place. In essence, legitimation is the collection of ways in which an institution is explained and justified to its members."[35] "Legitimation" appeals to other beliefs, assumptions, myths, or elements of the audience's "symbolic universe," a concept that is very important for the sociology of knowledge. As Esler explains:

> A symbolic universe is a body of theoretical tradition which integrates different provinces of meaning and encompasses the institutional order in a symbolic totality. . . . Within such a universe, the members of the institution have an experience of everything in its right place and also of the various phases of their biography as ordered. . . . Over the institutional level as well, symbolic universes operate as sheltering canopies. The symbolic universe also orders history; it locates all collective acts in a cohesive unity that includes past, present and future.[36]

Having set forth his theoretical assumptions, Esler proceeds to investigate several traditional conundrums of Luke-Acts exegesis. In the last chapter, Esler explores a problem that has vexed many interpreters of Luke-Acts: the stance of the author toward the Roman Empire. Surely one of Luke's purposes is to portray Christianity as politically innocuous, as a movement that should be tolerated if not welcomed by Romans. Why, then, does Luke retain aspects of the tradition that could make Christianity appear revolutionary or at least socially problematic, such as the experiences of Jesus and Paul before Roman courts, the obvious corruptness of Roman officials like Felix and Festus, and Christianity's concern with the poor and oppressed? What precisely is Luke's position toward the Roman government, and whom does he want to influence with his depiction of it?

First, Esler argues that Luke modifies much of his inherited tradition to show that even though the new religious movement might appear politically dangerous, Jesus and his disciples were repeatedly pronounced innocent of breaking any Roman law. Furthermore, when the Christians found themselves in trouble, it was through the instigation of unbelieving Jews, whose occasional successes against the Christians were due to the weakness or self-aggrandizement of individual Roman officials, not to any problem with the system of Roman jurisprudence itself. Indeed, the Roman system often saved Christians from local, and in Luke's view, unfounded hostility.[37]

But why does Luke go out of his way to portray the Romans this way?

> There is only one answer which offers a satisfying explanation for the political theme in Luke-Acts, that among the members of Luke's community were a number of Romans serving the empire in a military or administrative capacity, and that part of Luke's task was to present Christian history in such a way as to demonstrate that faith in Jesus Christ and allegiance to Rome were not mutually inconsistent.[38]

Esler has thus come full circle in his book to return to the theme of legitimation. He concludes,

> Luke's two volumes may be described as an exercise in the legitimation of a sectarian movement, as a sophisticated attempt to explain and justify Christianity to the members of his community at a time when they were exposed to social and political pressures which were making their allegiance waver. Luke represents traditions relating how the gospel was initially proclaimed by Jesus and later preached throughout the Roman East in such a way as to erect a symbolic universe, a sacred canopy, beneath which the institutional order of his community is given meaning and justification.[39]

Garrett and Esler are scholars who use social-scientific approaches rather freely, eclectically appropriating sociological or anthropological perspectives when they seem heuristically useful. A different practice is exemplified by the recent work *The Social World of Luke-Acts: Models for Interpretation*, edited by Jerome Neyrey. The book includes articles by several scholars who meet regularly and collaborate in their use of explicit social-scientific models and methods.[40] This particular collection of essays by "the Context Group," as the scholars call themselves, includes studies of Luke-Acts centering on "honor and shame," personality in the first century, urban social relations of the preindustrial city, sickness and healing, and patron-client relations. One feature setting this collection of essays apart from those of most other social approaches to the New Testament is that each of the authors begins with a clearly expressed social-scientific model and proceeds to apply that model to the text of Luke-Acts. Some of the essays are more successful than others in blending social-scientific methods with textual interpretation, but the collection nevertheless serves as a valuable resource, even if only to spur theoretical and methodological discussion among biblical scholars.

An especially interesting article in *The Social World of Luke-Acts* is that by Douglas E. Oakman, "The Countryside in Luke-Acts." Oakman begins with a "conflict" model of social interaction, as opposed to a structural-functionalist model. (Conflict models tend to analyze social structure and change by concentrating on the way different groups within a society pursue their own interests; the approach thus emphasizes the conflicts between different worldviews and ideologies rather than accepting the functionalist view of society as a self-maintaining organism. The opposition between these two approaches has been important in sociological theory in past years, but the clean demarcation between them has now been generally blurred.) Oakman also outlines an agrarian social stratification model to demonstrate the way land and its resources are controlled in preindustrial peasant economies. By carefully noting how Luke portrays the countryside and peasant activity in Luke-Acts, Oakman is able to address a concern that we already have seen dealt with in Esler's book above: the political implications of Luke's writings. Oakman notes that although Luke does seem concerned about the poor, his apparent solutions to social inequalities center on voluntary charity within the church, never on a questioning of the land distribution system that sustained the economic injustices of the Roman Empire. Therefore, what might initially appear to be Luke's revolutionary inclination against the oppressive nature of early imperial economy turns out to be politically conservative. As Oakman concludes,

> What was originally a radical social critique by Jesus and his followers of the violent and oppressive political-economic order in the countryside under the early empire becomes in Luke's conception a rather innocuous sharing-ethic ambiguous in its import for rural dwellers. The countryside is apparently idealized by Luke as a

place particularly receptive to this message. . . . No dramatic social reconstruction—such as the elimination of the preindustrial
city or Roman imperium—is to be expected or is necessary.[41]

Oakman's article demonstrates the interesting results that can be obtained
by combining detailed social-scientific models with historical and exegetical
research.

A tight consensus, it is evident, does not exist among social-scientific critics
regarding epistemology or methodology. Thus it is difficult to predict what the
future will bring for this much-divided subdiscipline of biblical studies. Some
opine that, due to the scarcity of data and evidence, we have *already* said most
of what can be said about the social history of early Christianity. But most
scholars believe that new directions in scholarship will emerge more from new
questions and perspectives on the part of scholars than from new "raw" data
(if such can theoretically be said to exist). Antoinette Wire, for example,
points out that feminist scholarship has long led the way in understanding that
"historical research reflects its own time." So the future of social-scientific
criticism "depends on our history and what the trends are in our world."[42] As
Andrew Overman puts it, "In all areas of academic study, especially religion,
there is a synergistic relationship between our contemporary reality and the
research we do on antiquity. Our reading is nuanced and sometimes changed
radically, based on changes in our contemporary world." Of course, more historical discoveries and a better knowledge of the materials we do possess
would be welcome. "A broader and more sophisticated use of the Roman
world—archaeology, epigraphy, realia—needs to come about to fill out this
approach," Overman concludes.[43]

Beyond the question of data, however, I would like to note a few new
theoretical directions being taken in the field. First, most scholars engaged in
social approaches to the New Testament claim to find sociology less and less
helpful and anthropology and ethnography more and more interesting.[44] Second, many scholars recognize the importance of various literary methods and
are attempting in their study of the New Testament to combine insights of
literary critics with those of social critics. This movement in biblical studies
perhaps reflects the burgeoning of "cultural studies" in many universities.[45]
Third, the studies by Esler and Oakman mentioned above share a concern to
analyze the social and political ramifications of religious language, texts, and
movements. Such studies may be the harbingers of a growing interest in what
may loosely be called "ideological criticism." Now that scholars have some
social historical material ready to hand, it may be time to interrogate that
evidence more carefully to ascertain what structures and operations of power
are reflected in the early church's texts. How do the theological debates of the
New Testament relate to ideological conflicts or struggles for power among

early Christians? What are the social and political positions of various Christian groups in relation to the dominant Greco-Roman culture or to the Roman Empire? With several literary-critical circles turning to ideological issues (I have in mind various forms of poststructuralist criticism, the "New Historicism," feminist criticism, and gay and lesbian theories, besides the many different embodiments of Marxist analysis), it is to be expected that biblical scholars, especially those just emerging from university graduate schools, will bring similar interests to their study of early Christianity.

Whatever the future may bring, it is clear that after a twenty-year deluge of articles and books employing social-scientific methods for the study of the Bible, the approach has now arrived at a certain maturity. Different schools of thought even within this subdiscipline of biblical studies vie for the attentions and approval of the guild as a whole. Social-scientific criticism, which only recently enjoyed the reputation of a maverick among methods, is now a staid and respectable (and predictable?) member of the neighborhood. Whether it continues to provoke controversy and interest probably depends more on the ingenuity of its practitioners than on any specific characteristic of the method itself.

Notes

1. Interview, May 23, 1991. This essay is based on a series of telephone interviews as well as published documents. Between May 22 and 27, 1991, the following people were interviewed, with transcriptions of those interviews providing the sources for many of the quotations in this essay: L. William Countryman, John H. Elliott, Elisabeth Schüssler Fiorenza, John Gager, Susan R. Garrett, Wayne A. Meeks, Jerome H. Neyrey, Andrew Overman, and Antoinette Wire. The reader should keep in mind that these quotations are from oral interviews and therefore should not be expected to display the polished prose that characterizes the written works of the scholars quoted.

2. For the theological influences on Weber, see Gilbert A. Greggs, Jr., "Priest, Prophet, and Apocalyptic: The Authoring of Religious Identity in the Period of the Restoration" (Ph.D. diss., Yale University, 1991), pp. 74–114; see also Peter Burke, *Sociology and History* (London: Allen & Unwin, 1980), pp. 20, 24; Fredric Jameson, "The Vanishing Mediator: or, Max Weber as Storyteller," in *The Ideologies of Theory, Essays 1971–1986*, Vol. 2 of *The Syntax of History* (Minneapolis: University of Minnesota, 1988), pp. 23–34.

3. F. Engels, "On the History of Early Christianity," in *Marx and Engels on Religion* (Moscow: Progress Publishers, 1957); Karl Kautsky, *Foundations of Christianity* (New York: International, 1925).

4. Ernst Troeltsch, *The Social Teaching of the Christian Churches* (Chicago: University of Chicago, 1976); Adolf Deissmann, *Light from the Ancient East* (New York: George H. Doran, 1927).

5. See Werner George Kümmel, *The New Testament: The History of the Investigation of Its Problems,* trans. S. McLean Gilmour and Howard C. Kee (Nashville: Abingdon, 1972), pp. 206–324.

6. Martin Dibelius, *The Message of Jesus Christ: The Tradition of the Early Christian Communities* (New York: C. Scribner's Sons, 1939), Rudolph Bultmann, *The History of the Synoptic Tradition,* 2nd ed. (Oxford: Basil Blackwell, 1968).

7. Shailer Mathews, *The Social Teaching of Jesus: An Essay in Christian Sociology* (New York: Macmillan, 1897); Shirley Jackson Case, *The Evolution of Early Christianity* (Chicago: University of Chicago, 1914); *The Social Origins of Christianity* (Chicago: University of Chicago, 1923).

8. Wayne Meeks, interview, May 22, 1991.

9. John Elliott, interview, May 24, 1991.

10. John Gager, *Kingdom and Community: The Social World of Early Christianity* (Englewood Cliffs, N.J.: Prentice-Hall, 1975).

11. John H. Elliott, *A Home for the Homeless: A Sociological Exegesis of 1 Peter, Its Situation and Strategy* (Philadelphia: Fortress, 1981).

12. Bryan R. Wilson, *Sects and Society: A Sociological Study of the Elim Tabernacle, Christian Science, and the Christadelphians* (Berkeley, Calif.: University of California, 1961).

13. Gerd Theissen, "Itinerant Radicalism: The Tradition of Jesus' Sayings from the Perspective of the Sociology of Literature," *Radical Religion* 2 (1975):84–93; originally published in German, *Zeitschrift für Theologie und Kirche* 70 (1973):245–71; see also *Sociology of Early Palestinian Christianity* (Philadelphia: Fortress, 1978); *The Social Setting of Pauline Christianity: Essays on Corinth* (Philadelphia: Fortress, 1982) (the essays in the latter were written from 1973 to 1975). For a survey of critiques of Theissen's work, see Bengt Holmberg, *Sociology and the New Testament: An Appraisal* (Minneapolis: Fortress, 1990), pp. 44–54, 119–25, 140, and the works there cited.

14. Wayne Meeks, "The Man from Heaven in Johannine Sectarianism," *Journal of Biblical Literature* 91 (1972):44–72.

15. Ibid., p. 70.

16. Bruce Malina, "The Social Sciences and Biblical Interpretation," *Interpretation* 37 (1982):229–42, at p. 231.

17. The "group-grid" model, articulated by Mary Douglas, plots social groups on a chart depicting four quadrants arranged around two axes, one horizontal ("group") and one vertical ("grid"), based on the worldview of the group and the members' attitudes toward issues like purity, ritual, the body, and boundaries. The axis called "group" gauges the pressures put on individual members to conform to the group's norms and the degree to which individuals submit to those pressures. The "grid" axis measures the degree to which the society utilizes, on the one hand, a shared system of values and beliefs or, on the other hand, whether classification systems are "privatized." See *Natural Symbols: Explorations in Cosmology* (New York: Vintage, 1973; originally published in 1970), esp. pp. 82–86.

18. For use of the group-grid model see Bruce Malina, *Christian Origins and Cultural Anthropology: Practical Models for Biblical Interpretation* (Atlanta: John Knox, 1986); Bruce Malina and Jerome Neyrey, *Calling Jesus Names: The Social Value of Labels in Matthew* (Sonoma, Calif.: Polebridge, 1988). For criticism, see Susan R. Garrett, Review of *Christian Origins and Cultural Anthropology, Journal of Biblical Literature* 107 (1988):532–34; and "Christianity, Sociology of Early," in *The Anchor Bible Dictionary,* vol. 6, pp. 88–89 (New York: Doubleday, 1992).

19. Wayne Meeks, interview, May 22, 1991.

20. John Elliott, interview, May 24, 1991.

21. William Countryman, interview, May 25, 1991.

22. Bengt Holmberg, *Sociology and the New Testament: An Appraisal* (Minneapolis: Fortress, 1990), pp. 18, 66. The latter terms are embedded in a quotation of James Beckford, *The Trumpet of Prophecy: A Sociological Study of Jehovah's Witnesses* (New York: Wiley, 1975), pp. 154–58.

23. Almost every essay in a recent book on Luke-Acts make such a claim: Jerome H. Neyrey, ed., *The Social World of Luke-Acts: Models for Interpretation* (Peabody, Mass.: Hendrickson, 1991), pp. 64, 95, 128, 149, et passim.

24. John Elliott, interview, May 24, 1991.

25. Susan R. Garrett, interview, May 22, 1991.

26. John Gager, interview, May 27, 1991.

27. Susan R. Garrett, *Demise of the Devil: Magic and the Demonic in Luke's Writings* (Minneapolis: Fortress, 1989).

28. Ibid., p. 29, citing several different theories in a brief section.

29. Ibid.

30. Ibid., p. 35; she is quoting Clifford Geertz, *Local Knowledge: Further Essays in Interpretive Anthropology* (New York: Basic Books, 1983), p. 58.

31. Ibid., p. 86.

32. Philip Francis Esler, *Community and Gospel in Luke-Acts* (Cambridge: Cambridge University Press, 1987).

33. Ibid., p. 1.

34. Ibid., p. 16.

35. Ibid., pp. 16–17. See Peter Berger and Thomas Luckmann, *The Social Construction of Reality: A Treatise in the Sociology of Knowledge* (Garden City, N.Y.: Doubleday, 1967); see also Berger, *The Sacred Canopy: Elements of a Sociological Theory of Religion* (Garden City, N.Y.: Doubleday, 1969).

36. Ibid., p. 18.

37. Ibid., pp. 204–5.

38. Ibid., p. 210.

39. Ibid., p. 222.

40. See note 23 above.

41. Oakman, "The Countryside in Luke-Acts," p. 177.

42. Antoinette Wire, interview, May 23, 1991.

43. Andrew Overman, interview, May 23, 1991.

44. In interviews this sentiment was expressed explicitly by Wayne Meeks, Susan Garrett, and Jerome Neyrey; but a perusal of studies also gives the impression that particularly sociological (as opposed to anthropological or ethnographic) theories are on the wane among scholars of early Christianity.

45. See, for example, Jeffrey C. Alexander and Steven Seidman, eds., *Culture and Society: Contemporary Debates* (Cambridge: Cambridge University Press, 1990).

For Further Reading

Alexander, Jeffrey C., and Seidman, Steven, eds. *Culture and Society: Contemporary Debates.* Cambridge: Cambridge University Press, 1990. An interesting anthology of different authors from anthropology, sociology, literary studies, and social history, showing how various disciplines have approached what is known in some circles as "cultural studies."

Bauman, Zygmunt. *Thinking Sociologically.* Oxford: Basil Blackwell, 1990. Very readable introduction to the basic issues in traditional sociology.

Burke, Peter. *Sociology and History.* Controversies in Sociology 10. London: Allen & Unwin, 1980. Entertainingly written, brief discussion of the intersection between sociological and historical methods.

Elliott, John H., ed. *Social-Scientific Criticism of the New Testament and Its Social World. Semeia* 35 (1986). A collection of essays primarily by New Testament scholars who use the more rigorous social-scientific approach concentrating on explicit models.

Garrett, Susan R. "Sociology of Early Christianity," *The Anchor Bible Dictionary,* vol. 6, pp. 89–99 (New York: Doubleday, 1992). An in-depth introduction to social-scientific methods in New Testament studies, addressing the theoretical issues underlying differences in method.

Holmberg, Bengt. *Sociology and the New Testament: An Appraisal.* Minneapolis: Fortress, 1990. A critical survey of the field, especially useful for its attention to German and Scandinavian scholarship. This book covers many important subjects but is rather shallow in its handling of theoretical issues.

Kee, Howard C. *Knowing the Truth: A Sociological Approach to New Testament Interpretation.* Minneapolis: Fortress, 1989. A brief survey of the field with suggestions for further work; a prolegomenon for a future book on possible theological significances of New Testament sociology.

Osiek, Carolyn. "The New Handmaid: The Bible and the Social Sciences." *Theological Studies* 50 (1989):260–78. An excellent, brief survey of the relevant literature.

7

CANONICAL
CRITICISM

Mary C. Callaway

O NE significant factor distinguishing biblical texts from similar ancient
Near Eastern writings is that they were not dug up from the ground
by archaeologists but have been interpreted and handed on from the
beginning by communities who define themselves by them. Tradition history
has demonstrated that Israelite traditions were transmitted and reinterpreted
by successive generations to respond to new situations, and the Bible is the
result of layer upon layer of these resignified traditions and stories. At certain
historical moments, notably the sixth century B.C.E. and the first century C.E.,
the process of shaping traditions ceased and the finished text became canonical. However, even when the boundaries were fixed, the form of the text remained fluid for centuries, as text critics have shown. Further, the process of
recontextualizing and actualizing traditions that had been informing Israel
since at least the tenth century B.C.E. continued unabated in Israel's heirs,
Judaism and Christianity. Although we know very little about how canonization occurred, it is clear that the canon represented formalization of an ancient
phenomenon: a core of traditions that was continually contemporized for the
benefit of the community.

It is this dynamic quality of scripture in interactive formation with believing
communities that canonical criticism addresses. In its narrow sense "canon'"
refers to lists of authoritative books, found in both Judaism and Christianity
from the beginning of the first century C.E., and a concern with what is included in the boundaries of the official text and what is excluded. But the
Dead Sea Scrolls, the Septuagint, and the New Testament all bear witness to
the diversity of canons in the first century C.E. Even today, the major faiths for
whom the Bible is of central importance represent five different canons. Canonical criticism does not address the history of these lists or the councils that
may have formalized them; those concerns properly belong to the history of
canon. Canonical criticism begins instead with the assumption that biblical

texts were generated, transmitted, reworked, and preserved in communities for which they were authoritative, and that biblical criticism should include study of how these texts functioned in the believing communities. Source, form, and redaction criticism focus on stages in the development of the biblical text prior to its final form, whereas canonical criticism analyzes the text as it was received in its final form. The emphasis may be on the function of the fixed text in the first communities to receive it, or on the process of adaptation by which the community resignified earlier traditions to function authoritatively in a new situation and thereby produced the final text. In either case, the focus of canonical criticism is on the two-way process by which the tradition functioned to define the communities and the communities continued to shape the traditions. Hence the emphasis is on communities, rather than individual authors or sources, and on the final form rather than on earlier stages in its development. Canonical criticism understands the exegetical task to be constructive as well as descriptive.

Historical Background

A brief sketch of three factors giving rise to the canonical approach may help clarify its relation to biblical criticism. First, the attempts to write a biblical theology, ongoing since at least the 1940s, began to unravel in the early 1960s. The task of biblical theologians had been to find the locus of biblical authority in a single, controlling theological construct of the scriptures. Two criteria were essential: The idea must be distinctive to the scriptures (i.e., not found in the literature outside Israel), and the Bible must be so suffused with it implicitly or explicitly that at least a tinge of it could be detected in every book. Like a variety of garments dyed various shades of the same hue, the books of the Bible could be unified by their tincture with a unifying theological concept. For Walter Eichrodt this concept was covenant, for Oscar Cullman the biblical idea of time, for Gerhard von Rad salvation history.[1] But the multiplicity of theories, and the failure of any of them to construct a roof wide enough to cover all of the idiosyncratic residents of the Bible, began to suggest that the search for the unifying idea of scripture was ill-conceived. The recalcitrant books of the Bible were made of different fabrics and would not all take a single dye.

Brevard Childs responded to this situation in his *Biblical Theology in Crisis* (1970), in which he suggested that exegesis should not stop with relating a pericope to its original historical context but should explore the dialectic between individual text and full canonical context. At the same time, he was working on parts of the Old Testament seen by others as intrusions into the text, such as Psalm superscriptions, asking how these "late" additions functioned, and what they could tell scholars about the ways in which the earliest communities unified their diverse authoritative traditions.[2] The development of the canonical approach moved the quest for the locus of biblical authority from the Bible's content to its shape.

A second factor influencing the development of canonical criticism was growing dissatisfaction with the results of historical-critical scholarship. What had promised to be an objective analysis of the biblical texts in their original settings had proved impossible because it was based on the assumption that the scholar could stand outside of history in order to analyze it. A review of critical work over a period of years shows how emphases change because the exegetes' own historical contexts inevitably color their work. It is easy from a distance to see the effect of Darwin's theory on Wellhausen's reconstruction of Israel's religion, of existentialist philosophy on Bultmann's reading of the New Testament, or of anti-Semitism on some Christian Old Testament scholarship. The growing suspicion that value-free, objective historical work is impossible has posed one of the most serious challenges to the historical-critical method.

Symptomatic of this problem was the hidden assumption of many biblical critics that authority rested in the earliest version of a biblical tradition. The work of later tradents and redactors was called "accretions," a term suggesting hardened deposits encrusting and distorting the original text, implicitly understood to be of lesser authority than the earliest tradition. The judgment that certain verses were "not genuine" ostensibly referred to their provenance but functionally came to mean "not authoritative." Authority was located in individuals, such as the Yahwist, Isaiah of Jerusalem, or Jeremiah, over against the communities that preserved, interpreted, and shaped the traditions about the individuals. Such a bias toward the earliest over the later and the individual over the community represented the values of Western post-Enlightenment societies read back into early Israel. Ironically, both liberals and fundamentalists based their reading of scripture on the shared assumption that the individual author represents the authoritative voice of the text.

By focusing on the early communities that preserved and shaped the traditions, canonical criticism resisted the unspoken hermeneutical assumption of historical criticism that biblical authority resided at the level of the "original author." On the other hand, canonical criticism was also a logical development of historical-critical work, whose history was a movement from smaller (sources) to larger (redaction) units of tradition. Canonical criticism can be understood as the next logical step after redaction criticism, moving from the last stage of redaction to the early stages of reception as scripture. James Sanders notes the necessity of canonical criticism by arguing that "criticism had skipped over the crucial link, jumping from redaction to conciliar decision."[3] Canonical criticism attends to this rich stage in the formation of the Bible.

Converging with growing disenchantment in the academy was the disillusionment in the churches that methods promising to make the Bible accessible had in fact locked it into the past. Further, by fragmenting the text into ever-smaller units that could only be read diachronically, some thought that biblical scholars had made the Bible virtually unreadable and unpreachable. In the words of a one-time colleague of both Childs and Sanders, scholars have effectively "decanonized" the Bible.[4] By reading the Bible as scripture, which meant emphasizing the continuity between the reading of canonizing communities and contemporary believing communities, canonical criticism tried to bridge this gap. Sanders refers to canonical criticism as "the beadle who carries the critically studied Bible in procession back to the church lectern from the scholar's study."[5] The origins of canonical criticism, then, lie in both the academic and the ecclesiastical communities. Its history is germane to an understanding of its nature, which can be characterized as a hermeneutical approach grounded in the historical-critical method.

Canonical Context and Canonical Hermeneutics

Canonical criticism has been defined by the work of two scholars, Brevard Childs of Yale University and James Sanders of Claremont Graduate School, whose approaches differ in significant ways.[6] The very term "canonical criticism" embodies the problem and is a good place to begin the discussion. The term was coined by Sanders in 1972 in *Torah and Canon*, in which he raised the question of why the Torah ends with Deuteronomy rather than Joshua. Since the most ancient traditions appear to have been a story of God's promise to the fathers and its fulfillment in the conquest of Canaan, the omission of Joshua—the fulfillment of the promise—is a startling reinterpretation of Israel's foundational story. In its final, canonical shape, the Torah in effect reinterprets Israel's story. Tradition history and form criticism have recovered the lineaments of the original story, climaxing with Israel's entry into Canaan (see, e.g., Exod. 15:1–18; Deut. 26:5–9; 33:1–29); yet the authoritative version preserved in Israel ends with Israel encamped in the enemy territory of Moab, leaderless after the death of Moses. The results of redaction criticism indicate that the final editing of the Torah was accomplished by Priestly editors in sixth-century Babylon. The work of canonical criticism begins with the results of redaction criticism, asking how the shape of the Torah resignified the traditions embedded within it. In Sanders's analysis, the canonical shaping of Israel's story into the Torah produced a radical new interpretation of the promise-fulfillment tradition by truncating the original story. For the exiles in Babylon who had lost the land, the Torah offered a new reading of traditions that must have seemed dead, for it situated the fulfillment of the promise in the future. Further, the Torah moved the focus from the land, which Israel had lost, to the law, which it could never lose.

Sanders used the term "canonical criticism" purposely to underscore the nature of canonical criticism as a critical pursuit, building on tradition history and comparative midrash. Its goal is to recover the hermeneutics of those who interpreted older traditions into what became the authoritative version. Using the metaphor of inflected languages, Sanders refers to the canon as a paradigm by which the believing community can learn to conjugate the verbs of God's activity. Scripture does not offer eternal truths or theological doctrines but a set of stories, along with the various ways in which the believing communities have found life in those stories. The very nature of canon is to be simultaneously stable and adaptable, a fixed set of traditions infinitely adaptable to new contexts by successive communities of believers. Hence, for Sanders, it is not the final form of the text but the process by which the community arrived at that form that is canonically significant. Canonical criticism helps close the gap between what it meant and what it means by retrieving canonical hermeneutics, the underlying theological presuppositions by which ancient communities applied old traditions to new situations.

Brevard Childs, on the other hand, rejects the term "canonical criticism" precisely because it implies that here is another technique that can take its place alongside source, form, and redaction criticism. Canonical criticism for him is "a stance from which the Bible is to be read as sacred Scripture."[7] Childs uses the term "canon" to emphasize "that the process of religious interpretation by a historical faith community left its mark on the literary texts which did not continue to evolve and which became the normative interpretation of those events to which it bore witness."[8] Characterizing scripture as canon also avoids the idea of an authoritative text whose meaning resides in the mind of God, for canonical texts imply an authority resulting from transmission and reception of traditions that have been shaped in the communities of faith.

Unlike redaction criticism, which investigates the editorial processes leading up to the final form of the text, canonical criticism seeks to understand the effect of redaction on the final form of the text and to investigate its theological dimensions. Childs has shown, for example, how the canonical context of Isaiah 1–39 within Isaiah 1–66 shifts the original emphasis of Isaiah's message of doom for Jerusalem to a movement from judgment to salvation.[9] Although the historical context of First Isaiah is important for exegesis, for Childs this context has been subsumed into the larger literary context of the canonical book of Isaiah. While an exegetical understanding of First Isaiah begins with eighth-century Judah, a canonical reading proceeds from there to analyze how the words of the eighth-century prophet first functioned as scripture when they were preserved on a scroll with the words of the anonymous prophet of sixth-century Babylon. Significant for Childs is the way the original oracles are "loosed from their historical moorings" and thereby made available for successive generations. Reading the oracles of First Isaiah canonically, therefore, means reading them synchronically in the literary and theological context of the whole book of Isaiah. For Childs the focus is not the process of reinterpretation or the hermeneutic leading to the final form of the text but its theological shape. The term "canonical" signifies both the historically final as well as the normative form of the text.

From these two approaches it is possible to distill some basic features characterizing the emerging discipline of canonical criticism. First, while using literary and historical methods, canonical criticism is primarily theological in its nature. Its underlying concern is to find the locus of authority in the biblical texts by analyzing the ways in which the texts were authoritative for the believing communities that received them as scripture. Second, canonical criticism focuses on the dynamics by which the communities of faith and the developing traditions shaped each other. The biblical text is seen as the product of the believing community, but at the same time the community's identity has been shaped by reflection on its religious traditions. The voices of individual authors preserved within the text are of less significance than the "voice" of the text received by the community. Third, canonical criticism assumes that hermeneutics by which the scriptures can be appropriated need not (indeed, should not) be imported from philosophical or theological systems but are to be found within the scriptures themselves. The discipline of canonical criticism attempts to tease them out, either in the hermeneutics of the communities adapting the tradition (Sanders) or in the shape of the canonical text (Childs). Childs expresses this succinctly when he says, "There is no one hermeneutical key for unlocking the biblical message, but the canon provides the arena in which the struggle for understanding takes place."[10]

Fourth, canonical criticism insists that authority resides only in the full canon, which is the context in which every biblical text finally must be read. The voice of a particular tradition is read canonically against other voices and points of view; no position is absolute. Canonical criticism views scripture not as a treasury of stories but as a lively discussion in which theological ideas are constantly being reformulated in response to new data. Childs notes:

> One of the important aspects within the shaping process of the Old Testament is the manner by which different parts of the canon were increasingly interchanged to produce a new angle of vision on the tradition. The canonical process involved the shaping of the tradition not only into independent books, but also into larger canonical units, such as the Torah, Prophets and Writings. For example, law was seen from the perspective of wisdom; psalmody and prophecy were interrelated; and Israel's narrative traditions were sapientialized (cf. Sheppard). The canonical process thus built in a dimension of flexibility which encourages constantly fresh ways of actualizing the material.[11]

Reading in a Canonical Context

Genesis 1–2 offers an opportunity to explore how canonical criticism relies on the results of historical criticism yet approaches the text with a different set of questions. Source criticism has demonstrated that Genesis 1–2 is a composite work, comprised of Priestly traditions in Gen. 1:1–2:4a and Yahwistic traditions in Gen. 2:4b–25, while redaction criticism suggests that P has subordinated the J tradition by subsuming it under the framework established by Genesis 1. P's editorial technique here appears to be asyndetic, setting one text alongside another without any link. As a result scholars refer to "the two creation accounts" in Genesis 1–2 and are interested in differentiating the two accounts by their reliance on earlier traditions, theological presuppositions, and relation to the purposes of J and P.

But the shape of the biblical text before the reader does not suggest that it is offering two contradictory accounts of a single event. The canonical approach tries to make sense of the text as it appears (i.e., the Masoretic text) and to hear in it a single voice, while at the same time affirming that literary-historical analysis has recovered two independent traditions. Since the believing communities transmitted only the text as we have it, scholarly reconstructions of earlier authoritative traditions embedded in the text are pertinent to the prehistory of the text but not to an understanding of its canonical meaning. The canonical text speaks with a single voice, and that is not the voice of the earliest tradent, nor of the redactor, but a new voice that transcends even the intentions of the final redactor.

A canonical approach can legitimately seek the unity of the text in this new voice. Hence Gen. 2:4b, "These are the generations of the heavens and the earth," can be understood not as the end of the P creation account, forming an inclusion with Gen. 1:1, but rather as the introduction to the J account.[12] In this reading, J's account is absorbed into P's and read as an elaboration of it. The creation of heavens and earth in Genesis 1 points to the creation of human beings and their intimate relation to YHWH in the garden. Whatever the striking shift in language and literary style from Genesis 1 to Genesis 2 may suggest about original sources, it now functions to alert the reader to the relationship between the two chapters. Similarly, by reading Genesis 2 as an elaboration of the creation of the heavens and the earth in Genesis 1, the reader is encouraged to hear the language of Genesis 2 as figurative rather than literal.

In wrestling with the problem of the two names for the deity, the ancient rabbis determined that whenever the text said Elohim (God), it referred to the just aspect of the deity, and whenever it said YHWH (Lord), it referred to the deity as merciful. They did not posit two sources behind the text of the Torah, but they did hear two opposing tendencies, and drew from them the lesson of the inscrutability of the Holy One, paradoxically both just and merciful. Reading the text as a unity, the rabbis nevertheless heard the echoes of two voices and tried to maintain their distinctive emphases even as they harmonized them. One of the benefits of canonical criticism is its recovery of the history of interpretation as a legitimate aid to exegesis.

A somewhat different way of reading canonically is to highlight the multivalence in the final shape of the text. If Gen. 2:4a is read as an *inclusio* with Gen. 1:1 and is the end of the Priestly tradition, then a distinctive shift in perspective occurs at 2:4b. As has often been noted, P's term "the heavens and the earth" signifies primary interest in the cosmos and its order, while J's "the earth and the heavens" indicates emphasis on the earth and its inhabitants. The different semantic fields and literary forms employed by the two chapters strengthen the perception that here are two different perspectives. Finally, the different sequence of events and mode of creation in each chapter might well lead a reader to ask why the canonical form of the creation story is so confusing and contradictory. The canonical shape of Genesis 1–2 encourages the reader to attend to the peculiar diction and timbre of each voice in turn. To read Genesis 1–2 canonically is to allow the play of perspectives without insisting on a resolution. Perhaps the "canonical intention" is to remind the believing communities that creation is God's business. One account standing by itself could encourage a literal reading, leading the community to believe that it had the facts of how God created the world. Two conflicting accounts set back to back suggest that all language about the process of creation is figurative.

This understanding of Genesis 1–2 is supported when we broaden the canonical context to include the entire canon of the Hebrew Bible. Most other creation texts are poetic and often highlight the very aspects notably absent from Genesis 1. The battle between the creator god and the waters/dragon of chaos, so prevalent in the literature of Israel's neighbors, does not occur in Genesis 1. The absence of the traditional battle is particularly noticeable because the text opens with uncreated waters and darkness, and God spends the first two days of creation separating off and containing these forces. The creation of light and of the firmament seems to deal with problems posed by preexistent "stuff" whose presence impedes the created order. Of course, no battle takes place; God speaks, and the light and the firmament appear to cordon off the darkness and the waters. Yet P's insistence that God was alone at creation and met no opposition is challenged by poetic traditions (Pss. 74:2–17; 89:5–11; Job 38:8–21) and again in the eschatological visions of the prophets (Isa. 51:9–11) and the apocalyptic belief that the ultimate battle will recapitulate God's victory at creation (Isa. 27:1; most vividly apparent in Revelation 12). The canon bears witness to a variety of creation traditions, some describing a bloody battle between YHWH and chaos, others picturing a calmly majestic artist calling the world into being.

Another creation text, Prov. 8:22–31, provides an alternative to the solitary deity of Genesis 1–2. In Proverbs, Wisdom (Hebrew: *hochma,* Greek: *sophia*) helps YHWH draw up blueprints for the cosmos and delights in the newly created works day by day. She is "the first of YHWH's works," preceding the creation of the world, yet Genesis 1–2 is silent about her. The figure of Wisdom is minor in the canon of the Hebrew Bible, yet becomes indispensable in the development of Christological formulations about the preexistence of the Logos and its role in creation (e.g., in John 1:1–3 and Col. 1:15–17).

Genesis 1–2 reflects the ambiguity of the larger canonical treatment of creation, suggesting that no version of creation can be read as absolute. Since scripture is a canon and not a compendium, a faithful reading cannot select the text most conducive to the reader's own predisposition but must maintain the multiplicity of traditions in all their ambiguity and contradiction. The most significant theological contribution of canonical criticism is the axiom that no voice of the canon should be privileged over others; there is no text by which all other texts must be interpreted. Biblical texts only become the Word of God in their full canonical context.

Canonical Hermeneutics

Reading Genesis 1–2 for its canonical hermeneutics illuminates another significant dimension of the text. The tradition that creation followed a bloody battle between a young deity and the primordial waters of chaos, portrayed as the dragon Tiamat, dominated Babylonian theology. The story of Marduk's victory over Tiamat and his subsequent creation of the world and enthronement as king was read in public celebration at the Babylonian New Year festival. A comparison of this story with Genesis 1 suggests that P incorporated the Babylonian cosmology and some of its storyline into the Israelite creation account, but with a distinctive shift in emphasis. By presenting the waters as a neutral, nameless presence, without history or power, P has transformed the old story into a monotheistic one. But the monotheizing hermeneutic creates the theological problem of theodicy. If there is no Tiamat, who is responsible for the evil we experience in creation?

Genesis 1 maintains a carefully ambivalent stance toward the waters. They have been drained of personality and divine status; nevertheless they remain in their appointed places. On the one hand, they had to be dealt with before God could create the world. On the other hand, they could be contained by the power of the divine word. Contained, but not exterminated. The waters remain, albeit in check behind the firmament and under the earth, a potential threat to creation. This ambivalence toward the power of the waters is seen in P's version of the Flood narrative (Gen. 7:11), in which God temporarily allows the primordial waters to reclaim their original power, devastating the whole creation except the occupants of a single boat designed to withstand the waters. P calls attention again to the hostile nature of the waters in the Noachic covenant, when God promises never again to let the waters destroy the earth. Yet they remain, encircling the world from above, on the other side of the firmament, and from below, lapping at the pillars supporting the earth.

Elsewhere in the canon, the menacing nature of the waters is graphically evoked. The use of the deep as an image of peril in the Psalms (Pss. 18:–19; 69:1–3; 130:1) and the description of wicked enemies as "waters" (Isa. 17:12–14, S. of Sol. 8:7) testifies to the link made between the primordial waters and the human experience of evil. The interpretation of the ancient Babylonian story with a monotheistic hermeneutic results in a text in which the potential for evil in a good creation becomes a way of describing the freedom of God. It turns the question of theodicy around to view it from God's perspective, and what we are shown is the impenetrable mystery of the uncreated waters checked by the divine word.[13]

For those in Babylon who had lost their land and for whom God's promise seemed dead, the question of evil was not an academic one. The book of Lamentations and Psalms 74 and 137 eloquently bear witness to the genuine despair that threatened to overcome the exiled Judeans whose theological framework was inadequate to contain their experience. Either God had been defeated by Marduk or he had ruthlessly abandoned his people and promises. Even the theological explanation that eventually dominated, construing the exile as punishment for Judah's sins, was not wholly adequate. In the exile, apparently, the innocent had been swept away with the guilty.

In the context of this experience of cognitive dissonance between the official theology and the experience of the exile, the hermeneutics by which the ancient traditions were resignified in Genesis 1 are significant. Our reading suggests that theirs was a hermeneutic that above all presupposed the freedom of God. Not only is God not bound by any other powers in the universe, he is not even bound by Israel's theology. By placing Genesis 1 at the beginning of the Torah, the canonical shapers provided a lens through which the ensuing stories could be read. God is God, and is not limited by any human understanding of what a deity ought to do. The unthinkable had happened to Israel, and it threatened its most cherished doctrines about God. In this context of devastation, P fashioned a new way of reading the old stories, teaching the Judahites that their understanding of God had been inadequate; they needed to do a new reading of their entire history.

The Limits of Canonical Readings

Canonical criticism is in its formative stages, and its originators are still the most significant practitioners, but even at this stage misreadings demonstrate that reductive understandings are a serious problem. Some critics mistakenly construe canonical criticism to be akin to the New Criticism in literary analysis, an interest in the literary text without reference to any historical context. This misunderstanding arises from focusing on Childs's emphasis on interpreting the text in its final form and fails to grasp the importance of the believing communities as the context in which the text has been shaped.[14]

A second misunderstanding sees in canonical criticism an attempt to return to precritical reading, casting aside the gains of historical-critical work. This reductive view fails to see the foundations of historical-critical exegesis on which canonical criticism is based, and the tendency of canonical criticism to favor multiple readings of every biblical text. It is ironic that canonical criticism is attacked by some as akin to fundamentalism and by others as leaning toward deconstruction. And there may be cause for concern. Childs's work is extensive and highly nuanced. But in lesser hands canonical criticism could become simply a way of avoiding the arduous process of exegesis and returning to precritical reading of scripture.

An unresolved theological problem resulting from the hegemony of the historical-critical method is the relation of history to the biblical witness. Canonical criticism assumes that scripture resulted from the believing communities' reflection on Israel's religious traditions. Because the act of shaping loosened the traditions from their original moorings, the original historical contexts of passages recoverable by historical-critical methods have been subordinated to the canonical context in which they have been preserved. The actual events that gave rise to the religious traditions in the first place are not only for the most part unrecoverable but also secondary. It is the witness of the believing community that is canonical, not the historical event itself. Canonical criticism resists dethroning the biblical witness as only one source of historical information among many. Here, canonical criticism has raised a most significant theological issue: What is the relation between historical-critical study of the Bible and its use as religious literature?[15]

On the other hand, canonical criticism as practiced by Childs tends to absolutize the historical moment crystallized in the final form of the text, without much regard for the historical factors that may have influenced its formation. The moment of canonization, like earlier moments in the development of the text, was motivated by immediate concerns of the community; it was not directed at unborn generations centuries away. The canonical shapers of Isaiah may have loosed the oracles of First Isaiah from their historical moorings to attach them to the oracles of an anonymous exilic prophet, but they did so in response to a particular historical situation. Any move away from understanding the biblical writings in their historical context, at any stage in their development, opens the risk of absolutizing the words at the expense of the Word.

Another potential danger in canonical criticism is the tendency to read texts as a unity and therefore to prefer harmonization to dissonance and uncertainty. Reading a biblical book canonically is like walking a tightrope, because it means attending to the subordinated voices even while hearing them in the context of the dominant voice. When a canonical-critical reading subordinates earlier sources to later ones, it risks flattening out the text in order to make it more accessible to the reader. Yet it is precisely in the nature of the canon to protect the ancient voices and to create dissonances within the texts. The canon has a peculiar double effect, encouraging the reader to find unity in the texts, yet at the same time checking those attempts by its plurality of voices. Even if earlier traditions are intentionally recontextualized and subsumed in the final form of the text, they still remain part of its fabric. Sometimes the "fabric" of the text works against its final shape; in such cases, the tension is a critical part of the authoritative voice of the text, transcending the agenda of any one historical group, including the canonical shapers, but preserving them all.[16] The sum is truly greater than the parts, but it will not tell the truth unless the parts function in it. Because of this peculiar nature of the canon, "the Bible contains its own self-corrective apparatus."[17] Further, "with its affirmation that many have been given glimpses of God's purpose and none has the entire, complete and final answer, the canon calls us to continue to study the text."[18]

Perhaps here is the genuine theological issue of canonical criticism as a hermeneutical approach to the text. Childs says that "the use of the term 'canonical integrity' is not to be identified with literary, historical, or conceptual unity. It refers rather to the effectiveness of the literature to function coherently within a community of faith."[19] Elsewhere he says:

> I do not wish to suggest that the canonical shaping provides a full-blown hermeneutic as if there were only one correct interpretation built into every text which a proper canonical reading could always recover. The canonical shaping provided larger contexts for interpretation, established the semantic level, and left important structural and material keys for understanding. Nevertheless, exegesis also involves the activity of the interpreter who from his modern context must also construe the material. There is an important dimension of "reader competence" which reacts to the coercion exercised by the text itself.[20]

Ideally, canonical shaping provides a guide to interpretation, not the assumption of a single "correct" reading. In practice, however, by finding a hermeneutical key in the final shape of the text, canonical criticism gives the impression of offering at least the parameters of a theologically definitive reading. The frequency of the term "normative" in canonical criticism further encourages the conclusion that the readings of canonical criticism are somehow authoritative ones. The variety of possible readings of Genesis 1–2 proposed above attempts to show that canonical criticism properly leads not to one normative reading but to a variety of canonical possibilities in a text. Perhaps the future of canonical criticism lies in the work of staking out the parameters within which a multiplicity of readings can function for the believing communities.

Notes

1. For a discussion of the relation between biblical theology and canonical criticism see James Barr, *Holy Scripture: Canon, Authority, Criticism* (Philadelphia: Westminster, 1983), pp. 130–44; Childs's review of Barr's book in "Childs vs. Barr," *Interpretation* 38 (1984):66–70; and James Sanders, *From Sacred Story to Sacred Text* (Philadelphia: Fortress, 1987), pp. 155–63.

2. Brevard Childs, "Psalm Titles and Midrashic Exegesis," *Journal of Semitic Studies* 16 (1971):137–50.

3. James Sanders, *From Sacred Story to Sacred Text*, p. 165.

4. Gerald Sheppard, cited in Brevard Childs, *Introduction to the Old Testament as Scripture* (Philadelphia: Fortress, 1979), p. 79; James Sanders, *From Sacred Story to Sacred Text*, p. 158.

5. James Sanders, *Canon and Community: A Guide to Canonical Criticism* (Philadelphia: Fortress, 1984), p. 20.

6. For an interchange between Childs and Sanders see the responses to Childs's *Introduction to the Old Testament as Scripture* and the rejoinder by Childs in *Horizons in Biblical Theology* 2 (1980):113–211.

7. Childs, *Introduction to the Old Testament as Scripture*, p. 82.

8. "Childs vs. Barr," p. 68.

9. Childs, *Introduction to the Old Testament as Scripture*, pp. 325–33.

10. Brevard Childs, *Old Testament Theology in a Canonical Context* (Philadelphia: Fortress, 1985), p. 15.

11. Childs, *Old Testament Theology in a Canonical Context*, p. 13.

12. *Introduction to the Old Testament as Scripture*, pp. 148–150.

13. For a fuller exploration of the relation between the motif of the waters and the problem of evil see John Levenson, *Creation and the Persistence of Evil* (San Francisco: Harper & Row, 1988).

14. John Barton's *Reading the Old Testament* (Philadelphia: Westminster, 1984), in which he presents canonical criticism as essentially a form of literary analysis, is a prime example of such a misunderstanding.

15. See Childs's remarks in "Response to Reviewers of *Introduction to the Old Testament as Scripture*," *Journal for the Study of the Old Testament* 16 (1980):52–60; and *Introduction to the Old Testament as Scripture*, p. 15.

16. A careful reader of 1 Samuel 7–31 cannot help seeing that the voice of the "early source," which is pro-Saul, cannot be readily harmonized with the redactor's

voice, which is pro-David. Because the early Saul traditions and Saul's demise are so intertwined with David's rise, the canonical shape of the text suggests something of the dark side of God. As Childs repeatedly insists, a canonical reading is not coterminous with the agenda of the last redactors.

17. Sanders, *Canon and Community*, p. 46.

18. Donn F. Morgan, *Between Text and Community: The "Writings" in Canonical Interpretation* (Minneapolis: Fortress, 1990), p. 147.

19. Childs, "Response," p. 55.

20. "Childs vs. Barr," p. 69.

For Further Reading

Childs, Brevard. *The Book of Exodus.* Philadelphia: Westminster, 1974.
———. *Introduction to the Old Testament as Scripture.* Philadelphia: Fortress, 1979.
———. *Old Testament Theology in a Canonical Context.* Philadelphia: Fortress, 1985.
Sanders, James. *Canon and Community: A Guide to Canonical Criticism.* Philadelphia: Fortress, 1984.
———. *From Sacred Story to Sacred Text.* Philadelphia: Fortress, 1987.

8

RHETORICAL
CRITICISM

Yehoshua Gitay

G OD'S complaint against the nation of Israel, which starts Isaiah's first address, is rhetorical speech:

> Hear, O heavens, and listen, O earth
> for the LORD has spoken:
> I reared children and brought them up,
> but they have rebelled against me.
> The ox knows its owner,
> and the donkey its master's crib;
> but Israel does not know,
> my people do not understand.

This speech seeks persuasion—to persuade the eternal witnesses, heaven and earth, that the people of Israel have betrayed God. Isaiah's argument avoids abstraction, using instead concrete, indisputable examples. A common argumentative ground is thus established between the speaker and his audience; both sides share the fundamental premise that animals are faithful to their masters. Therefore, the accuser may draw the conclusion that the people of Israel, in contrast, are unfaithful to their God, who is their father and owner—a paradox. The argument contained in this prophetic "proof" is quasi-logical rather than scientific. It occupies a middle ground between rational, mathematical proof and emotional appeal.[1] This kind of argumentation is typical of religious rhetoric.[2]

This passage from Isaiah illustrates the oratorical appeal of prophetic address as a whole, which has as its goal persuading an audience to change its thinking patterns. It also illustrates the communicative nature of biblical discourse, which seeks in numerous cases to appeal to its readers/listeners. The search for effective communication invites a specific literary method that will enable the critic systematically to study the discourse's strategy and tech-

135

niques of effective communication. This method is known as "rhetorical criticism" or "rhetorical analysis." For reasons discussed below, the term "rhetorical analysis" is preferred for the approach described in this chapter.

Rhetoric, according to Aristotle's classical definition, is "the faculty [power] of discovering in the particular case what are the available means of persuasion."[3] Rhetoric is the art of putting a thought over in a particular manner. Rhetorical study is a pragmatic method of analysis that integrates the three dimensions of a literary work: the author, the text itself, and the audience.[4] The author/speaker establishes his or her thematic goal through the transmission of his or her thought into a text (speech). The listener's/reader's situation, ways of perception, and set of mind are also taken into consideration by the author/speaker. The discourse is structured and shaped thematically and stylistically in order to capture the audience's interest. Rhetoric, the art of persuasion, is concerned with an audience who may not share or may even oppose the speaker's/author's ideas, concepts, or ideologies. Rhetorical analysis reveals the speaker's strategy of appealing to or mastering the audience's mind.

Since rhetoric is argumentative in nature (with certain modifications to be discussed below), the study of rhetoric requires a reconstruction of the argumentative situation: the condition that gave birth to a given discourse. In other words, the rhetorical utterance is a response to a specific argumentative situation (also known as the rhetorical situation). "It is the situation which calls the discourse into existence. . . . We need to understand that a particular discourse comes into existence because of some specific condition or situation which invites utterance."[5]

This definition of rhetorical analysis requires further clarification. James Muilenburg's renowned call for an extension of form criticism[6] is what many biblical scholars, following Muilenburg's own terminology, mean by "rhetorical criticism." But Muilenburg's approach is an expression of stylistic-formalist awareness rather than a systematic study of early Hebrew rhetoric, the biblical art of persuasion, which is the concern of the present chapter. Muilenburg's "rhetorical criticism" focuses on stylistic phenomena such as figurative language and relationships of sounds as ends in themselves. Therefore, biblical scholarship regards Muilenburg's school of rhetorical criticism as a synchronic approach that aims to reveal the art of the final product, that is, the aesthetic dimension of the text. However, "rhetorical analysis" or "rhetorical study," as described in this chapter, is a pragmatic analysis that seeks to reveal the mutual relationship of the author(s), the text, and the audience. Style is just one aspect of rhetoric, which endeavors to reach the audience effectively.

Rhetorical analysis is also frequently associated with reception theories such as reader-response criticism. There is, however, a significant difference between the two approaches. Receptionists focus on the act of reading and the audience's imagination and self-interpretation.[7] Rhetoric, however, attempts to bring the audience into agreement with the thinking of the author. Thus the analysis of rhetoric focuses on the text itself, regarding the audience as an element in the deliberate communicative endeavor and not as a subjective commentator.

Rhetorical Analysis of Prophetic Literature

The Israelite prophets challenge the fundamental assumptions as well as the political and religious institutions of their society. But a close reading of prophetic speech shows that condemning the people's deeds is not an end in itself. The prophets also seek persuasion: explaining to their audience the consequence of their deeds and calling them to choose the right way. It is thus no accident that the discussion of biblical rhetoric starts with the prophets, whose speeches present their rhetorical endeavor to deliver persuasively a disputable message.

Amos 5:18 illustrates this rhetorical endeavor:

> Alas for you who desire the day of the LORD!
> Why do you want the day of the LORD?
> It is darkness, not light.

Here Amos contradicts the religious consensus of his time by questioning the popular concept of God as savior and arguing instead for a concept of God as judge. He thus denies a religious premise that is fundamental for his audience. It is doubtful that Amos would be able to change his audience's mind about that premise merely by denying it. A specific strategy of appeal needs to be employed. Therefore, Amos must choose a thesis agreed upon by his opponents as his point of departure. Then from this established common ground, he may argue for his specific point of view.

Chaim Perelman, the noted rhetorician, illuminates the general nature of the argumentative process:

> Lest he fail in his mission, the speaker should depart from his premises only when he knows that they are adequately accepted; if they are not, the speaker's first concern should be to reinforce them with all the means at his disposal. This transfer of adherence is accomplished only through the establishment of a bond between the premises and the theses whose acceptance the speaker wants to achieve.[8]

A common perspective shared by the speaker and the audience is essential for effective communication. The prophet, therefore, avoids abstraction, beginning instead with particular points of agreement.

Amos's long series of rhetorical questions, which comprise his speech of 3:1–15, reveals his rhetorical concern. He affirms a universal truth or law of nature: Two people who walk together surely planned their meeting in advance (3:3); a lion will not roar in the forest unless it has prey (3:4). Then, after he has established a common-ground agreement with his audience, Amos turns to the disputable issue:

> Does disaster befall a city
> Unless the Lord has done it? (3:6)

This is not mathematical proof but a sound quasi-logical argument that draws its conclusion based on the principle of cause and effect. The prophet's religious concept of God's punishment, based on his religious thesis of cause and effect, is founded on the law of nature that rejects the incidental: *ex nihilo nihil fit* ("nothing comes from nothing").

Turning our attention back to the prophet Isaiah, we can see that he differs from his audience regarding the question of true worship. Isaiah challenges his listeners' religious assumption that sacrifice is the proper means of satisfying the divine:

> What to me is the multitude of your sacrifices?
>   says the Lord;
> I have had enough of burnt offerings of rams
>   and the fat of fed beasts;
> I do not delight in the blood of bulls,
>   or of lambs, or of goats. (1:11)

Isaiah's goal is to convey the notion that cult is secondary while moral-ethical behavior is the primary religious requirement:

> Wash yourselves; make yourselves clean;
>   remove the evil of your doings
>   from before my eyes; cease to do evil. (1:16)

Isaiah thus seeks to introduce a new concept that challenges popular practice. This new concept is difficult for his listeners to accept. Hence, he employs specific rhetorical means to ease the task of persuading his audience. He argues his case, avoiding the abstract and emphasizing the particular, in order to present his view of Israel's misbehavior:

> The ox knows its owner,
>   and the donkey its master's crib;
> but Israel does not know,
>   my people do not understand. (1:3)

The prophet compels the attention of his audience by employing the quasi-logical argument of comparison, which is an effective rhetorical means of persuasion, described in the classical handbook on rhetoric known as *Ad Herennium:* "It is, moreover, presented in the form of a contrast. For a comparison in the form of a contrast is used when we deny that something else is like the thing we are asserting to be true. . . . Thus the comparison is used for the purpose of proof."[9]

Isaiah compares Israel to animals who understand certain rules of behavior; absurdly, concludes Isaiah, Israel rejects this law of nature. But logic itself is insufficient: "It is not enough to know what we ought to say; we must also say it as we ought . . . the way in which the thing is said does affect its intelligibility."[10] That "how" (style, form) is as important as "what" (message, content) as an essential rhetorical premise. A study of Isaiah's language in 1:3 reveals a specific intentional stylistic device. The use of the first person pronominal suffix *)ammi* ("my people" in v. 3b) instead of the abstract noun *)am* ("people") intends to strengthen the tension in this passage: The ox and the ass are referred to abstractly, while God's nation is alluded to personally ("my"). The language points out the absurdity of the people's actions—those whom God personally brought up ignore him. The sudden turn from the third person indirect approach ("Israel") to an intimate first person approach ("my people") dramatically highlights the people's disloyalty.

Style is the weapon that any speaker employs to reach an audience. "We must assign to each style the figures that are appropriate to it," claims Demetrius, the great classical theoretician of effective style.[11] The following examples illustrate the contribution that a consideration of style in rhetorical analysis can make to the critical study of prophetic literature.

1. It is almost an axiom in modern prophetic research that the prophets were poets.[12] Hence, prose sentences in the prophetic books are frequently regarded as secondary editorial additions. A close reading of Isa. 1:18–20, for instance, indicates a dramatic stylistic shift in the address. The previous lines in vv. 16–17 are short and rhythmical, representing the condensed characteristic biblical verse:[13]

> Wash yourselves, make yourselves clean;
> > remove the evil of your doings
> > from before my eyes;
> cease to do evil,
> > learn to do good;
> seek justice,
> > rescue the oppressed;
> defend the orphan,
> > plead for the widow.

However, vv. 18–20 read:

> Come now, let us argue it out, says the LORD. . . . If you are will-
> ing and obedient, you shall eat the good of the land; but if you
> refuse and rebel, you shall be devoured by the sword; for the
> mouth of the LORD has spoken.

The latter represents a change from the dramatic, rhythmical, condensed
structure of poetry. The language of vv. 18–20 is characteristic of biblical
prose. Should we conclude, then, that the prose lines are non-Isaianic, a later
scribal addition?

The answer is no, since the prophet should be viewed as both a poet and a
prose narrator who adapts his style skillfully to the audience's perception.
Thus prose sections may be seen as part of the original prophetic text. The
emotional poetic tone of vv. 16–17 seeks to capture the audience's mind;
there is no room for contemplation as the prophet's words strike his listeners.
Verses 18–20, however, call for consideration, as Isaiah appeals to his listeners
to think further. The change in style reflects a new rhetorical situation: The
style moves more slowly, with lines now joined (unlike vv. 16–17) by the
conjunction "and," and reflecting considerably less emotion. The switch from
emotionally tense language to a balanced contemplative style is rhetorically
functional. It does not necessitate the assignment to two different authors
(contrary to what form-critical analysis might contend) but stems from considerations of rhetoric.[14]

2. It has long been established that biblical verse consists primarily of parallel units. It is usually claimed, therefore, that the unparalleled line of
Isa. 1:4d, "Who are utterly estranged," indicates an accident in the transmission of the text. But this line is rhetorically functional; the unresolved parallel
is particularly striking for the listener who expects its fulfillment. Curiosity,
and therefore concentration, is raised to the breaking point. As a contemporary
biblical critic has observed, "The process of literary creation . . . is an unceas-
ing dialectic between the necessity to use established forms in order to be able
to communicate coherently and the necessity to break and remake those forms
because they are arbitrary restrictions and because what is merely repeated
automatically no longer conveys a message."[15] Since Isaiah's aim is to attract
the attention of a hostile audience, he must arm himself with the appropriate
stylistic techniques for capturing his listener's ears.

3. The mixture of styles, the breaking of literary patterns, and the employment of long asymmetrical verses call attention to the crucial question of the
nature of prophetic speech. Since Hermann Gunkel's pioneering form-critical
studies, which emphasized the conventional, impersonal nature of biblical discourse, there has been a general consensus among critics that the prophets
delivered short oracles rather than lengthy orations. Each individual literary

form, argued Gunkel, is an independent prophetic oracle.[16] According to this approach, Isa. 1:10–17 bears the form of a priestly instruction, a *torah*, which isolates it as a single oracle.[17]

Rhetorical analysis, however, reveals that prophetic speeches are fluent, oratorical addresses. They are usually divided into four or five functional parts or paragraphs: an introduction (prologue), a statement of facts, a thesis (which the prophet may confirm with specific examples), and an epilogue. This structure is flexible, and certain speeches do not contain every part. Isaiah 1:2–20 contains an introduction (vv. 2–3), a statement of facts (vv. 4–9), a confirmation (vv. 10–17), and an epilogue (vv. 18–20). This structure allows the prophet to introduce gradually his notion of the relationship between God and the people. Thus he can appeal to his audience rather than simply provoking them by challenging concepts that are fundamental to them. The structural argumentative order intends "to persuade, and the crux of the problem is not, ordinarily, to establish valid terms but to establish a persuasive relationship between them."[18]

Rhetorical analysis differentiates three kinds of oratory: (1) *judicial* (legal), (2) *deliberative* (political), and (3) *epideictic* (ceremonial).[19] In *judicial* speech the speaker seeks to persuade the audience to make a judgment about events occurring in the past; a speech is *deliberative* when the speaker seeks to persuade the audience to take some action in the future and *epideictic* when the speaker celebrates or denounces some person or quality. Prophetic address, because of its generally polemical nature (e.g., Isa. 1:2–20 and Amos 3:1–15) corresponds primarily to *deliberative* speech. But a number of speeches of rejoicing and salvation may be categorized as *epideictic* (e.g., Isa. 8:21—9:6 and 10:33—12:6). Also, many of the Psalms (e.g., Pss. 6; 23; 29) belong to the category of *epideictic* oratory. The rhetorical methods described above apply to all categories of oratory. In short, due to their views, which oppose the religious standards of their audience, prophetic speeches are the main object of rhetorical study. Nevertheless, other parts of the Bible that display a polemical or argumentative intention are also the subject of rhetorical analysis.

Rhetorical Analysis of Other Biblical Poetry

Since biblical poetry is mainly a form of speech, the criteria for rhetorical analysis exemplified earlier are useful in analyzing all biblical poetic utterances. The book of Job, for instance, is a desperate rhetorical appeal by Job and the friends to persuade one another. Job's speech of chapter 3 is a rhetorical attempt to convey his feeling of emptiness. There is no meaning, claims Job, in the present world, which ought to function according to moral cause and effect. He presents a full speech, twenty-three verses long, in order to demonstrate the controversial view that it is better not to be born at all, and existence in the world of darkness is preferable, since there is neither suffering nor injustice there.

> "Let the day perish in which I was born,
>   and the night that said, 'A man-child is conceived.'
> Let that day be darkness.
>   May God above not seek it,
>   or light shine on it.
> Let gloom and deep darkness claim it.
>   Let clouds settle upon it;
>   let the blackness of the day terrify it." (3:3–5)

Thus Job argues his point not by employing an argument of strict reason or by challenging God in a philosophical manner but by a graphic articulation of his emotional state, which is meant to remain on the mind of the audience.

God's response to Job (chapters 38–41) is also characteristic of the biblical art of religious rhetoric:

> "Who is this that darkens counsel by words without knowledge?
> . . . .
> Where were you when I laid the foundations of the earth?
> . . . .
> Who determined its measurements—surely you know!"
>   (38:2–5)

This is not the answer that Job (or the reader) expects. God neither answers Job's accusations nor responds to the friends' apologetic reasoning. God's rhetorical questions sharpen the difference between the human and the divine. There is no common language, and Job appears foolish for trying to argue "reasonably" against God! Through rhetoric, speakers portray their opponents in a ridiculous way, one which does not allow a reasonable answer. God does not need to apologize or prove his innocence. The rhetoric of the passage demonstrates Job's ignorance. The rhetorical questions manipulate him into confirming God's uniqueness and hence God's unchallengeable nature.

The use of rhetorical questions, as in Job, is an important tool in speech. "The rhetorical question is one of the most forceful and effectual ways employed in speech for driving home some idea for conviction. Because of its impressive and persuasive effect the hearer is not merely listener; he is forced to frame the expected answer in his mind, and by doing so, he actually becomes the coexpressor of the speaker's conviction."[20]

An analysis of Psalm 1 may demonstrate the impact of rhetorical study on the Psalms. Form critics point out that Psalm 1 is didactic poetry: "We should expect to find the writer of the psalm in the circles of teachers of wisdom and

Torah."[21] This determination of the thematic formalistic category of the psalm is helpful. However, rhetorical analysis is concerned with the specific, pragmatic dimension of the psalm. The question is how the psalmist delivered his message to his audience. The message is plain: God will support the righteous but diminish the wicked. This is a conventional theme, one that is in danger of becoming a cliché. The psalmist seeks to avoid the cliché and to attract his audience's attention. The way in which he may effectively appeal to his audience is the major rhetorical concern. In this case the psalmist employs an extended metaphor:

> They (righteous people) are like trees
> planted by streams of water,
> which yield their fruit in its season,
> and their leaves do not wither.
> In all that they do, they prosper. (v. 3)

In contrast:

> The wicked are not so,
> but are like chaff which the wind drives away. (v. 4)

The function of this metaphor is to express a contrast between the poet's point and reality. The poet wishes to paint an optimistic picture of the success of the righteous, a picture that is not self-evident in real life. Hence, rather than arguing the case theologically, the poet employs a metaphor. The metaphor exhibits the known reality of nature, which is undeniable. A picture from the sphere of nature is applied to the theological sphere of reward and punishment as a fact that speaks for itself.

Rhetorical Criticism of Biblical Narrative

Biblical narrative is constructed of two literary components: (1) narrative reports in the third person and (2) dialogues or speeches. By exploring the mutual relationship between author, text, and audience, the study of rhetoric seeks to reveal the message (content, theme) of a narrative and then to investigate its means of communication (style, form). Thus rhetorical study is not limited to sporadic literary episodes and their literary history. Sometimes the message of a text is not revealed explicitly in a single literary episode but is conveyed vis-à-vis the structure of the whole. The individual episode dramatizes the overall message or plot so as to capture the audience's interest. That is to say, rhetorical study must search for the message or plot of the entire composition as well as the dramatic devices in individual episodes. Hence, rhetorical study of narrative is concerned with two questions: "what" (content, plot, message) and "how" (form, style, literary means). Thus rhetorical analysis obviously applies only to dynamic narrative texts, texts that deliver a specific thematic/ideological message, and not to schematic genealogical, administrative, or geographical lists.[22]

An example is the *Akedah* or story of the "binding" of Isaac in Genesis 22. In contrast to form criticism, rhetorical analysis does not focus on its preliterary history but treats it in light of the major theme of the Abraham stories as a whole—the promise of many descendants through Isaac and the obstacles to the fulfillment of this promise. The chain of stories about Abraham carries a specific didactic intent. The fulfillment of the promise is not an earthly matter that can be achieved by human beings, however outstanding they may be. The promise has been given by God. Abraham, the carrier of the promise, received his son Isaac, the object of the promise, not by the power of nature but by the interference of God. The *Akedah* provides tension within the theme of the promise, raising curiosity and increasing the audience's attention to the difficult question of fulfillment. The *Akedah* is the climax to the series of obstacles to the promise: the childlessness of Abraham and Sarah, their age, the birth of Ishmael, and his exclusion as heir. The sacrifice of Isaac would make the promise of a nation through Isaac impossible to fulfill. Together with these other obstacles, the story makes clear that the fulfillment of the promise depends on God alone.

The *Akedah*, therefore, is a rhetorical endeavor to dramatize the question of God's fulfillment of the promise to Abraham. God's command that Abraham sacrifice Isaac increases the tension in the narrative and for the narrative's audience. Does God regret the promise (as he regretted creating humankind before the Flood)? The direct question of the son ("where is the lamb for the sacrifice?") and the ambiguous response of the father ("God himself will provide the lamb for a burnt offering") are followed by long silences. These are broken by short dialogues that utilize the intimate language of "father" and "son" (vv. 7–8). The form and structure of this passage are designed to create tension and to communicate a message in the most dramatic manner.

Speeches by nature reflect a specific polemical situation. The effective speech of Hushai, who succeeded in refuting the more rational recommendation of the wise counselor, Ahithophel (2 Sam. 17:1–14), demonstrates the oratorical-rhetorical nature of speeches employed in narrative.[23] Hushai faces a rhetorical problem: how to refute Ahithophel's brilliant advice (17:1–3). Hushai immediately opposes Ahithophel, emphasizing, however, that as a rule Ahithophel's advice is good; only this time it is not good. Thus Hushai does not directly challenge Ahithophel but describes an alternative.

Hushai's argument consists of two parts. First, he claims to have an intimate knowledge of David and his plans for the war. Thus he begins by confirming what Absalom knows—that David and his warriors are stubborn fighters. He employs a metaphor to drive home the point to Absalom:

> You know that your father and his men are warriors, and that they are enraged like a bear robbed of her cubs in the field. Besides your father is expert in war; he will not spend the night with the troops. (v. 8)

Hushai's advice has been countered. Nevertheless, he continues, appealing to Absalom's character. He realizes that Absalom is still unsure of himself and that the image of David, the father and the king, still moves the son, Absalom.

> Then even the valiant warrior, whose heart is like the heart of a lion will utterly melt with fear, for all Israel knows that your father is a warrior, and that those who are with him are valiant warriors. (v. 10)

This is psychological reassurance. Hushai assures Absalom that if he chooses to disregard Ahithophel's advice and does not attack right away, it is not due to cowardice but to reason; everyone fears David. Again, Hushai employs a metaphor to communicate the fear David inspires.

Now Hushai submits his own advice, which is also expressed metaphorically. Absalom should bring together all Israel "like the sand by the sea for multitude" (v. 11) " . . . and we shall light on him as the dew falls on the ground" (v. 12). Hushai's goal is to give David time to escape, a goal he achieves thanks to his shrewd rhetoric. Indeed, according to the narrator, Husahi's rhetoric saves David and his faithful men. Speech can be powerful; rhetoric can affect the outcome of important situations!

Is there a fixed paradigm of ancient Hebrew persuasion or effective communication? The instances presented here are characteristic. Emotions, exaggerations, repetitions, sound effects, examples, and parables are all used to appeal to an audience. Roland Barthes, the noted French structuralist, has recently called for a systematic study of structure, a "model" of rhetoric that would address this question. He writes:

> The literary message can and must be subjected to a systematic exploration, without which we can never confront it with the History which produces it, since the historical being of this message is not only what it says but also the way in which it is fabricated. Of course, the linguistics of connotation—which we cannot confuse with the old stylistics, for the latter studying means of expression, remained on the level of speech [*parole*], while the former, studying codes, takes its place on the level of the language [*langue*]—is not yet constituted.[24]

While Barthes's call is significant, we must recognize that each case is specific. Therefore, the rhetorical critic must systematically study the nature of a given literature and its codes of communication. This systematic communicative study brings to light stylistic conventions. Then the same conventions can be sought in specific instances, which are unique in their particular situations and thus exclusive in their literary structure and stylistic shape. Accordingly, style is a tool for achieving effective communication and must be studied as an integral part of the message and the rhetorical situation of a given text; the study of style is never an end in itself.

Because it plays a part in the author's ideology and the audience's condition, rhetoric is a study that impinges on the three dimensions of literary discourse: the literature itself, its readers, and its author. This integral study allows one to see more clearly the nature of biblical literature, the author's and audience's perception. Prophecy, wisdom, and narrative in the Bible are all complex literatures. Each is comprised of varieties of stylistic genres and incorporates long harmonic literary units that have been shaped in order to communicate effectively to the readers/listeners. Recent interest in the text itself rather than its literary history contributes significantly to the study of biblical rhetoric. It calls attention to the uniqueness of a given biblical narrative rather than focusing on its impersonal formulaic language.

The Hebrew Bible is oratorical in nature. The speeches and the dialogues take place either between human beings or between God and humankind. All speeches seek communication; they seek either to persuade (i.e., to obtain results) or to communicate emotions such as rejoicing and thanksgiving. This sacred oratory is didactic in nature. The speeches intend to teach; a lively, dynamic literature is in process. Rhetorical analysis reveals this didactic character of biblical literature. The study of rhetoric enables the modern critic to reconstruct the didactic matrix in its historical-cultural circumstances. Rhetorical analysis provides the means of restoring the natural tone of biblical oratory, its logic of argumentation, and its emotional atmosphere. The systematic study of rhetoric opens the window for understanding the polemical nature of biblical literature, its argumentation, and its modes of effective communication.

Notes

1. For the question of rhetorical argumentation consult Chaim Perelman and Lucie Olbrechts-Tyleca, *The Realm of Rhetoric* (Notre Dame, Ind.: University of Notre Dame, 1982), pp. 53–80.

2. On the nature of religious rhetoric see Ernesto Grassi, *Rhetoric as Philosophy* (University Park, Pa.: Pennsylvania State University, 1980), pp. 102–14.

3. Aristotle, *The "Art" of Rhetoric*, trans. H. E. Butler, Loeb Classical Library (Cambridge, Mass.: Harvard, 1926), 1355b.

4. Consult Edward P. J. Corbett, *Rhetorical Analyses of Literary Works* (New York: Oxford University Press, 1969), p. xxvii.

5. Lloyd F. Bitzer, "The Rhetorical Situation," in *Rhetoric: A Tradition in Transition,* ed. W. R. Fisher (Ann Arbor: Michigan State, 1974), p. 247.

6. James Muilenburg, "Form Criticism and Beyond," *Journal of Biblical Literature* 88 (1969):1–18.

7. See the chapter by Edgar V. McKnight on reader-response criticism in this book. See also Terry Eagleton, *Literary Theory* (Minneapolis: University of Minnesota, 1983), pp. 54–90; and Hans Robert Jauss, *Toward an Aesthetic of Reception* (Minneapolis: University of Minnesota, 1982).

8. Perelman and Olbrechts-Tyleca, *Rhetoric,* p. 21.

9. *Ad Herennium,* trans. Harry Caplan, Loeb Classical Library (Cambridge, Mass.: Harvard, 1954), 4.46.

10. Aristotle, *Rhetoric,* 1403b–1404a.

11. Demetrius, *On Style,* trans. W. Rhys Roberts, Loeb Classical Library (Cambridge, Mass.: Harvard, 1953), p. 76.

12. Bishop Robert Lowth, professor of poetry at Oxford, inaugurated the modern, systematic study of biblical poetry more than two hundred years ago. See his *De sacra poesi Hebraeorum* (1753) (*Lectures on the Sacred Poetry of the Hebrews* [New York: Garland, 1971]).

13. See James Kugel, *The Idea of Biblical Poetry* (New Haven, Conn.: Yale University Press, 1981).

14. The issue is discussed at length in Yehoshua Gitay, "Oratorical Rhetoric," *Amsterdamse Cahiers* 10 (1989):72–83.

15. Robert Alter, *The Art of Biblical Narrative* (New York: Basic Books, 1981), p. 62.

16. See Hermann Gunkel, *What Remains of the Old Testament* (New York: Macmillan, 1928); "The Israelite Prophecy from the Time of Amos," in *Twentieth Century Theology in the Making,* ed. J. Pelikan (New York: Harper & Row, 1969), pp. 48–75; "Jesaia 33, eine prophetische Liturgie," *Zeitschrift für die alttestamentliche Wissenschaft* 42 (1924):63–88.

17. See Joachim Begrich, "Die priesterliche Tora," *Beihefte zur Zeitschrift für die alttestamentliche Wissenschaft* 66 (1936):232–60.

18. W. J. Brandt, *The Rhetoric of Argumentation* (Indianapolis: Bobbs-Merrill, 1970), p. 61.

19. See Aristotle, *Rhetoric,* 1358a.

20. J. C. Labuschagne, *The Incomparability of Yahweh in the Old Testament* (Leiden: E. J. Brill, 1966), p. 23.

21. Hans-Joachim Kraus, *Psalms 1–59* (Minneapolis: Augsburg, 1988), p. 114.

22. Examples of such lists include Gen. 5:1–32; Josh. 13:2–32; 1 Kings 4:1–19.

23. For an impressive rhetorical analysis of Hushai's speech see Shimon Bar-Efrat, *Narrative Art in the Bible* (Sheffield: Almond, 1989), pp. 70–72.

24. Roland Barthes, *The Rustle of Language* (Berkeley: University of California, 1989), p. 85.

For Further Reading

Classical Rhetoric

Aristotle. *The "Art" of Rhetoric.* Trans. H. E. Butler. Loeb Classical Library. Cambridge, Mass.: Harvard, 1926.
Bizzell, Patricia, and Herzberg, Bruce. *The Rhetorical Tradition.* Boston: Bedford, 1990. A useful anthology of readings from classical times to the present.
Demetrius. *A Greek Critic: Demetrius on Style.* Ed. G. M. Gruber. Toronto: University of Toronto, 1961.
Quintilian. *The Institution Oratoria.* Trans. H. E. Butler. Loeb Classical Library. 4 vols. Cambridge, Mass.: Harvard, 1921.

Secondary Literature

Corbett, Edward P. J. *Classical Rhetoric for the Modern Student.* New York: Oxford University Press, 1971.
Perelman, Chaim, and Olbrechts-Tyleca, Lucie. *The New Rhetoric.* Notre Dame, Ind.: University of Notre Dame, 1969.
Vickers, Brian. *In Defense of Rhetoric.* Oxford: Clarendon, 1988.

The Bible as Rhetorical Discourse

Bühlmann, W., and Scherer, K. *Stilfiguren in der Bibel.* Biblische Beiträge 10. Freiburg: Schweizerisches Katolisches Bibelwerk, 1973.
Bullinger, Ernest W. *Figures of Speech Used in the Bible.* Grand Rapids, Mich.: Baker, 1968. A comprehensive analysis of biblical figures catalogued on the basis of classical rhetoric.
Frye, Northrup. *Anatomy of Criticism.* Princeton: Princeton University Press, 1957.
———. *The Great Code.* San Diego, Calif.: Harcourt Brace Jovanovich, 1982.
Gitay, Yehoshua. *Prophecy and Persuasion.* Forum Theologicae Linguisticae 14. Bonn: Linguistica Biblica, 1981.
———. "Reflections on the Study of the Prophetic Discourse," *Vetus Testamentum* 33 (1983):207–21.
Kennedy, George A. *New Testament Interpretation Through Rhetorical Criticism.* Chapel Hill, N.C.: University of North Carolina Press, 1984.
König, Eduard. *Stilistik, Rhetorik, Poetik.* Leipzig: Dieterich'sche, 1900. A monumental study that occasionally refers to the pragmatic rhetorical aspect of the figures.

Leon, Judah Messer. *The Book of the Honeycomb's Flow*. Ithaca, N.Y.: Cornell
University Press, 1982. This book, originally published in 1475 in Mantua,
Italy, establishes a precedent in the history of Hebrew letters; it is a system-
atic study of rhetoric and the Bible.
Sternberg, Meir. *The Poetics of Biblical Narrative*. Bloomington, Ind.: Indiana
University Press, 1985.

PART THREE
OVERTURNING THE TRADITION

9

STRUCTURAL
CRITICISM

Daniel Patte

The Origin of Structural Criticism

A Method Developed Out of
Semiotic and Semantic Theories

STRUCTURAL criticism (or exegesis) is self-consciously developed on the basis of semiotic theories—that is, the theories that extend structural linguistic theories[1] (how meaningful communication takes place in and through language; the grammar of sentences)[2] to encompass all means of human communication (including through entire discourses and texts)[3] and semantic theories (how meaning is produced and communicated). It is called "structural" because, according to these theories, a text is meaningful for readers only insofar as they recognize (1) *different* features in this text and (2) an interrelation—a *structure*—among these different features.

The basic principles of this method can be readily understood. In the same way that one cannot truly appreciate "good health" (its meaning and value) as long as one has not experienced "sickness" (and thus does not know the difference and relation between being healthy and sick), so a word ("blue") is meaningless as long as one does not recognize that it is *different* from other words ("blew," "red") and how it is *related* to other words, either in the text (e.g., in a sentence) or in the language (e.g., it belongs together with words about colors, and not with verbs of action). So it is with all the features that can be perceived in a text, from the smallest features—such as letters, syllables, words, their denotations (what they refer to), their connotations (the values associated with them)—to larger features, such as sentences, paragraphs, parts; characters, actions, situations, subplots, and plots; metaphors and other figures, allusions to other texts, figurative units, and the like. Since quite different kinds of features can be recognized in a text, different "structures" and thus different "meanings" (or "meaning-producing dimensions") are per-

153

ceived in a text. Since, in a given study, one usually focuses the analysis on one or a few of these structures, structural criticism takes several different forms (see bibliography). However, in the limits of this chapter, only one of its forms can be presented.

A Method for the Study of the "Faith" Expressed by a Religious Text

Among several other possibilities, structural criticism provides the means for studying the main characteristics of the "religion" or "faith"—the author's[4] "convictions"—expressed by a text. This meaning-producing dimension (which is present in any text, but is particularly important in religious texts) should not be ignored in biblical studies.

The "religion" of biblical texts was studied, in the nineteenth century and beginning of the twentieth century, with the method of "history of religions," by comparing biblical texts with other religious texts of the period (e.g., Babylonian, Assyrian, Egyptian, Jewish, Hellenistic). Although such comparisons are still done for other purposes (cf. form and tradition criticisms), at present the method of "history of religions" per se is less frequently used in biblical studies, because its results are often difficult to evaluate. Practitioners of this method argued that biblical texts are comparable to, and influenced by, other religious texts and traditions of their time—both Hellenistic[5] and Jewish,[6] in the case of New Testament texts. The difficulty was how to determine which specific features of very different religious texts and traditions are truly comparable.

Structural criticism offers the possibility of reopening this quest, because semiotic theories (and especially Greimas's structural semiotics) provide the possibility of identifying several sets of features (meaning-producing dimensions) in a given text that have different functions in the communication of its religious message. This includes the features that most directly express the basic religious message, which is one of the things the author "wants to convey:"[7] the author's own "faith" or system of "convictions."[8] Yet these convictions should not be confused, for instance, with the "figures" (symbolism) of the text,[9] through which the author's convictions are expressed in terms of the intended readers' old views, so as to better convince them to adopt new views (the author's convictions).[10] Thus the use of Hellenistic or Jewish "figures" (e.g., "sacred meal," "Son of man") in a given New Testament text is not *necessarily* a sign that the text expresses a "religion" that is fundamentally Hellenistic or Jewish. This might be the case, as the "history of religions" school often insisted. But these figures might also have been used to convince readers to abandon their undue reliance on Hellenistic or Jewish views for conceiving the Christian faith. One way to adjudicate the case is to elucidate the dimension that expresses the basic characteristics of the "religion" (system of convictions) of that text, and to compare these results with those of similar studies of Hellenistic or Jewish texts. Then one compares what is truly comparable: a dimension that, in each of these texts, has the same function.

By itself, the study of the "system of convictions" of a text reaches important exegetical results. It reveals basic characteristics of the religious message of this text, even though the full significance of these results only appears when they are compared with the results of similar studies of other texts or with those of the studies of other dimensions of the same text (something we cannot do here).

Structural Criticism and the Other Methods of Biblical Criticism

Structural criticism, in agreement with the other exegetical methods, takes as its starting point the general observation that biblical texts, like any text, were written in order to communicate something to a specific audience, and thus with the hope that they would *make sense for* that audience. They also *make sense for* readers in other times, including today, each time they are read. The fact that biblical texts are religious texts that, in certain instances, emphasize that their goal is to transmit "revealed" or "inspired" knowledge[11] does not prevent them from being instances of *human* communication. Even though they are, for believers, "Word of God," they remain "human words."

Consequently, all the exegetical methods have been developed, implicitly or explicitly, on the basis of "theories of communication"[12]—including theories about "language" (linguistics) and about "meaning" (semantics). The diversity of methods is due, in part, to differences in theories.

It makes sense to develop exegetical methods on the basis of ancient theories of communication, such as classical rhetoric, and theories about specific forms of oral communication and literary conventions of the time of the biblical texts.[13] Yet, ultimately, all exegetical methods (including the preceding ones) presuppose that communication is a "human" phenomenon that obeys similar rules through the centuries, despite cultural and other differences. If this were not the case, there would be no hope of understanding ancient texts.[14] Thus each method presupposes one or another general theory of human communication as a "universal" phenomenon. These general theories of communication, and their corresponding critical methods, can be viewed as belonging to two groups.

Certain theories consider that *what is truly significant* in any given instance of communication (e.g., a text) is *what is new* in it, that is, how the language, the sources, the traditions, and so forth, have been *transformed* in this given instance. This is what is presupposed by the so-called historical methods (source, form, tradition, redaction criticisms), for which it is essential to establish the place of a given word, tradition, or text in the *linear* flow of history.

This "diachronic" approach elucidates what is "new," and thus truly signifi-cant, in a given instance by showing how it differs from what precedes and follows it in time.

More recent theories[15] consider that *what is truly significant* in any given instance of communication is *how its features are interrelated in a system,* that is, how various words are interrelated with other words in the language (viewed as a system); how the different features of a text are interrelated to form a coherent whole; how a text is interrelated with its literary, social, religious, and political environment (other kinds of systems); how a text participates with its readers in producing meaning (the system being all the features of the reading process). This is what is presupposed by the newer methods (structural, narra-tive, reader-response criticisms), as well as by sociological, canonical, and some rhetorical criticisms.

Structural criticism belongs to this latter set of methods, in which it distin-guishes itself by making explicit the general theory of communication—semi-otics—upon which its methods are developed. As a consequence, structural exegetical studies are often unduly theoretical and methodological—using a quite technical vocabulary (i.e., jargon). While at first this was necessary to clarify the difference with earlier methods, it is no longer necessary, as we shall see below.

A second difference with other methods is that even when it studies a single dimension, semiotic theory informs structural criticism that a text involves *several* meaning-producing dimensions, which can give rise, in the process of reading, to quite different "meanings." Together with reader-response criti-cism, structural criticism acknowledges that a specific meaning is perceived in the text by certain readers because of their specific social, cultural, and reli-gious locations. Yet it emphasizes that this meaning is not projected upon the text by these readers, except in the case of "illegitimate" readings. Because of their specific preoccupations and concerns at the time of a given reading, read-ers focus their attention on one or another of the several coherent meaning-producing dimensions of the text, which becomes the meaning of the text for them. The different "meanings" arise from the selection of different meaning-producing dimensions and their appropriation as the coherent meaning of the text for the readers.

Finally, because it self-consciously uses a "theory," structural criticism re-mains fully aware that it is culturally conditioned (as any "theory" is), a point emphasized by poststructuralist criticism.[16] This means that structural criti-cism views the other methods, including the so-called historical methods, as complementary to itself. Different methods, based on different theories, study different meaning-producing dimensions, each of which can be legitimately perceived as the meaning of the text, according to specific standpoints of read-ers. Thus whatever method one uses, one should not pretend that one elucidates *the* (single) meaning of the text. This undue claim has the disastrous ethical consequences of denying, without any true examination, the legitimacy of other readings and thus the legitimacy of the interests and concerns of other readers who perceive other "meanings" in the text, because their readings are focused upon other dimensions.

A Structural Exegesis of Luke 24

Procedures for the Elucidation of Convictions Expressed by a Biblical Text

The specific method of structural criticism presented here studies a single meaning-producing dimension of a biblical text: its "system of convictions." The following twofold definition[17] provides the basis for the procedures of the exegesis.

1. Convictions as basic characteristics of the "faith" of the author are "self-evident truths," in contrast with "ideas," which are "demonstrated truths." Convictions impose themselves upon believers (and are often viewed as "revelations") instead of being learned or deduced by reasoning, as ideas are. They provide a vision of human experience that defines a believer's fundamental identity and thus orients his or her behavior.

2. Convictions form a "system" in the sense that they are organized according to a peculiar "structure"[18] (distinct from the structures of other dimensions) characterized by a fundamental pattern[19] that is repeatedly applied to the different domains of human experience. This is why, for example, one can use family language (father, children) to speak about the relationship between God and human beings; the domains of human family and of God-human relationships are perceived as being "alike" because they follow the same pattern. Consequently, although a given passage deals with only one or a few domains of human experience, its study elucidates the fundamental pattern of the entire system of convictions—that is, basic characteristics of the faith of the author.

Since, when authors express their convictions, they cannot afford to be misunderstood—their identity is at stake!—they make their convictions unambiguous by stating both "what they mean to say" and also "what they do not mean to say." Thus the structure of a system of convictions and its fundamental pattern appears in a text as a set of *explicit* semantic oppositions. Furthermore, since convictions govern the way believers act, and since writing a religious text is an act through which an author-believer seeks to convey his or her convictions to readers, the semantic oppositions that most directly express the author's convictions are linked with (1) the *"inverted parallelisms"* through which the author organizes the discourse and each of its "thematic units" so as to transform the readers' views[20] and (2) *"oppositions of actions"* (because actions of characters are meaningful actions according to the author's convictions).

Thus in order to elucidate basic characteristics of the system of convictions expressed in a biblical text (be it narrative, as Luke 24 is, or not), it is essential to identify a complete thematic unit and the "inverted parallelisms" that delimit it; to analyze its "oppositions of actions"; and then to interpret the results of these formal procedures by clarifying the organization of the convictions.

Luke 24:1–53 as a Complete Thematic Unit

Since we have chosen to study a thematic unit at the end of the Gospel of Luke, its end is already identified: 24:53. But does it truly begin in 24:1?

In a narrative text, thematic and narrative units do not necessarily correspond to each other. A thematic unit often contains several narrative units that function as thematic subunits; yet its beginning coincides with that of a narrative unit. Thus we first note that Luke 24:1* is the beginning of a narrative unit, since it describes the women in a new time ("on the first day of the week"),[21] going to a new space (the tomb), where they are joined by new characters (the "two men," 24:4) (note the three criteria used to identify narrative units). The narrative unit about the women that begins in 24:1 ends in 24:11. Luke 24:1–11 is also a thematic subunit defined by inverted parallelisms: The description in 24:9–11 of the women going away from the tomb and interacting with other characters (the apostles) is in inverted parallelism with the description in 24:1–4.[22] The question is, Could this subunit be the introduction of a larger unit ending in 24:53? To demonstrate this, we need to consider whether or not it is in inverted parallelism with the end of the chapter.

In Luke 24:53, the apostles are "continually in the temple blessing God"; that is, they are presented as performing a Jewish (in the "temple") ritual of thanksgiving. In 24:1 the women, who had been described as resting on the sabbath "according to the commandment" (23:56b), are also presented as attempting to perform a Jewish ritual—ritual of mourning (with "spices and ointments"). This observation is confirmed by the presence of other inverted parallelisms. Both in 24:3 and 24:52–53, Jesus is absent (parallel features); yet it is a cause of perplexity and fear for the women at the tomb in 24:3–5, and a cause of "great joy" for the apostles at Jerusalem in 24:51–53 (inverted

---

*Scripture quotations in this chapter are from the Revised Standard Version.

features). Furthermore, both in 24:6-7 and in 24:44, 46, we find, almost in the same words, a reference to what Jesus told his followers regarding his crucifixion and resurrection (parallel features), but in 24:44-49 these words are explained (inverted features).

Such multiple inverted parallelisms demonstrate that 24:1-53[23] is a complete thematic unit, which includes three subunits: 24:1-11, the introduction; 24:12-35,[24] the Emmaus story; and 24:36-53, the conclusion.[25]

The inverted parallelisms we noted between the beginning and the end of 24:1-53 allow us to identify the theme of the unit in general terms. Since they contrast people who do not believe that Jesus is risen (the mourning women going to the tomb to anoint his body, 24:1) with people who believe that he is risen (the apostles with "great joy" who "bless" God, 24:52-53), *the theme concerns the process of becoming true believers in the (crucified and) resurrected Christ*. The parallelisms show that belief in the crucified and resurrected Christ (1) is in continuity with Judaism (Jewish rituals in both 24:1 and 24:52-53), (2) is held when people remember Jesus' words (prophecies) during his ministry about his death and resurrection, and (3) is held in the absence of Jesus (24:3 and 24:51). The inversions show that in order to have such a true belief, one needs (1) to be in the right place—among the living, in society (Jerusalem, 24:52) rather than "among the dead" (the tomb, 24:5)— and (2) to understand the significance of Jesus' death and resurrection—understanding why he "must" die and rise (cf. 24:7) with the help of the scriptures (24:45-49). In addition, the inversions show that true belief involves a positive evaluation of Jesus' absence (great joy), rather than a negative one (mourning).[26] Surprisingly, in view of the central subunit (24:12-35 and also 24:36-53, which emphasizes the recognition of the risen Jesus' presence), the inverted parallelisms underscore that true belief in Jesus' resurrection is not a belief that the risen Christ is present, since the great joy associated with this belief occurs in the absence of Jesus (after "he parted from them," 24:51).

Such seem to be the surprising convictions regarding the process of becoming believers expressed by the overall theme of Luke 24:1-53. Yet their identification is still quite general and tentative. This theme and its convictions need to be clarified through a study of the convictions expressed by each subunit.

The Convictions Expressed in Luke 24:1-11

Since the inverted parallelism between 24:1-4 and 24:9-11 (the introduction and conclusion of this subunit) concerns the women going to (24:1) and returning from (24:9) the tomb and being associated, respectively, with "two men" (24:4) and with the eleven apostles and "all the rest" (24:9), the theme of the subunit concerns convictions about *locations and relations with people*.

Two explicit oppositions of actions (here, cognitive actions) underscore and specify these convictions. A first one contrasts the women's (negative) action, being "perplexed" (lacking knowledge, *aporeisthai;* 24:4), with their (positive) action, "remembering" (having knowledge; 24:8), following the two men's instruction. The underscored convictions appear when one compares the subjects (agents) and effects of the positive and negative actions. Here the question is, What distinguishes the women in 24:4 and 24:8? In brief, in 24:8 they have been instructed by the two men. Note that the validity of the women's will[27] to find Jesus is not challenged. But at first, the women *do not know how to find Jesus,* because they lack a knowledge of Jesus' words about his death and resurrection and thus have a wrong knowledge about Jesus; they believe he is to be found among the dead, rather than among the living. *Knowing how to find Jesus involves remembering his words.*[28] Furthermore, at first, the empty tomb does not make sense for the women; they are perplexed by it. In sum, *the empty tomb is meaningless as long as this extraordinary event is not interpreted in terms of Jesus' words about the necessity ("must") of this death and resurrection* (cf. 24:7).

This first set of convictions (in italics) explains why "locations" is part of the subtheme of 24:1–11. In order to find the resurrected Jesus, one needs to be at the right place: among the living, that is, in society, rather than among the dead, at the tomb, or more generally, outside of society. This is also part of the theme of 24:1–53. Note that in 24:36–53 (see also 24:33–34), the apostles are "in society" (at Jerusalem) when they meet the resurrected Jesus. Yet the opposition also shows that the fundamental problem (which turns out to be the fundamental human predicament for Luke) is more general: People *do not know how to* find Jesus, or *how to* make sense of situations (here, the empty tomb), or as we shall see, *how to* recognize Jesus in these concrete situations. In order to overcome this predicament, a first condition is stipulated: One needs to remember Jesus' words. Yet this is certainly not enough; note that the text does not say either that the women believed or that they found Jesus.

A second opposition of actions contrasts the women telling "all this" to the eleven (24:9–10) and the negative response of the apostles who "did not believe them" (24:11). The conviction concerns the relationship between "women" (positive subject) and "men" (apostles, negative subject). The women accept the words of the "two men" as trustworthy, since they act accordingly. By contrast, for the apostles, the women's report is not trustworthy (as "idle tale"), even though the text emphasizes that their report was complete ("all this") and thus trustworthy—a point underscored by the fact that the women are honored by being named (24:10). In brief, the *men-apostles' patriarchal attitude* (not accepting as trustworthy a report by women, even though it is trustworthy) *is marked as negative.* Yet it remains that the women's report is unable to overcome this patriarchal attitude; the women lack something so as to be in a position to be effective "witnesses."

This second set of convictions explains why "relationships" are part of the subtheme of 24:1–11. Taking the words of witnesses as trustworthy—as the women did, and as the apostles did not do—is an essential step for believing in the resurrected Jesus. The theme of 24:1–53 also underscores this point by specifying what makes witnessing (cf. 24:48) effective: In addition to reporting the event and Jesus' words, one also needs to explain the significance of these as fulfillments of the scriptures (cf. 24:46–47) and to be "clothed with power from on high" (24:49).

Convictions Underscored in Luke 24:12–35

The theme of this second thematic subunit is marked by two sets of inverted parallelisms.

A first set concerns Simon Peter. In 24:12 he went to the tomb, where "he saw the linen clothes by themselves" and thus did not see Jesus and was as perplexed as the women were. After he departed from the tomb (cf. 24:12b), and thus when he was back in society, possibly in Jerusalem (24:33), it is reported that the risen Lord "was seen by Simon" (24:34; lit. trans.).[29] Thus once again, *in order to see Jesus, one needs to be in society.*

The second set of inverted parallelisms, about the two disciples of Emmaus, underscores a point concerning *recognizing Jesus and believing that he has risen.* In 24:13–16, when they are on the road with Jesus, "their eyes were kept from recognizing him." In 24:29–31, "their eyes were opened and they recognized him," and as a consequence they believe, together with the other disciples, that "the Lord has risen indeed" (24:34). This latter theme is clarified by three oppositions.

The first opposition is set by the polemical exchange between Jesus, who inquires about their conversation (24:17), and Cleopas, who rebukes him (24:18). The irony is that Cleopas and his companion accuse Jesus of not knowing what happened in Jerusalem and thus assume that they themselves truly know it. Thus a first thing that *prevents them from recognizing Jesus is their false confidence in having a true and complete knowledge of the situation,* although in fact their knowledge is incomplete. Such an incomplete knowledge results in a negative evaluation (they are "sad") of a situation (Jesus' crucifixion and the empty tomb) that should be assessed positively (as joyful).

The second opposition is another polemical exchange between the two disciples, who explain the situation (24:19b–24), and Jesus, who rebukes them (24:25–27). What is wrong with the two disciples and their statement is made explicit in 24:25: They are "foolish," that is, they do not understand the situation and events they describe. Why? Because they are "slow of heart to believe all that the prophets have spoken," and therefore fail to interpret these events in terms of the scriptures and the scriptures in terms of these events (24:27). As a consequence, instead of understanding that it was "necessary that the

Christ should suffer these things and enter into his glory" (24:26), they view Jesus' crucifixion as the failure ("we had hoped," 24:21) of a "prophet" (24:19). And despite a more positive assessment of the women's account (because it has been partially confirmed by "men," 24:24), they still take their report that Jesus is "alive" as resulting from a dubious "vision of angels" (similar to women's "idle tale"). In sum, the main problem with the two disciples, their "foolishness," is that they *do not know how to interpret* the situation, because they do not interpret it in terms of scriptures; as a consequence, they do not recognize Jesus and have a negative evaluation of the situation (they are "sad"). Positively, *in order to recognize Jesus' presence and to have a positive evaluation of Jesus' crucifixion and empty tomb, one needs to interpret the situation in terms of the scriptures, something one knows how to do if one "believe[s] all that the prophets have spoken."* Yet this is not sufficient, since after Jesus has "interpreted to them in all the scriptures the things concerning himself" (24:27), they still do not recognize him.

The third opposition contrasts the (negative) action that Jesus "appeared" to want to take, going further (24:28b), and the (positive) action of staying with the two disciples (24:29b). It concerns the establishment of Jesus' will. The fact that in 24:28 Jesus is said to have "appeared" ("made as if," *prosepoesato*) to be going further, however this term might be interpreted, shows that the text presents the disciples' perception of Jesus' will. Thus what is at stake is the role of the disciples in establishing Jesus' will to stay. For them, it is important to convince this stranger ("they constrained him") not to continue his journey at night (cf. 24:29); they are concerned for his welfare. In other words, they are themselves characterized by a will to take care of the needs of this stranger for shelter and also for food; indeed, they give him the seat of honor at the table, since he is the one who says the blessing and breaks the bread (24:30). Then, they recognize him. Why? It is certainly because they remembered that he had performed the same symbolic gestures before them during his ministry (cf. 9:16 and 22:19)—they have already expressed that they remembered his deeds and words (cf. 24:19).

Yet none of this would have happened if they had not taken care of the needs of the stranger and had not honored him, as Jesus taught them to do by means of parables (e.g., 10:25–37). In fact, by so doing, they initiate and participate in a symbolic act that, as the parables did, teaches them how to interpret (e.g., the parable in 10:25–37 teaches the lawyer how to interpret the law he has just recited).

In sum, what are, according to this subunit, the necessary conditions for recognizing the resurrected Christ and thus believing that "the Lord has risen indeed" (24:34)? *Confidence that one understands the situation by oneself needs to be overcome, by being taught to interpret it in terms of the scriptures; but according to Jesus' instruction, one must also care for the needs of and honor the stranger who provides such a teaching; then, as one remembers Jesus' deeds and words during his ministry and participates in a symbolic act, one recognizes the resurrected Christ's presence.*

Convictions Underscored in Luke 24:36–53

This passage is marked as a complete thematic subunit by two sets of inverted parallelisms. The first set concerns the disciples who, at first, "were startled and frightened, and supposed that they saw a spirit" (24:37), and at the end have a great joy and bless God (24:52–53), an expression of true belief. The second set of inverted parallelisms concerns Jesus, who was present with the disciples in 24:36–37 but had parted from them in 24:52–53 (see 24:51).

Since there is no opposition of actions, the convictions are exclusively expressed by the inverted parallelisms. These show that the theme concerns *the transformation of fear and wrong belief in Jesus' presence into great joy and true belief in his absence.* Thus we need to consider closely the initial situation and how it is progressively transformed.

Initial Situation

The new subunit is linked with the preceding one by the phrase, "As they were saying this" (24:36), which refers to the disciples' preceding words, which include the declaration, "The Lord is risen indeed" (24:34). But knowing and believing that Jesus is risen do not prevent them from being startled and frightened when he stands among them, and from disbelieving (cf. 24:38). Why? Because they do not recognize Jesus and/or have a wrong understanding of what it means that he is risen. Once again, disciples do not know how to interpret a situation. More specifically, they think he is a spirit, and for them, being in the presence of a spirit is dangerous.

First Step of the Transformation

By showing them his hands and feet, Jesus dispels their misunderstanding that he is a spirit (24:38–39) and therefore cancels their fear, which is replaced by "joy" (24:41; not yet a "great joy"!).

Second Step of the Transformation

Yet they still disbelieve (24:41). In order to dispel this disbelief, Jesus eats before them the food they give him (24:41–43; cf. 24:30), reminds them of what is written about him in the scriptures, and teaches them how to interpret the scriptures ("opens their minds," 24:44–46; cf. 24:25–27, 32). The process of bringing the disciples to recognize Jesus and thus to acknowledge that he is risen is therefore the same as in the case of the disciples of Emmaus (although in reverse order).

Third Step of the Transformation

But this recognition and the belief that Jesus is risen are not enough to bring about the "great joy" that characterizes the disciples in 24:52–53 (and is not mentioned regarding the Emmaus disciples), even as Jesus departs from them. Contrary to our expectation, it is not the presence of Jesus and its recognition that give them this "great joy." What is it then? The answer lies in 24:47–51, verses that are no longer parallel to the experience of the Emmaus disciples. We find four reasons for their "great joy." First, 24:47 begins to explain the significance of Jesus' death and resurrection: They mean that "repentance" should be and can be preached "for the forgiveness of sins" "to all the nations." Thus forgiveness of sins is now available to all the nations. Second, his death and resurrection mean that they now have a vocation as "witnesses of these things" (24:48). Third, his death and resurrection mean that the disciples will receive "the promise of the Father," "the power from on high," that is, the Holy Spirit. And finally, they are blessed (24:50); this is a true and effective blessing, since it is given by the risen Christ.

Convictions about the Process of Becoming True Believers According to Luke 24:1–53

What is the result of structural exegesis? It is the elucidation of a part of the author's system of convictions, that is, of a vision of a domain of human experience, here what we call "the process of becoming true believers," which the author aims at sharing with readers. The events that took place during the days following Jesus' death and that involved the women, the two disciples of Emmaus, the apostles, and the resurrected Christ are "images"[30] that together express a vision of the process of becoming true believers, whatever might be the circumstances. Would-be believers (with whom readers are invited to identify themselves) are *like* the women, *like* the two disciples of Emmaus, *like* the apostles, and the process that they collectively went through in order to become true believers is *like* the process any believer needs to go through.

Summarizing our findings, we seek to understand the different steps of this process. The ultimate step of the process is that true believers are effective "witnesses" of Jesus' crucifixion and resurrection (24:48) who preach repentance and forgiveness of sins "to all nations, beginning from Jerusalem" (24:47). The question is, What is necessary for being such a witness?

1. First, like the two disciples (24:19–24) and the women (24:6–7), one needs to know (and remember) the events that took place—that is, the story of Jesus' death and of the empty tomb, as well as the story and words of Jesus during his ministry. One can be a firsthand witness of these events, or know them through the reports of such witnesses (reports of the "two men," 24:6–7; of the women, 24:9–11, 22–24; of

Peter, 24:24, 34)—the latter case being like the situation of believers in the time of the church.

2. Then, one needs to believe that the reported events mean that "the Lord has risen indeed." For this, the empty tomb and the crucifixion need to be interpreted (1) in terms of Jesus' words (24:6–7) and (2) in terms of the scriptures (24:25–27, 44–45). The fundamental problem is that would-be believers do not know how to interpret these events, even though (and because!) they self-confidently think they truly know them. They need to be taught not only the fact that these events fulfill Jesus' words and the scriptures but also how to make this interpretation themselves (and thus how to appropriate it), by acting out what they have been taught (the women doing what the "two men" told them; 24:8–9) or by taking care of the teacher's needs and honoring the stranger (24:28–31, 41–42). This amounts to acting out Jesus' teaching and participating with him in a symbolic act.

3. Yet this knowledge-belief that "the Lord is risen indeed" is not sufficient. Once again with the help of the scriptures and of Jesus' teaching during his ministry, one also needs to understand that Jesus' resurrection means that forgiveness of sins is available to all the nations, and that, as a believer, one has the vocation to be a "witness of all these things." One also understands that one will be given the means (power from on high and effective blessing by the risen Christ) to carry it out (24:47–50)—and not that one should expect the presence of Jesus with oneself. In order to carry out this vocation, one needs, of course, to be in society (and not to look for Jesus "among the dead").

4. Then, as a consequence, one can have "great joy" in the absence of Jesus (who has departed for heaven); one is a true believer, in that one can continually bless God (true worship) and this in continuity with Judaism (in the temple)—continuity that is marked all along, since without the help of the Jewish scriptures one would not know that Jesus is risen and would not understand the meaning of his resurrection.

Limitations of Structural Criticism

The limitations of a structural exegesis are clear. We have left out many features of the text. Actually, our structural study was limited to the study of a single meaning-producing dimension, and thus we bracketed out its other meaning-producing dimensions. For instance, we have not studied Luke 24 as a "figurative system," a study usually concerned with the "theology" (rather than the "convictional vision" or "religion") of the text and entailing the study of each figure in terms of its "intertexts" (the texts and traditions to which the text alludes); as a story (characterized by the unfolding of its plot); as a realistic narrative (characterized by the features that give to Luke 24 a "historical" character); or as a discourse through which the author (enunciator) seeks to affect the reader (enunciatee) in certain ways. These and other dimensions can be studied by other structural methods, since each of these dimensions is characterized by a specific "structure."[31] But in most instances they can also be studied by means of other methods (e.g., historical, literary, and rhetorical methods). This is what led me to choose to focus the above presentation on a method of structural criticism aimed at elucidating the system of convictions of the text (characteristics of its "religion"), a dimension neglected by other methods, even though structural criticism has much to contribute to the study of the other dimensions.

As we have underscored above, it is essential to acknowledge the strict limitation of the method one uses. Although, as is also the case of each of the other dimensions, the meaning-producing dimension elucidated by this exegesis (its convictional vision, "faith," or "religion") can become for certain readers "the" meaning of the text that they implement and find meaningful for their lives as believers (or for the purpose of comparing the basic characteristics of the "religion" of different religious texts), as with any type of exegesis, one must make explicit that it merely elucidates one of the possible meaning-producing dimensions of the text. Otherwise, as we have argued above, the structural exegesis will have the disastrous ethical consequences of denying, without any true examination, the legitimacy of other readings and thus the legitimacy of the interests and concerns of readers who perceive other "meanings" in the text, because their readings are focused upon other dimensions.

Notes

1. The main semiotic theories are those of Charles S. Peirce (e.g., *Collected Papers*, 2nd ed., ed. C. Hartshorne and P. Weiss [Cambridge: Harvard University Press, 1960]); Umberto Eco (e.g., *A Theory of Semiotics* [Bloomington, Ind.: Indiana University Press, 1976]); and A. J. Greimas (e.g., with J. Courtes, *Semiotics and Language: An Analytical Dictionary* [Bloomington, Ind.: Indiana University Press, 1982]). This latter theory, which is more explicitly a "structural semiotics," is the basis of structural exegesis. Greimas's technical vocabulary, to which I refer in notes, is defined in this dictionary.

2. See the many linguistic theories developed out of the seminal work of F. de Saussure at the beginning of the twentieth century, published in English as *Course in General Linguistics* (New York: McGraw-Hill, 1966).

3. Actually, all cultural artifacts are means of communication, as Lévi-Strauss em-

phasized in his anthropological study of Native American culture. The publication of C. Lévi-Strauss's *Structural Anthropology* (Garden City, N.Y.: Basic Books, 1963) proved to be a decisive step in the early development of structuralism, which led to the progressive elaboration of structural semiotic theories.

4. Technically, the "enunciator's" or "implied author's" convictions. Semiotics and structural criticism emphasize in this way that, when studying a text, one only discovers the way in which the "author" presents himself or herself *in the text*—that is, one discovers the "enunciator" and not the "real author." Even if this presentation is sincere, it is always partial (incomplete and biased); the real author only presents that part of himself or herself that is appropriate for the topic at hand. Whether or not one acknowledges this distinction, it is a fact that, in biblical studies, all that is known about the author is usually derived from the text itself. Thus what is meant by "author" is the "enunciator" or "implied reader." In order to avoid distracting technical vocabulary, I will use here the term "author" in that sense.

5. The history of religions school can be represented by the works of Wilhelm Bousset (see his book on the "religion of Judaism," in German, 1903, and *Kyrios Christos* [Nashville: Abingdon, 1970]; German edition, 1913), who argued that Palestinian Judaism was influenced by Hellenistic religions and that Paul and his disciples were strongly influenced by Hellenistic Oriental religions; and Richard Reitzenstein (see his book on *The Hellenistic Mystery Religions,* German edition, 1910), who claimed that Paul's Christ myth was borrowed from Hellenistic mystic and pre-Christian Gnostic redeemer myths. Both Dibelius and Bultmann were proponents of this comparative approach before using it to develop "form criticism."

6. Although the designation history of religions is usually reserved for the studies in the preceding note, one should not overlook that this type of research also included comparisons of the New Testament with Apocalyptic Jewish literature. Thus Johannes Weiss *(Jesus' Proclamation of the Kingdom of God* [Philadelphia: Fortress, 1971; German, 1982]) argued that late Jewish Apocalyptic expectations (of the kingdom, of the Son of man) were the framework for Jesus' proclamation.

7. Especially in a "religious" text. Note that since this "author" is the "enunciator," we are not speaking of the "intention" of the real author (which is an "illusion" created by readers) but technically of the "intentionality" of the text. Note also that, for structural semiotics, a text is perceived as having a plurality of "intentionalities." Besides wanting to convey a religious message (one meaning-producing dimension) through a given text, the author (enunciator) might also want to convey exhortations to moral life (another meaning-producing dimension) and the like.

8. What Greimas calls the "semantic universe" or "narrative semantics" of a text— one kind of semantic meaning-producing dimension—and what Lévi-Strauss calls the "mythical structure" or "deep structure" (this latter designation is quite misleading; for readers, this structure is not "deeper" for any other structure!). This structural dimension is studied in most structural studies, although in many cases, this is only as a means to elucidate another dimension. The method I will present here is greatly sim-

plified yet still reliable, as compared with its earlier formulations, which included the use of complex models such as Greimas's "semiotic square" and Lévi-Strauss's formula and model for the mythical structure.

9. Another kind "semantic" meaning-producing dimension that Greimas calls "discursive semantics."

10. Similarly, the author's "convictions" should not be confused with his or her "theological," "ethical," or narrative expressions. These are different dimensions of the "syntax" of a text, each of which can take two different forms (in Greimas's terminology, that of a "narrative or argumentative syntax" and that of a "discursive syntax").

11. For example, the many oracles of the Prophets, the teaching of Jesus as divine revelation in the Gospels, Paul's references to revelations he had received (e.g., Gal. 1:11–17).

12. This phrase is used here in a broad sense to designate all the theories concerning how people communicate meaningfully with one another, including "epistemology" (how do we know and understand) and "semantics," as well as theories concerning the means (e.g., language, text, oral speech) or conditions (e.g., social contexts, literary conventions) of communication.

13. The cases, respectively, of rhetorical criticism (although it can also be based on modern rhetorical theories), form criticism, and certain kinds of literary criticism. The same could be said about the ancient view of religious texts (implied by the formation of the canon) in canonical criticism.

14. This is one of the three basic principles of historical-critical studies that E. Troeltsch called the "principle of analogy" in his seminal essay "On the Historical Dogmatic Method in Theology" (German, 1898). See its discussion in Van Harvey, *The Historian and the Believer. A Confrontation Between the Modern Historian's Principles of Judgement and the Christian Will-to-Believe* (New York: Macmillan, 1966), pp. 102ff.

15. Ushered into biblical studies by James Barr, *The Semantics of Biblical Language* (London: Oxford University Press, 1961), in which the author denounces the "diachronic" interpretation of biblical language prevalent in exegesis, and represented by Kittel's *Theological Dictionary of the New Testament.*

16. Note that what is rejected by "poststructuralism" is "structuralism," that is, the views of early "structuralist" scholars (e.g., Lévi-Strauss) who claimed universal value for the "structural theory"—a claim that semiotics and structural criticism also reject.

17. For a more detailed discussion and definition of "convictions," see D. Patte, *Paul's Faith and the Power of the Gospel: A Structural Introduction to Paul's Letters* (Philadelphia: Fortress, 1983), introduction, and *The Gospel According to Matthew: A Structural Commentary on Matthew's Faith* (Philadelphia: Fortress, 1987), introduction.

18. This is what the anthropologist Claude Lévi-Strauss called the "mythical structure." See Lévi-Strauss, *Structural Anthropology,* ch. 11.

19. Greimas calls it an "axiology."

20. These concepts will be illustrated below through the study of Luke 24. Semiotic theory defines a "thematic unit" as a passage that (1) begins with an "inverted

content," where a theme is posited so as to be readily recognizable by the readers, and thus primarily expresses the readers' view of that theme, and (2) ends with a "posited content," where the theme is restated in a way that most directly expresses the author's conviction. Thus a thematic unit aims at transforming the readers' vision of a theme. Its beginning and end are in "inverted parallelisms," in the sense that they have something (the topic of the theme) in common (so "parallelisms"), but also a different way of viewing this topic (so the inversions).

21. It is also possible to begin the narrative unit at 23:56b; the mention of the Sabbath can be viewed as belonging to the present unit (introducing the actual time reference, which allows one to make sense of the "first day") as well as to the preceding unit.

22. Unlike "inclusions" (which mark figurative units), "inverted parallelisms" are not necessarily expressed by the same vocabulary, *and* include both semantic features that are similar or parallel and other features that are different or inverted. Here, at the beginning and the end of 24:1–11, the features that are *parallel* include "the women in movement (during the first day of the week)." The features that are *inverted* include "going to the tomb" versus "going away from the tomb" and "being with the two men" versus "being with the apostles."

23. Exactly, Luke 23:56b–24:53, so as to include the mention of resting on the sabbath "according to the commandment." To avoid this cumbersome formulation we shall simply refer to 24:1–53.

24. We shall see that our structural exegesis provides an argument for including 24:12, which is not found in certain manuscripts but is found in other important manuscripts.

25. The inverted parallelisms that justify the claim that these last two passages are complete thematic subunits will be discussed below.

26. Another inversion seems to be that false belief is associated with "women" and true belief with "men." But, as we shall see, the text underscores that this distinction between women and men is irrelevant and even in contradiction with true belief (see the study of 24:1–11).

27. Since, in order to perform an action, a subject needs "will," "ability," and "knowledge," the convictions that contrast two subjects necessarily concern how one or several of these are established. The question is, What is understood by the text?

28. Note that convictions are formulated in relatively general terms. As parts of a system of convictions, they reflect a general pattern that applies to the various domains of human experience.

29. The fact that two different verbs of "seeing" are used (respectively, *blepo* and *horao*) does not invalidate an "inverted parallelism"! It contrasts *semantic features*.

30. "Images" (or "thematic expressions") should not be confused with "figures" (which form another meaning-producing text). These "images" are exclusively constituted by the features of the text that are in inverted parallelisms and in oppositions.

The many other features of the text that do not participate in inverted parallelisms and oppositions contribute to form the "figures" (that are the combination of these other features with the "thematic expressions" or "images").

31. Respectively, what Greimas calls the structures of the "discursive semantics" (figurative system), of the "semio-narrative syntax" (story), of the "discursive syntax" (realistic narrative), and of the "enunciation" (discourse) of the text.

For Further Reading

The specific method of structural criticism introduced above is presented in the following books (the first one being focused upon the semiotic theory on which the method is based).

Patte, Daniel. *Religious Dimensions in Biblical Texts: Greimas's Structural Semiotics and Biblical Exegesis.* Society of Biblical Literature Semeia Studies. Atlanta: Scholars, 1990.

——— *Structural Exegesis for New Testament Critics.* Guides to Biblical Scholarship. Minneapolis: Fortress, 1990.

For the use of structural criticism for the study of meaning-producing dimensions other than the system of convictions (and often several of them at once, including the system of convictions), see, for example, the following:

Boers, Hendrikus. *Neither on This Mountain nor in Jerusalem: A Study of John 4.* Society of Biblical Literature Monograph Series 35. Atlanta: Scholars, 1988.

Group of Entrevernes. *Signs and Parables: Semiotics and Gospel Texts.* Trans. G. Phillips. Pittsburgh: Pickwick, 1978.

Leach, Edmund. *Genesis as Myth and Other Essays.* London: Cape, 1969.

Polzin, Robert M. *Biblical Structuralism: Method and Subjectivity in the Study of Ancient Texts.* Semeia Supplements. Philadelphia: Fortress, 1977.

——— *Moses and the Deuteronomist: A Literary Study of the Deuteronomic History.* New York: Seabury, 1980.

Malbon, Elizabeth Struthers. *Narrative Space and Mythic Meaning in Mark.* San Francisco: Harper & Row, 1986.

10
NARRATIVE
CRITICISM

David M. Gunn

T HE term "narrative criticism" in biblical studies is a loose one, more
found in New Testament than in Hebrew Bible studies. Since the late
seventies, it has sometimes been used broadly of literary-critical, as
opposed to historical-critical, analysis of biblical narrative, from a variety of
methodological standpoints. That has usually meant interpreting the existing
text (in its "final form") in terms primarily of its own story world, seen as
replete with meaning, rather than understanding the text by attempting to
reconstruct its sources and editorial history, its original setting and audience,
and its author's or editor's intention in writing. More specifically, the term has
been used of formalist analysis, especially in New-Critical vein, where the
critic understands the text to be an interpretable entity independent of both
author and interpreter. Here meaning is to be found by close reading that
identifies formal and conventional structures of the narrative, determines plot,
develops characterization, distinguishes point of view, exposes language play,
and relates all to some overarching, encapsulating theme. Unlike historical
criticism, which in practice has segmented the text, formalist narrative criticism has often been an exercise in holism.

In the past decade narrative critics of the Bible, influenced by secular criticism, have begun to pay more attention to the place of the reader in the making of meaning (see Chapter 11, on reader-response criticism). One important
upshot of this attention is a growing recognition that no system of reading can
ever guarantee the "correct" interpretation of a story, no matter how highly
trained and "competent" readers may become. There will always be differing
interpretive methods, just as there will always be interpreters who read from
different places and who find significance in different elements of the text.
Most recently, and mostly in Hebrew Bible studies, some reader-oriented approaches to narrative are showing the influence of secular strategies known as
deconstruction (see Chapter 12, on poststructuralist criticism) and ideological

criticism (see Chapter 13, on feminist criticism). They are, for example, confronting seriously the view that language is infinitely unstable and thus that meaning is always deferrable; they are radically foregrounding the reader's values as determinative of interpretation; they are arguing that criticism is not anchored in fixed texts but in fragile communities of interpreters; and they are recognizing that criticism is social construction, or persuasion, if you will.

While developments in New Testament narrative studies over the past two decades could be said in general terms to parallel work on the Hebrew Bible, the two fields have also remained distinctive. Narrative criticism of the Gospels and Acts has tended to be relatively conservative in its methodology, concerned with observing the mechanics or artistry of literary construction and often still haunted by historical criticism's need to know the author's "intention" and the text's "original" readership if it is to speak legitimately of the text's meaning. While centering interest on the story, especially its plot and characters as elements of an artistic whole, Gospel critics have been reluctant to take a literary approach that unravels unity and/or places the reader in an ideologically exposed position in relation to the text. But this is a Hebrew Bible critic speaking, and, indeed, the rest of this essay is focused on Hebrew Bible criticism. I hope, however, that those primarily interested in New Testament narrative will still find here a pertinent discussion. They might also peruse first the eminently readable book by David Rhoads and Donald Michie, *Mark as Story: An Introduction to the Narrative of a Gospel* (Fortress, 1982). They should then dip into a more difficult, but even more elegantly written, account of New Testament literary (narrative) criticism, namely, Stephen Moore's *Literary Criticism and the Gospels: The Theoretical Challenge* (Yale, 1989). These works mark two turning points. The former book offered accessibility to this new kind of criticism as well as comprehensibility—it showed how the method worked and it took this approach through a whole Gospel. The latter situates New Testament studies in relation to the larger world of (secular) literary theory and criticism and challenges New Testament critics to respond.

Literary-critical studies of narrative in the Hebrew Bible have been more varied and adventurous than their New Testament counterparts. It should also be remembered that the study of poetry, though afforded much less attention than narrative, has been an integral part of literary-critical developments in connection with the Hebrew Bible. I think, for example, of Francis Landy's brilliant work on Song of Songs which he intimately connects with the Garden story in Genesis 2–3 (*Paradoxes of Paradise*, Almond, 1983). Indeed, for this reason alone (there are others), the narrative-oriented survey that follows relates a somewhat skewed story.

Current literary-critical study of Hebrew Bible narrative has disparate roots. As early as 1965 Edwin Good at Stanford was writing essays of literary criticism, though his book was to stay out of print for over a decade (*Irony in the Old Testament*, Westminster, 1965; 2nd ed. Almond, 1981). In the crucial formative period of the seventies a number of significant contributors worked in relative isolation from one another. Meir Sternberg, in comparative literature at Tel-Aviv University, was little known in the United States before the end of the decade and had limited impact here until the publication of his major work in English in 1985 (*The Poetics of Biblical Narrative*, Indiana University Press), though his important initial paper (with Menakhem Perry) on reading "gaps" in the story of David and Bathsheba appeared in modern Hebrew in 1968 (English translation in *Poetics Today* 7 1968). Also teaching Hebrew and comparative literature at the University of California, Berkeley, Robert Alter published a series of articles (mostly in *Commentary*, a journal unfamiliar to many biblical critics) between 1975 and 1980. It was not until the publication of his book in 1981 (*The Art of Biblical Narrative*, Basic) that his work came to have widespread influence. It took some time, too, before several other innovative books received due attention in North America: Jan Fokkelman's detailed study of style and structure in Genesis, published in the Netherlands in 1975 (*Narrative Art in Genesis*, Van Gorcum; reprinted in JSOT, 1992); Jonathan Magonet's analysis of literary technique in Jonah, published in Switzerland in 1976 (*Form and Meaning*, Lang; 2nd ed. Almond, 1983); and Shimon Bar-Efrat's extensive survey, *Narrative Art in the Bible*, published (in Hebrew) in Israel in 1979 (Sifriat Poalim; ET Almond, 1989).

David Clines (*The Theme of the Pentateuch*, JSOT, 1978) and myself, at the University of Sheffield in England, on the other hand, had broader ties to the North American biblical studies guild, especially to active members of the Society of Biblical Literature, who opened valuable avenues of support and stimulation. My own first literary-critical essay on Hebrew narrative (which became a key chapter in my 1978 book, *The Story of King David*, JSOT), somewhat after the fashion of F. R. Leavis and British practical criticism learned in Australia in the late fifties and sixties, was commissioned by Robert Culley of McGill University in Montreal for an early issue of *Semeia*. This journal, founded by Robert Funk in Missoula, Montana, for the Society of Biblical Literature, has proved to be of central importance for biblical narrative criticism. The particular issue (number 3, 1975), for example, also contained papers and comment by, among others, Culley himself, George Coats (Lexington Seminary, Kentucky), Burke Long (Bowdoin College, Maine), Robert Polzin (Carleton University, Ottawa), David Robertson (University of California, Davis), and Hugh White (Rutgers University, Camden, New Jersey), all of whom have played significant, though very different, roles in shaping the field of study. Later, Coats's invitation to me to speak to a consultation on narrative at the Society of Biblical Literature in 1979 was germinal for my next book, on Saul.

At Indiana University Kenneth Gros Louis, an English literature professor, and James Ackerman, in the religion department, collaborated to publish in 1974 a pioneering collection of essays (*Literary Interpretations of Biblical Narratives*, Abingdon), which would be followed in 1982 by a further volume, by this time reflecting a considerably expanded repertoire of texts and critics. Like Culley, Ackerman has been an influential figure, as much through his encouragement of others as through his own finely nuanced writing. At Union Theological Seminary in New York in the early sixties, Ackerman had been a student of James Muilenburg, who coined the term "rhetorical criticism" for a study of literary features of texts, in New-Critical mode, that offered an alternative to traditional source and form criticism. Muilenburg's legacy shows in the work of other students of his, such as Walter Brueggemann and Phyllis Trible. Brueggemann, at Eden Theological Seminary in St. Louis, wrote imaginatively on the David stories in Samuel between 1968 and 1974 (and again in the eighties). Trible, at Andover Newton Theological School and then Union Theological Seminary in New York, wrote meticulous rhetorical criticism from a feminist perspective that was groundbreaking in a profoundly new way, issuing in a book of essays of signal importance, *God and the Rhetoric of Sexuality* (Fortress, 1978).

From Canada, David Jobling at St. Andrew's College, Saskatoon, published in the same year that Trible's book came out another set of essays that reflected the first really successful attempt to convey the power of structuralist readings of biblical narrative texts (*The Sense of Biblical Narrative*, JSOT, 1978; 2nd ed. 1986). In 1978, too, Vanderbilt professor James Crenshaw wrote a book of what he termed "aesthetic criticism" (*Samson*, John Knox). From St. Thomas Seminary in Denver, Peter Miscall began to explore in article form the subject of "narrative analogy," influenced by Robert Alter among others.

At the heart of the shift to these new explorations of narrative was a shift in publishing outlets for innovating scholars and reorganization of the Society of Biblical Literature. In 1974, as already noted, Robert Funk founded and edited *Semeia*, "an experimental journal for biblical criticism," for the society. Focused for some years on structuralist work, it yet contrived to give voice to a plurality of alternatives to conventional historical criticism. My own contribution, with colleagues David Clines and Philip Davies, was to found and edit *The Journal for the Study of the Old Testament* in 1976, which from its outset offered a home to literary-critical work. As in the case of *Semeia*, accompanying the journal was a monograph series also receptive to new methodology. At the Society of Biblical Literature forums were established for cultivating contacts and discussion on the new narrative studies. Especially important were the Rhetorical Criticism Section, the Consultation on Narrative, the Structuralism and Exegesis Section, and the Biblical Criticism and Literary Criticism Section.

By about 1980 a threshold was crossed. That year Robert Polzin published *Moses and the Deuteronomist* (Seabury), a highly innovative study of Deuteronomy-Judges utilizing Bakhtin's account of narratorial voices and dialogic narrative, and I published my (more New-Critical) close reading of the Saul story, which unapologetically cut through source-critical boundaries in the interests of an extended, final-form interpretation (*The Fate of King Saul*, JSOT). Cheryl Exum of Boston College published the first of a series of papers on the Samson story, a prelude to many more to come on various texts, increasingly feminist in orientation. The next year (1981) saw the founding of *Prooftexts*, "a journal of Jewish literary history" with serious commitment to literary-critical study of the Bible and often the vehicle for important contributions on narrative from Edward Greenstein of Jewish Theological Seminary in New York. The same year saw the publication of the inaugural volume of essays in my Bible and Literature series with newly founded Almond Press, *Images of Man and God: Old Testament Short Stories in Literary Focus*, edited by Burke Long; also Fokkelman's massive study of King David, *Narrative Art and Poetry in the Books of Samuel*, vol. 1 (Van Gorcum). Most important, however, for the immediate impact of literary studies on the field of biblical studies, Robert Alter's *The Art of Biblical Narrative* was published and received wide and favorable publicity.

In 1982 Northrop Frye's massive analysis of the Bible from the perspective of archetypal criticism made its appearance (*The Great Code: The Bible and Literature*, Academic), though, at least among professional biblical critics, it had surprisingly limited impact for a work from a critic of such reputation in English literature scholarship. In other developments, Peter Miscall's *The Workings of Biblical Narrative* (Fortress/Scholars, 1983) took a major new step in its exploration of the "undecidability" of texts, using texts from Genesis and 1 Samuel as a proving ground, while Adele Berlin at the University of Maryland offered students and scholars interested in entering the new field a lucid presentation of the "mechanics" of narrative composition, especially character and point of view, in her *Poetics and Interpretation of Biblical Narrative* (Almond, 1983). Phyllis Trible brought out a second influential book of feminist readings, starting from the same New-Critical (rhetorical) reading method as before but now more reader conscious and troubled by the text (*Texts of Terror*, Fortress, 1984). At about this time Esther Fuchs began to write her hard-hitting, "text-resisting" feminist readings of Hebrew Bible narratives.

Perhaps the culmination of this phase of growth came with Meir Sternberg's book, *The Poetics of Biblical Narrative* (Indiana University Press, 1985), and the collection of essays edited by Robert Alter and English literature critic Frank Kermode, *The Literary Guide to the Bible* (Harvard, 1987). The former book represented the outcome of more than a decade of work on a system of interpretation claimed to comprehend all Hebrew Bible narrative. Central (and problematic) is Sternberg's view that God and the narrator are omniscient and that the coincidence of their omniscience helps make irresistible the meaning of the text, "the point of it all." The work basically derives from modernist assumptions about textual meaning, with clear links to formalist and New-Critical methods. (It was published—with help from James Ackerman—as the first volume of an important new series from Indiana University Press, eventually to be called Indiana Studies in Biblical Literature, and edited by Robert Polzin and Herbert Marks.) The latter book (*The Literary Guide*) indicated the growing numbers of scholars working in the field but also, following the editors' agenda, reflected a fairly conservative, formalist approach. Several significant scholars, particularly those pursuing feminist criticism—Exum, Fuchs, and Trible, for example—were noticeably absent.

Since the mid-eighties major studies and collections have appeared with increasing frequency. Alex Preminger and Edward Greenstein edited *The Hebrew Bible in Literary Criticism* (Ungar, 1986), and Greenstein has since brought together some of his own work in *Essays on Biblical Method and Translation* (Scholars, 1989). David Clines, too, has a volume of very readable essays on a range of texts (*What Does Eve Do to Help?* JSOT, 1990). David Jobling furnished another volume of structuralist-influenced essays (*The Sense of Biblical Narrative*, vol. 2, JSOT, 1986). Joel Rosenberg (Tufts University) explored political allegory in Genesis and Samuel (*King and Kin*, Indiana University Press, 1986). The books of Samuel have continued to be favorites: previously established critics Fokkelman (*Narrative Art*, vols. 2 and 3, Van Gorcum, 1986 and 1990), Miscall (*1 Samuel*, Indiana University Press, 1986), and Polzin (*Samuel and the Deuteronomist*, Harper & Row, 1989) have all written extensively on this material, along with Brueggemann in a more theological vein (for example, *David's Truth*, Fortress, 1985, and *Power, Providence and Personality*, Westminster/John Knox, 1990) and trenchant Canadian critic Lyle Eslinger (*Kingship of God in Crisis*, Almond, 1985). Eslinger has since treated the Deuteronomic history as a whole (*Into the Hands of the Living God*, Almond, 1989). Written in Sheffield, Australian Barry Webb's close reading of the whole book of Judges (*The Book of the Judges*, JSOT, 1987) was the first of several extended studies of this previously relatively neglected material. Thomas Mann, formerly at Princeton Theological Seminary, has explored the "narrative integrity" of Genesis-Deuteronomy (*The Book of the Torah*, John Knox, 1988). Ezra-Nehemiah has been the subject of a book-length study, *In an Age of Prose* (Scholars, 1988), by Tamara Cohn Eskenazi (now at Hebrew Union College–Jewish Institute of Religion, Los Angeles), and Daniel 1–6 has been read as a narrative whole, rather than as discrete tales according to form-critical designations, in a close reading with deconstructive sympathies by Emory graduate (now at Perkins School of Theology, Southern Methodist University) Danna Nolan Fewell (*Circle of Sovereignty*, JSOT, 1988; 2nd ed. Abington, 1991).

Also from Emory, Daniel Hawk (now at Centenary College, Shreveport,

Louisiana) has written on plot in Joshua (*Every Promise Fulfilled,* Westminster/ John Knox, 1991). The book is one of the first in a new series edited by Danna Fewell and myself, Literary Currents in Biblical Interpretation, designed to bring contemporary literary scholarship to students as well as scholars. Another title, on a biblical book that has received significant attention from narrative and feminist critics (including both Bal and Trible), is the study of characters in Ruth by Danna Fewell and myself (*Compromising Redemption,* Westminster/John Knox, 1990). We use the device of retelling the story as a way of giving narrative expression to an interpretation which we also present analytically. Such recourse to narrative (and poetry) in critical writing has precedents outside biblical studies and may become more common in our own field.

One cutting edge of current studies of Hebrew Bible narrative is to be found among those exploring texts from a reader-oriented perspective, particularly where they are taking account of the ideological dimensions and deconstructive possibilities of reading, though serious and sustained deconstructive criticism is still in its infancy. A powerful influence since the mid-eighties has been Dutch narratologist Mieke Bal (*Narratology,* ET Toronto, 1985), working with what was then for her an unfamiliar language (Hebrew) and text (the Bible). Her books include *Lethal Love* (Indiana University Press, 1987), *Murder and Difference* (Indiana University Press, 1988), and *Death and Dissymmetry* (Chicago University Press, 1988). Schooled in critical theory and wielding interpretive tools borrowed widely from, for example, semiotics, psychoanalysis, and anthropology, she has challenged biblical critics to take a broader, "interdisciplinary" view of their work. Bal is adamant that her own narratology, which has structuralist roots, does not produce the only "correct" interpretation. (Here she differs from another professional narratologist in the field, Sternberg.) Rather, she believes that working with a given set of concepts for describing a text makes the discussion accessible to others. In a sense, the distinctions that narrative theory formulates are heuristic—they have no essential reality in themselves but they enable interpretation to proceed in a consistent and discussable manner. As a feminist reading strategy, Bal often makes particular use of the concept of point of view, what she calls "focalization." Another strategy, characteristic of deconstruction, is to build a reading around some puzzling element in the text that is usually bypassed or harmonized. By exposing the different and the discordant, she can often expose at the same time the patriarchal stamp of traditional interpretation.

Of other narrative critics currently working with ideological dimensions of reading, David Jobling has probably the most sophisticated grasp of the theoretical issues. Phyllis Trible continues to develop feminist readings. Others include Alice Bach (Stanford), Randall Bailey (Interdenominational Theological Center, Atlanta), Walter Brueggemann (Columbia Seminary), Claudia

Camp (Texas Christian University), David Clines (Sheffield), Cheryl Exum (Boston College), Danna Nolan Fewell (Perkins, Southern Methodist University), Esther Fuchs (Arizona), Sharon Pace Jeansonne (Marquette), Susan Niditch (Amherst), David Penchansky (College of St. Thomas, St. Paul), Ilona Rashkow (State University of New York, Stony Brook), Lori Rowlett (Southern Methodist University), Regina Schwartz (Duke), Renita Weems (Vanderbilt), and James Williams (Syracuse), as well as myself, often writing with Danna Fewell. The list, representing very varied stances, could be much larger (my apologies to the excluded) and draws from a group that is growing rapidly as younger scholars add their energies—for example, significant published work will increasingly be seen from Emory graduate students Timothy Beal, Alice Hickcox, Deborah Krause (now at Eden Theological Seminary, St. Louis), Tod Linafelt, Mary Shields, and Jan Tarlin.

A mark of current narrative criticism in Hebrew Bible studies is its considerable diversity. The lack of an obvious institutional center (as my location notes indicate) is paralleled by the lack of an obvious theoretical or methodological center. That, it seems to me, is probably a healthy, if sometimes confusing, state of affairs.

How do I go about reading a narrative text myself? Let me try reading the story of Lot at Sodom in Genesis 19 as an example—only an example, not a strict paradigm, for I go about the craft of interpretation in various ways, depending upon the particular text, my familiarity with it, why I am reading it, and who (if I am to write about it) my audience is going to be. In the present case this is not a text with which I have worked closely before, though it has been the subject of class discussion once or twice in the past year or so. Why choose it? Our text choices are not usually innocent, though often we may think so. In the present case it is clear to me what some of my interests are. Feminism leads me to ask questions about the interpretive possibilities for Lot's daughters and to see a deconstructive opportunity (see Chapter 12) in the cursory mention of Lot's wife being turned to a pillar of salt. As part of an ongoing literary-critical project, I am also interested in the part played by God in the story. In fact, this latter interest (in the character of God) is related directly to the former (in feminist reading of the Bible). Thus to say that I am reading the story of Lot at Sodom is hardly accurate, though Lot of necessity will be a significant part of my discussion.

A crucial decision needs to be made. What are the boundaries of the text I am reading? From beginnings and endings we make meaning, no less than from middles. Chapter 19 neatly bounds the immediate account of Lot and his family, beginning with Lot sitting in the gate of Sodom and seeing the two visitors arrive and ending with him lying, unknowing, with this daughters, who subsequently give birth to two sons. On the other hand, the chapter, like Lot's story in general, is clearly interwoven with the surrounding story of Abraham. Moving back into Abraham's story, however, we reach at least 11:26, the genealogy of Terah, the patriarch's father. Moving forward into Abraham's story takes us at least to the account of his death in chapter 25. But beyond these boundaries, of course, are larger ones into which this story flows: in the final analysis the story stretches at least from Genesis to Kings, from the creation and expulsion from the garden to the monarchic state and exile from Judah. In practice, then, given the flexibility and extent of the possible boundaries to this account of Lot and his family, I shall focus mainly on chapter 19 and its immediate antecedents in chapter 18 but leave open the limits of the narrative.

Questions of plot and character are a staple of the study of narrative. Some narrative criticism highlights the one rather than the other: Certain structuralists and formalists, for example, regard characters as essentially functions of plot. These critics are interested in defining basic story types—the universal bones of narrative. Any complexity of characterization becomes subordinate to the character's place (as an "actant"—sender, object, receiver, helper, opponent, or subject) in a plot that is already dictated by the narrative genre. Other critics have seen character as the sine qua non of story, arguing that even when plots take readers into totally unfamiliar territory, readers reach out to identify characters in terms of their own world. Some critics try to accord no priority but rather recognize that plot and character are inseparable: We can only know characters through considering their actions and motivations, which constitute the plot; we can hardly talk of plot without considering the actions and motivations of its characters. In practice I find this last position to be true for me. Plot and character, on this understanding, are heuristic concepts, having no discrete reality in themselves but useful as starting points for making sense of narrative.

For entering this particular text, I am using plot. Here we are dealing with the organizing force or design, which we see as connecting events into some kind of comprehensible pattern. Readers are always struggling to make order out of what they read, and plot is one dimension of narrative order. We understand plot through different and incomplete sources—the voice of the narrator, the speech and actions of the characters. Often in biblical narrative, the relations between events are not made explicit. Our desire for order drives us to make connections. Even so simple a link as that made by many translators and commentators between God's remembering Abraham and his rescue of Lot is not unambiguously given to us by the narrator. Literally the narrator says, "And it happened, when God destroyed the cities of the district, that he remembered Abraham and he sent Lot out of the midst of the overthrow, when he overthrew the cities in which Lot dwelt" (Gen. 19:29).* To translate

---

*Scripture translations in this chapter are the author's own.

"so that he sent Lot out" is reasonable but nonetheless inferential. We read it that way in the interests of constructing the plot. That way, Abraham's earlier intercession becomes Lot's saving grace.

Plots may be conceived on a simple model of exposition, conflict, climax, and resolution. A situation is presented which is somehow disordered, incomplete, lacking, or harboring an unfulfilled desire. From this situation develops a conflict or complication which in turn produces a climactic turning point and some degree of resolution. Of course, there may be more than one conflict and more than one climax (though male writers and readers seem inclined to find satisfaction in a grand climax), and the longer stories in the Hebrew Bible are characteristically plotted in this more meandering way. Another way of asking about plot is to ask about desire. Who desires what and when? In what ways are the desires that drive the story fulfilled? Framed that way, the question about plot is also more obviously a question about character. It is also a question that applies to more than one character, thus freeing the interpretation of the story from being determined entirely by a decision about who is the "main" character—not as straightforward a matter as might initially be thought. (Is the main character the one who gets the most square inches of text? In chapter 19 that would cut out Yhwh, would it not?) Rather, each of the characters may be envisioned as having his or her own plot, one thread in a web of plots.

Since chapter 18 begins with the visitors' arrival at Sodom, we could start by asking about the visitors' desire. That would require going back into chapter 18. And then we would need to ask whether their desire was the same as Yhwh's desire—a question that becomes tied into another question, namely, whether we can sustain a clear distinction between the visitors and Yhwh. So given a need here to be succinct, let me turn straight to the latter character.

Yhwh enters the episode (18:17) persuading himself that he should disclose to Abraham "what he is about to do," an enigmatic intention which becomes clear when he goes on to speak of Sodom and Gomorrah and his need to know about their outcry of distress. Knowing each other is important, we learn, for both Yhwh and Abraham, for upon it appears to hang the agenda that the deity has marked out for the human. Abraham needs to know what Yhwh is involved in, as an object lesson. Thus the patriarch will command his sons and his house after him to keep Yhwh's way by doing righteousness (*tsedaqah*) and justice (*mishpat*). In turn, Yhwh can make good his promise that Abraham should become a great and mighty nation and a subject of blessing. Yhwh's speech not only brings Abraham into the new episode in terms of Abraham's needing to know more about Yhwh but also ties the episode firmly into the larger story of Yhwh and Abraham.

When the men (angels?) who are with Yhwh turn and go toward Sodom, Abraham confronts the deity. Will Yhwh, he asks, truly sweep away the righteous (or "innocent"—*tsadiq*) with the wicked? Should not the judge (*shophet*) of the earth do justice (*mishpat*)? Why Abraham should assume that Yhwh is going to destroy Sodom—the deity has said nothing about destroying—is unclear. Perhaps Sodom's evil reputation is known to Abraham, and perhaps he knows Yhwh as a god who will not hesitate to punish "great sin." Or at least he is taking no chances. (Yhwh makes no effort to disabuse him of his assumption.) Some critics, reading in terms of the larger narrative, would argue that Abraham is really concerned here not with the "innocent" in general but with his nephew Lot in particular, perhaps still regarded as his heir. Certainly in chapter 14 Abraham had mounted a major expedition to rescue his nephew; hence the possibility that Lot is the subtext of Abraham's concern makes some sense, despite the fact that he is not mentioned here at all.

On this reading, Yhwh enters the story desiring to deal with Sodom and Gomorrah's outcry but also desiring that Abraham learn something from what will transpire. Abraham enters the story desiring to save Lot. Precisely where Yhwh is to be found in the subsequent account is hard to say, since the two visitors ("messengers" or "angels") who speak mostly as "we" and are narrated as "they" become in v. 17 "he" and in v. 19 "you" (masc. sing.) and in v. 21 "I"—"I will not overturn the city"—as though Yhwh himself were speaking. (Such sliding identity is not unusual in the depiction of Yhwh in Hebrew Bible narrative—see, for example, the immediately preceding story of the visitors to Abraham's tent earlier in chapter 18, or the story of Gideon in Judges 6.) Whatever the case, there is little to suggest that the divinity, despite Yhwh's initial words in 18:20–21 about his needing to investigate, has any other intention than to destroy the city. The angels echo precisely Abraham's understanding of Yhwh's plan and speak as though the power to destroy were theirs: "For we are destroying this place, for their cry has grown great before Yhwh and Yhwh sent us to destroy it" (19:13). It is not even clear that the attempted assault on the visitors is the deciding factor, though that is usually how the plot is understood.* We may be left with the distinct suspicion that Yhwh's speech to Abraham in 18:20–21 was less than forthright.

With the overturning of the cities, both characters' plots find resolution. For Yhwh there will be no more outcries of distress from Sodom and Gomorrah, and Abraham will have learned—a salutary lesson—that his deity will not flinch from executing justice without fear or favor. For Abraham, his long journey with Lot has come to an end.

What does Lot desire? Confronted by visitors to the city, he desires to offer them hospitality in his own home. They decline. He insists. Then the complication arises. "But before they lay down, the men of the city, the men of Sodom, closed around the house, both young and old, all the people, to the last one [or 'on all sides']" (19:4). The men demand that Lot produce the visitors: "Bring them out to us that we may know [i.e., sexually] them." Perhaps premonitions about such treatment of strangers led Lot to insist in the first place that the visitors not stay in the street overnight. Perhaps he knew something of the violence awaiting visitors to Sodom from his own experience. At any rate his response suggests that his desire to sustain his hospitality now drives his action. "Please, my brothers, do not do evil. Please, look—I have two daughters who have not known a man. Please let me bring them out to you, and do to them whatever is good in your sight. Only do not do a thing to these men, for this reason: they have come under the shelter of my roof" (19:7–8). Possibly his offer of his daughters ("do what is good in your sight") is a desperate attempt to shock the assailants into a realization of the enormity of their demand ("do not do evil"), so that they desist altogether. The simpler reading is that Lot is callously willing to sacrifice his daughters in order to uphold his honor as a provider of hospitality. Certainly he has not willingly offered himself in place of the strangers!

For a moment resolution, of one sort or another, hangs in the air. Instead, for Lot, the complication becomes more acute. The men of the city have their own desire, for violence. "Come on, get closer!" they mock (the Hebrew means not "draw back out of the way" as most translations have it but "get close and then some more!"). "This one came to sojourn and he's busy being a judge! Now we'll do you more evil than them." The narrator continues: "So they pressed at the man, at Lot, hard, and came close to breaking the door" (19:9). A glance at the imagery of locking and unlocking, opening, latches, and doors in the Song of Songs is enough to suggest a perverse double entendre here. Rapidly Lot himself has become the rape object. With the next sentence the narrator mischievously maintains our focus on the rapists and their new victim—"And the men put out their hands and brought Lot to them"—before adding words which completely redefine the sense—"(in)to the house, and shut the door." The "men" therefore become the visitors, the reaching out a rescue instead of the inflicting of more abuse, and the door is again literally a door (though its closing against the attackers is also figuratively the closing of the door to Lot's body).

In terms of plot we could say that Lot's desire to show hospitality has been frustrated by the evil men of Sodom, to the point where Lot the sojourner is himself about to be abused along with the rules of hospitality. Put that way, plot and point of view go hand in hand. Since Lot's first sight of the visitors in 19:1, the story has been narrated predominantly from Lot's point of view. Now that changes. The visitors take charge (19:12–13). They strike blind the assailants, "both small and large," so that—a farcical touch—these wear themselves out trying to find the door. The visitors then ask whether Lot has any others with him—"son-in-law and sons and daughters and all who belong to you in the city"—in order to take them out of the place, "for we are destroying this place, for their cry of distress [or 'cry for help'] has grown great before Yhwh and Yhwh sent us to destroy it." ("It" is usually taken to be the city as in v. 14, but strictly its antecedent is the cry of distress!) Here we may see the plot of chapter 18 coming back into focus.

Lot does the visitors' bidding. He goes out and says to his sons-in-law, "his daughters' takers": " 'Arise, go out of this place, for Yhwh is destroying the city.' But in the eyes of his sons-in-law he was just fooling around." (The word *metsaheq* means laughing, jesting, playing the fool; perhaps there is a play on *metsa'eq*, crying in distress.) Having failed to impress his sons-in-law, he seems hardly impressed himself, for at dawn he is still at home. The visitors (now called "messengers" or "angels") urge him, "Arise, take your wife and your two daughters who happen to be here [literally: who are found (here); cf. Gen. 19:29, 30, 31, 32 referring to the righteous/innocent], lest you be swept away up [cf. 18:23, 24] in the iniquity of the city." Yet he still lingers.

"So the men [i.e., the visitors] seized his hand and his wife's hand and his two daughters' hands, through Yhwh's pity on him, and they brought him out and set him outside the city" (19:16). Having got him this far, they try again to make him follow their wishes and save himself: "Flee for your life! Do not pay attention behind you, and stop nowhere in the plain! Flee to the hills, lest you be swept away!" By now we may decide that the plot, seen as the visitors' desire to destroy the city and exercise Yhwh's justice and mercy/pity, is being further complicated by Lot. As Lot stalls, the visitors begin to lose charge, and Lot wrests readers' attention back to himself. Now once more he shows reluctance, though this time the reluctance begins to give shape to a new desire. Urged to flee to the hills, Lot objects, "No, my lords, if you please. Look here, your [sing.] servant has found favor in your [sing.] eyes, and you have made a great commitment [*hesed*] to me in saving my life [lit.: causing my life (*nephesh*) to live]. But I cannot flee to the hills, lest (the) evil cling to me and I die. Look now, this city is close to escape to, and it is tiny; please let me flee there—it is tiny, is it not?—and my life [*nephesh*] will be saved [lit.: will live]."

Lot's logic seems curious to me; and other commentators, where they have paused to comment, have generally found it puzzling, too. What is he saying? That despite the visitors' assurance he does not trust that they can guarantee his survival if he travels to the hills? But why should a city offer him any more protection? What evil is going to cling to him? The evil practiced in Sodom or the evil (destruction) that is to befall Sodom? Or is he speaking of evil more generally as the fate likely to be his, a townsperson living without support in the hill country? What is clear alone is that he desires, if he must flee at all, that it be to this little town of Zoar. And in response his interlocutor is willing to allow him to do what he asks, and to grant Zoar a reprieve since Lot will be in the town's midst. Thus Lot's desire apparently modifies the visitors' desire to destroy all.

The narrator now tells of what would seem to be the climax to the divine plot of punishment for evil: Yhwh rains brimstone and fire on Sodom and Gomorrah, "and he overturned those cities and all the plain and all dwelling in the cities, and the vegetation of the ground" (19:25). A brief comment about Lot's wife gazing behind him and being turned to a pillar of salt interposes. Then, following appropriately the account of the fulfillment of the divine desire, comes mention of Abraham, who went at dawn "to the place where he had stood before Yhwh" and, looking down, beheld the whole plain smoking like a furnace (19:27–28). Abraham, who had pressed God to spare the place if any innocent people could be found therein, now has his answer. There were none found. For Abraham that must include Lot, since he has no way of knowing that Lot has escaped.

Now the narrator concludes. "So it was, when God destroyed the cities of the plain, that God remembered Abraham. . . . " As we have seen, the sentence may be read as extending into the next clause: "and (so) he sent Lot from the midst of the overturning." Yhwh's remembering of Abraham turns out to be his reason for sparing Lot. The sentence, as it continues, however, quickly overturns any certainty about that motivation by attaching to the Lot clause a temporal clause of its own. We may then read two separate statements about God: "So it was, when God overturned the cities of the plain, that God remembered (his conversation with) Abraham. And (so it was, too, that) he sent Lot out of the midst of the overturning, when he overturned the cities where Lot dwelt" (19:29).

If now the divine plot seems at rest (if not clear resolution), the plot as it concerns Lot turns out to be still in motion. Lot's desire to find safety in Zoar is thrown into question. Without indication of any significant time elapsing after the destruction of the plain, the narrator tells us that "Lot went up from Zoar and dwelt in the hills, and his two daughters with him, for he was afraid to dwell in Zoar. So he dwelt in a cave, he and his two daughters" (19:20). In other words, after all his delaying and prevaricating he ends up where the visitors told him to go in the first place. All sorts of questions arise. Why did he say he wanted to go to Zoar if he was afraid to dwell there? Or did the fear arise after he arrived? Why was he afraid? Did he ever actually stay in Zoar? (Verses 23 and 30 say simply that he "came to" and "went up from" Zoar.)

Let me explore one possibility among several. I suggest that all along he knew Zoar to be, like the other cities, a place for visitors to fear, yet he pressed to go there nonetheless because he thought that he might thereby save it. Fearful places though these cities were, they were yet where he had lived, found sons-in-law, and survived to this point. Is the survival of Zoar, fearful though it be, Lot's gesture of humanity? Plainly unable to prevent the destruction of Sodom and Gomorrah, he tries for what he thinks is possible. Zoar is so tiny, a trifle, he insists to the divine visitors. Surely God can overlook a trifle for Lot's sake? Sensing his visitors' impatience to get on with the destruction and at the same counting on their desire to see to his own safety, Lot has played his cards well. On this reading, then, his delays are tactical in the service of a larger strategy. Lot saves a city where Abraham fails. Abraham's challenge hangs on the simple (I could say simplistic) binary categories of righteousness/innocence and evil. Lot's challenge is more subtle. It is based on his own personal involvement with his visitors: he capitalizes on what he sees (and makes sure they see he sees), namely, the *hesed* (faithfulness, commitment) they have shown him. His sons-in-law think that he is only playing the fool. If so, he is a significant fool, for he saves from destruction a whole, albeit tiny, city. Whether we judge that saving to be a good thing or not is, of course, another matter.

Thus I have construed Lot's plot in terms of his desire to belong to the city, to offer hospitality, and to extend his gesture of *hesed* even to a city he fears to dwell in. Though his desire to belong is frustrated, his story is not quite finished. If we jump to its end, we find him named as father of two nations. His belonging belongs to the future. A question hangs over my construal, however. What if God destroyed Zoar after all? Despite the visitor's assurance, the narrator does not single out Zoar as an exception to the depiction of destruction in vv. 25 or 29, and later Lot's elder daughter seems not to know of any remnant in the land (or "on the earth"). We have no certain way of settling the matter, though commentators as early as Ibn Ezra have argued that Deut. 29:22 (which fails to mention Zoar in its list of four destroyed cities) does so. Any reading of Genesis 19 must reckon with this uncertainty.

We have followed the plots of the divinity, of Abraham, and of Lot. Now we have found ourselves with another shift in point of view to that of Lot's daughters, in particular the firstborn. She convinces her sister that, as sole survivors, if they are to "make seed live," they must do so by their father. Over the next two nights they make their father drunk, and they go in and lie with him, first the elder, then the younger. Though the narrator interjects that Lot knew nothing of what happened to him those two fateful nights (vv. 33 and 35), the narrative otherwise is constructed from the daughters' perspective. Even the outcome retains that perspective, except for the phrase "to this day," which breaks the frame, as the narratologists put it, and draws attention to the narrator: "Thus they were pregnant, the two daughters of Lot, by their father. And the firstborn bore a son and she called his name Moab—he is the father of Moab to this day. And the younger, she also bore a son and she called his name Ben-Ammi—he is the father of the Bene-Ammon (Ammonites) to this day." Hence although I have claimed resolution for Lot's plot in his fathering of the two nations, my claim is tenuous. For Lot's hold on the end of the narrative is tenuous. His older daughter (literally) "lays" him, he has no knowledge of this carnal knowledge, and the children of his ignorance who bear his name (their names play on "By-

Father" and "Son-of-My-Father") are named not by him but by his daughters. The sons, not Lot, are called the fathers of their people. Thus Lot fades from the story, displaced by his daughters and by the sons he must have thought he would never have.

But I have almost displaced the daughters from view. Instead I wish to expand their plot just a little. They desire to make seed live (not "have children"). Where does their desire arise from? Of course, we can say that it is part of their social construction as women in patriarchy, where men's seed is a central theme of control and inheritance. We can also look back into their story in chapter 19 and glimpse them on their father's lips as exchange for two unknown men from who knows where. Even if, as I have wondered, Lot does not mean to be taken seriously in offering his daughters to be raped, nonetheless his rhetoric places them dangerously close to disposability. If he is literal in his offer, their marginality is made amply clear. The men, the visitors, ask Lot whether he has someone else with him: "Son-in-law, sons, daughters . . . " (v. 12). The order is interesting, an indication perhaps of Lot's desire to belong to the city. A son-in-law becomes more important than a son, for he signifies the community's acceptance of the father. Daughters are only a means to an end. Lot's sons-in-law are "takers of his daughters," an unusual phrase suggesting both Lot's marginal situation and the daughters' vulnerability in the power stakes of sojourning and citizenship. And where were the sons-in-law as all the men of the city gathered to assault the strangers, and the sojourner, in their midst? The logic of the text drives us to see them among the abusive crowd. English translations customarily transform "takers of his daughters" into something like those "who were about to marry his daughters," though such a stretch of meaning has no other warrant than to smooth this text. Taking the term "son-in-law" in its usual sense, we must assume either that the sons-in-law are not living with their wives, Lot's daughters, or that they are married to other daughters who rate no mention, either by their father or their husbands.

However we look at them, these daughters are on the margins of both their father's world and the larger social world in which their father in his quest for belonging has placed them. Given such marginality, we need hardly be surprised to find them, in extremity, constructing their remaining value in terms of their ability to bring (men's) seed to life, even if that has to be the seed of their own father. As though complicit with these values the narrator reports that the daughters bore sons, not daughters. (So, of course, Sarah, Rebekah, Rachel, Tamar, Hannah, and Naomi, to name a few, bear sons, not daughters.) Thus given that they are the most marginal of all the story's characters, it is ironic that Lot's daughters' plot finally supplants all the others. While Yhwh rains down brimstone and fire, overturns cities and wipes out whole populations, the most vulnerable and subordinate characters in the story take charge of their own lives, as they have been led to understand them, by doing what must be done to bring seed to life.

When the daughters were thrust out of Sodom, their mother was with them. We may have remarked on her palpable absence earlier in the chapter, at the visitors' arrival. Lot, we are told, "made them a feast, and baked unleavened bread, and they ate" (v. 3). But just as in the earlier scene of hospitality in chapter 18 where Abraham is credited with preparing the visitors' food, despite the narrator's having already detailed the preparation as essentially the work of Sarah and the servant, so here we may decide that Lot is no more likely to have made the feast and baked the bread than Abraham. The narrator, in patriarchal fashion, is recounting a man's story: the host offers the visiting men hospitality, so as far as the narrator, the visitors, and the implied reader are concerned, the meal is the host's. At least in the Abraham scene the narrator gave wife and servant a nod, if only perfunctorily. Here Lot's wife is visible only by inference.

We glimpse her next seized and expelled from home and city. Then, at some undetermined point in her expulsion, she looks behind Lot and becomes a pillar of salt. Why? That is, why does she gaze behind, and why is she turned to salt?

Commentators have little difficulty on the latter score. Why turned to salt? Because, they say, she disobeyed the angel's command. Few ask whether the command was heard by her, let alone addressed to her. In fact, having told us that the visitors had brought them out—Lot, wife, and daughters—the narrator continues with the visitors' command: "Flee [masc. sing.] for your [masc. sing.] life; do not look back [masc. sing.]" (19:17). The divine visitors are only concerned to talk to Lot, but the woman as subsumed in her husband is expected to obey. (It is the logic of the law in Exodus-Deuteronomy.) On the other hand, the narrator is not at all specific about the agency by which she becomes salt. Given the emphatic way in which the destruction unfolding before the woman is ascribed to Yhwh—"And Yhwh rained on Sodom and Gomorrah brimstone and from Yhwh in heaven"—coyness over her fate is curious. Is the narrator just a little nervous about signaling divine responsibility? Sandwiched between the big players, Yhwh and Abraham, Lot's "pillaried" wife may make for disturbing reading. As any journalist knows, an account of devastation in general (as in cities and inhabitants), no matter how massive the scale, may shock less than an account of devastation in particular (as in Lot's wife). Thus in the middle of the climax to both Abraham's and the divine plot stands a pillar of salt. A disturbance? A distraction? A seasoning? For salt surely makes a difference. We need to look further into this matter.

Why does Lot's wife turn her attention to what is behind Lot? Professional (male) critics have rarely asked the question, let alone attempted to answer it. Their sights are set firmly on the story's men. But women, poets, have asked and, in answering, recognized her humanity. She, in Kristine Batey's poem, is the one who cooked the meals in Sodom ("whoever is god—the bread must

still be made"), raised her daughters in Sodom ("The Lord may kill the children tomorrow, but today they must be bathed and fed"), and visited her
women neighbors in Sodom ("weren't they there / when the baby was born, /
and when the well collapsed?"):

> It is easy for eyes that have always turned to heaven
> not to look back;
> those that have been—by necessity—drawn to earth
> cannot forget that life is lived from day to day.
>
> . . . .
>
> On the breast of the hill, she chooses to be human,
> and turns, in farewell—
> and never regrets the sacrifice.*
>
> —Kristine Batey*

However, you may say, that is all very well, but in the story world of Genesis 18–19 Sodom is evil, in its totality. These are fictions, the poet's neigh-
borly, child-rearing, family-nurturing women; they are fictions invented
against the plain sense of the text. To which I reply that reading this text is not
quite so simple.

In chapter 18 God speaks first of the myriad "cry of distress" or "cry for
help" (ze'aqah) of Sodom and Gomorrah and of their grave "sin" (18:20–21).
Implied by the term "cry for help" are many oppressed people. Are they all at
the same time and equally oppressors deserving destruction? Neither the narrator nor God makes any attempt to clarify the matter. The term "cry for
help" remains, disturbing the notion of total depravity. On the other hand,
when Abraham (not the narrator or Yhwh) introduces the terms "innocent"
(or "righteous") and "wicked" to define the fate of the cities, he forces the
issue into a rigid choice between exclusive categories. For Abraham it is a
matter of either/or: people are either innocent or wicked. Yet given his earlier
treatment of Sarai (Gen. 12:10–20) and Hagar (Genesis 16), some of us may
surely be forgiven if we wonder where he would place himself on this grid. In
short, however we look at this discussion of prospective corporate judgment,
its terms are fraught with unclarity if not contradiction.

Another pointer to the text's inability to sustain a notion of total evil is a
simple verbal link between chapters 18 and 19 that has the potential to disturb
a reader alive to this issue. Having heard Abraham persist in asking what Yhwh
will do if forty righteous, or thirty or twenty or ten, "are found [there]"
(matsa'; Gen. 18:29, 30, 31, 32), I am struck by the way the angels speak of
Lot's daughters: "Arise, take your wife and your two daughters who are found
[here] [matsa'], lest you be swept away in the iniquity of the city" (19:15).

---

*"Lot's Wife," in Alive Now! January/February 1988, p. 27.

The daughters who are "found" recall the innocent/righteous who may be "found." So do the daughters signal the presence of "innocence" in the city?

The angels, however, no matter what their actions might suggest, noticeably fail to include the daughters in their spoken concern. "Arise," they say to Lot, "take your wife and your daughters . . . lest you [masc. sing.] be swept away." Likewise, the narrator's account of the angel's seizing by the hand Lot, his wife, and his daughter is punctuated by a parenthesis about Yhwh's compassion for him. It becomes clear, therefore, that just as the narrator has rhetorically excluded Lot's wife from her position as food preparer, so too the angels exclude wife and daughters from their own moral space as persons. Lot's offer of his daughters to the crowd gives us sufficient clue to the identity of at least some of the oppressed in Sodom, whose cries have reached heaven. How many daughters have already been raped? How many young men? And if the young men gather to rape other men (19:4), are they all there by choice in this violent city? But now we have another way of reading this story, for the excluded are beginning to appear and the included are beginning to look different. Turn back to the crowd gathered around Lot's house and read again. "The *men* of the city, the *men* of Sodom, both young and old, all the people to the last *man,* surrounded the house" (19:4). (Even the term "people" is routinely used of men as distinguished from women—for example, "there arose a great cry of distress of the people and of their wives" [Neh. 5:1]—so that this term cannot be adduced against my point.) These are the *men* of the city. So where are the women? Where are the young, not the young men but the *children*—the daughters and sons? Where are the *babies?* Where are all these in this facile talk of the innocent/righteous and the wicked?

I come back to the pillar of salt. Salt is seasoning for the food the woman prepares (Job 6:6), seasoning for the cereal offerings she makes ready for her man to take to the shrine (Lev. 2:13). Salt is for purifying when she finds the drinking water to be bad (2 Kings 2:20–21). The woman uses salt for preserving food; her menfolk—and her god, Yhwh—use it to prevent food being grown (Judg. 9:45; Deut. 29:23). Salt preserves Lot's wife as a monument which cries out in distress to heaven. For salt is tears, anguish for the women and children of Sodom.

> Who will weep for this woman?
> Isn't her death the least significant?
> But my heart will never forget the one
> Who gave her life for a single glance.
> —Anna Akhmatova*

---

*From "Lot's Wife," *The Complete Poems of Anna Akhmatova,* trans. Judith Henschemeyer (Zephyr Press, 1990), vol. 1.

Conventional readings of this story usually find in Yhwh and Abraham—rarely Lot—its redeeming message and models. Instead I find in Lot's wife its seasoning.

This interpretation has developed from asking questions about plot, framed as questions of desire. Inevitably some sense of the characters has emerged, though I have not formally addressed the issue of characterization. Were I to do so, I would find myself starting with another set of questions. I would seek clues in the way the narrator names, describes, or evaluates a character—though both personal description and evaluation are usually sparse in biblical narrative. What characters say and how they say it tell us much about the kind of people they are. And if we pay close attention to the context of a character's speech, the circumstances in which the speech takes place, we can better decide what to make of it. Biblical characters may be seen as bending their speech to their context, speaking obliquely rather than straightforwardly, or simply lying, no less than people in "real" life. Matching speech and action (as the narrator recounts it), or observing how speech and action are retold by characters, may enable us to see below surface simplicity to underlying complexity. Comparing and contrasting characters, taking note of how they speak to and about one another, may also help our definitions.

In all of this, as in the plot-based analysis above, careful attention to point of view, focalization, is crucial. Whose view is being presented at any given time? And what if we bestow on a character whose point of view has been subordinated in the narration our own focus? Bal does that by naming, for the purposes of analysis, an unnamed character—so "Jephthah's daughter" becomes Bath (Hebrew for "daughter") and thereby has focus in and of herself rather than being always a deflection of her father's focus. That move on the interpreter's part can make explicit what is implicit in another reading.

Three further observations need to be made on the practice of this kind of criticism. First, as I hope became clear above, any account of the text must take serious cognizance of it as a verbal construct, where words make worlds, where words lead us and tease us and plunge us into multiple possibilities of meaning. We can look for secure words, repeated or key words, for example, on which to anchor interpretation. On the other hand, we can seek to unsettle those securities by recognizing that words often participate in more than one pattern or concatenation, that words are always potentially on the move along a spectrum from literal to metaphorical. We can seek to exploit the multivalence of language. So we could talk of ambivalence, ambiguity, and irony (or of allusion and intertextuality—dialogue between texts—and so consciously see our text as a product of its relationships to other texts). Each of these discussions has the potential both to fix and to disrupt our reading.

Second, speaking of reading between texts, our reading of chapter 19 paid some attention to chapter 18 but scant attention to the wider matrix spoken of when I asked about the boundaries of the narrative. Set in the larger context of the Abraham story, this episode presents us with various interesting possibilities to pursue further. I could take up a thematic question about the relationships between the Abrahamic family and foreigners. Who is the subject and who is Other in the larger story? What value is placed upon the Other? Early in the story (Genesis 12), Abraham's xenophobia turns out in the case of Pharaoh to be seriously misplaced; so, too, later, in the chapter immediately following the Sodom story (20), with Abimelech, king of Gerar. Lot's attempt to assimilate, on the other hand, places him in the greatest jeopardy.

Or I could delineate Lot's character by a comparison with that of Abraham and soon conclude that each character has deeply problematic attitudes toward his family. Lot's offer of his daughters may recall Abraham's prostitution of Sarah, not only at the very beginning of his story (in Genesis 12) but again, despite Yhwh's insistence that Sarah is to bear the promised seed, in Genesis 20, immediately following the Sodom account. By the same token it may remind us of Abraham's preparedness to sacrifice Hagar and Ishmael (Genesis 16, 21) and, in due course, Isaac (Genesis 22). Lot can save (evil) Zoar but speak of giving his (innocent) daughters to the ravening mob. Abraham can plead for (evil) Sodom but say not a word in defense of his (innocent) son.

Or I could turn the question toward the character of Yhwh and suggest that the divinity's complicity in the death of Lot's wife is no less troubling than his sustenance of Abraham the family sacrificer or his wanton disregard for Isaac's well-being when making him the pawn in a "test." I could conclude that there is little blessing for either sons or daughters in God's grand program of making Abraham a great nation. Protecting the character of God has always been a major industry in biblical studies and the "new" literary criticism has not noticeably differed in this regard. Nevertheless, when the study of character becomes a key element of critical inquiry, it becomes difficult to avoid hard questions about a (the?) leading character in the story. (In this connection Harold Bloom's account of the deity in his *The Book of J* [Grove Weidenfeld, 1990] is refreshing.)

A further dimension of "intertextual" reading would involve bringing into interpretive play texts from farther afield than the Abraham story. Robert Alter and Laurence Turner, for example, have both explored connections between the Sodom story and the account of the Flood in Genesis 6–9. It seems to me that there are also strong verbal and thematic correspondences and contrasts with the account of the plagues and deliverance from Egypt in Exodus 1–15, especially the passover account in chapter 12. From outside the corpus of Genesis-Kings the book of Jonah, as others have observed, is an obvious candidate for a comparative reading.

My third and final point concerning my reading of biblical narrative concerns coherence. I believe that most readers, at least those likely to be reading this essay, have a powerful drive to form interpretations that offer an encompassing, comprehensive, and coherent account of their text. Postmodernist theory, in particular deconstruction, helps me to see that this "totalizing" drive is hardly inevitable or innocent. It places a premium on sameness (unity) and univocality and devalues difference (diversity) and multivocality. It leads to our ignoring or suppressing the very tensions and fractures in texts that may offer us enlivening insight or, indeed, escape from the tyranny of an interpretive tradition. Ironically, this is something that historical critics at the beginning of the modernist period knew and used to great effect as they sought out the verbal and conceptual discrepancies that crumbled the univocal divine voice of scripture into a very human amalgam of diverse voices and competing interests. Contemporary narrative criticism of the Bible would do well to cultivate a healthy suspicion of systematics.

Criticism of the new narrative studies has often taken the form of ignoring it, resisting its inclusion in curriculum or development in graduate schools, or suppressing its publication. Expressed criticism from historical critics has often been ill-conceived, argued on the basis of accusations about being subjective (as though historical criticism were not) and frequently both unwilling to acknowledge the discipline of literary criticism and unaware of the highly problematic nature of the subjective/objective distinction. "Traditional" historical critics have generally been even slower than many "new" literary critics (such as myself) to become fluent in the hugely important debate on critical theory that has gone on outside the boundaries of biblical criticism, though at least references to E. D. Hirsch (perhaps the most celebrated defender of "authorial intention"—a keystone of traditional historical criticism—as a fundamental category of criticism) seem to be on their way to becoming mandatory.

The question of literary criticism's relation to historical criticism has exercised many. A common strategy (indeed a commonplace of book reviews) of those willing to allow the former some place in the sun has been to insist that it must build on the achievements of historical criticism, as though the latter were "basic" to criticism. Few scholars, in practice, have demonstrated an ability to afford literary and historical criticism equally serious consideration in any sustained study of biblical narrative (David Clines [*The Esther Scroll*, JSOT, 1984], W. Lee Humphreys [*The Tragic Vision and the Hebrew Tradition*, Fortress, 1985; *Joseph and His Family*, South Carolina University Press, 1988], and V. Philips Long [*The Reign and Rejection of King Saul*, Scholars, 1989] are among the exceptions), and I would argue that usually the best literary criticism has been either largely independent of, or in controversy with, historical criticism. None of this is to say that these major kinds of criticism are or can be wholly independent of each other—on the contrary—but rather that claims by historical critics that theirs is the foundational discipline tend to be imperialistic.

On the other hand, the question of the relation of literature and history can be reformulated in cogent and challenging ways. Marxist criticism has viewed with deep suspicion theory and practice that leave out of account the production of the text. Interdisciplinary approaches now common in women's studies programs have also led critics to consider the interface (or reconstruction) of these particular disciplines. An acute problem remains in biblical studies, namely, that much of the data for any kind of historical discourse must come from texts whose provenance is, despite nearly two centuries of historical investigation, a matter of mere speculation. The question of literary criticism's relation to historical criticism therefore is an important one, but it requires a more sophisticated discussion than it has generally been afforded so far.

Another argument sometimes advanced is that literary criticism of biblical narrative confuses biblical and secular literature. Biblical narrative is claimed to be unique as narrative and so not subject to the kinds of critical analysis applied to other literature. The case has usually been made by apologists for traditional Jewish or Christian views of the Bible as scripture and as such is not, in my view, susceptible of constructive debate, since the position depends essentially upon an unarguable dogma or faith claim. This privileges the Bible against any kind of scrutiny that does not come from within the traditions of the faith community claiming the book as its own. Again it is noticeable that such argument against the new literary criticism is basically no different from that advanced by Jewish and Christian apologists against the inroads (or threat!) of historical criticism two centuries ago.

Finally I note a different kind of criticism that affects some kinds of narrative criticism more than others. Especially in its formative, New-Critical, phase narrative criticism has often deployed observations of formal patterning to substantiate pronouncements about meaning. Thus there exist numerous studies of the "chiasm," the abcba pattern, whether on a few verses or a whole book (so much so that, as a friend put it several years ago, any literary critic worth his or her salt could fake a chiasm). Nevertheless the very category of "form" is a problematic one, and the interpretive move from form to meaning is redolent with difficulties.

A list of criticisms could go on indefinitely. But it would involve much more discrimination between different kinds of narrative analysis than is possible here. I choose instead to urge that students of biblical narrative criticism take the trouble to learn of and reflectively apply current discussion in (secular) critical theory, exercise deep suspicion toward claims to a total or fundamental system by whomsoever, and to value imagination, intuition, joy, and pain as critical tools so that, when study of Hebrew Bible narrative becomes so technical and tedious that sleep is its only antidote, they have the courage to seek a new way.

For Further Reading

General

Brooks, Peter. *Reading for the Plot: Design and Intention in Narrative.* New York: Vintage Books, 1985.

Chatman, Seymour. *Story and Discourse: Narrative Structure in Fiction and Film.* Ithaca, N.Y.: Cornell University Press, 1978.

Fewell, Danna Nolan, ed. *Reading Between Texts: Intertextuality in the Hebrew Bible.* Louisville, Ky.: Westminster/John Knox, 1992.

Fewell, Danna Nolan, and Gunn, David M. *Gender, Power, and Promise: Ideology and Story in Genesis-Kings.* Nashville: Abingdon, 1993.

Greenstein, Edward L. "Deconstruction and Biblical Narrative." *Prooftexts* 9 (1989):43–71.

Gunn, David M., and Fewell, Danna Nolan. *Narrative in the Hebrew Bible.* Oxford: Oxford University Press, 1993.

Jobling, David, "Feminism and 'Mode of Production' in Ancient Israel: Search for a Method." In *The Bible and the Politics of Exegesis,* ed. David Jobling, Peggy L. Day, and Gerald T. Sheppard. Cleveland: Pilgrim, 1991.

———. " 'Forced Labor': Solomon's Golden Age and the Question of Literary Representation." In *Poststructuralism as Exegesis, Semeia* 54, ed. David Jobling and Stephen D. Moore. Atlanta: Scholars, 1991.

Lentricchia, Frank, and McLaughlin, Thomas, eds. *Critical Terms for Literary Study.* Chicago: University of Chicago, 1990. See especially Stanley Fish on "Rhetoric," Gerald Graff on "Determinacy/Indeterminacy," Myra Jehlen on "Gender," James H. Kavanagh on "Ideology," and J. Hillis Miller on "Narrative."

Longman III, Tremper. *Literary Approaches to Biblical Interpretation.* Grand Rapids: Academie Books (Zondervan), 1987.

Powell, Mark Allan. *What Is Narrative Criticism?* Minneapolis: Fortress, 1990.

Rimmon-Kenan, Shlomith. *Narrative Fiction: Contemporary Poetics.* London: Methuen, 1983.

Willett, Susan. "Coming Unstrung: Women, Men, Narrative, and Principles of Pleasure." *Proceedings of the Modern Language Association* 105 (1990): 505–18.

On Genesis 18–19

Alter, Robert. "Sodom as Nexus: The Web of Design in Biblical Narrative." In *The Book and the Text,* ed. Regina Schwartz. Oxford: Basil Blackwell, 1990.

Blenkinsopp, Joseph. "Abraham and the Righteous of Sodom." *Journal of Jewish Studies* 33 (1982):119–32.

Jeansonne, Sharon Pace. "The Daughters of Lot: Victims of Their Father's Abuse." In *The Women of Genesis.* Minneapolis: Fortress, 1990.

Turner, Laurence A. "Lot as Jekyll and Hyde: A Reading of Genesis 18–19." In *The Bible in Three Dimensions,* ed. David J. A. Clines, Stephen E. Fowl, and Stanley E. Porter. Sheffield: Journal for the Study of the Old Testament, 1990.

11
READER-RESPONSE CRITICISM

Edgar V. McKnight

R EADER-RESPONSE criticism approaches biblical literature in terms of the values, attitudes, and responses of readers. The reader, therefore, plays a role in the "production" or "creation" of meaning and significance. This attitude toward the role of the reader relativizes the conventional view that the meaning of a text is like the content of a nut, simply awaiting its extraction by a reader. Radical reader-response approaches also challenge conventional views concerning the autonomy of the critic and the scientific and objective nature of the process of reading and criticism.

Diversity in Reader-Response Criticism

Reader-response criticism is not a conceptually unified criticism; it is a spectrum of positions. Specific variants are defined in part by the prior literary and philosophical assumptions of those who practice reader-response criticism. My own project is the utilization of literary criticism in general and reader-oriented approaches in particular to carry out the goal of New Testament hermeneutics by enabling the discovery and creation of meaning-for-the-reader.[1]

Common to all reader-response approaches is the background of New Criticism, with its insistence on the structural unity of a literary work and the process of close reading that uncovers that structure. The elements that were highlighted in New Criticism's close reading also remain important. In fiction, for example, Cleanth Brooks and Robert Penn Warren specify that questions such as the following should be asked:

1. What are the characters like?

2. Are they "real"?

3. What do they want? (motivation)

197

4. Why do they do what they do? (motivation)

5. Do their actions logically follow from their natures? (consistency of character)

6. What do their actions tell about their characters?

7. How are the individual pieces of action—the special incidents— related to each other? (plot development)

8. How are the characters related to one another? (subordination and emphasis among characters; conflict among characters)

9. How are the characters and incidents related to the theme?[2]

Stanley Fish and Wolfgang Iser

A summary of the approaches represented by Stanley Fish and Wolfgang Iser will provide readers with a basic vocabulary and perspective for understanding the major variants of reader-response criticism.

Stanley Fish

The background for the work of Stanley Fish was New Criticism's view of the independence and self-sufficiency of the literary work of art and its attention to close reading of the literary work itself instead of to history, biography, and so on. Fish initiated his reader-response approach when he concluded that the essential factor in meaning is not the spatial form of the text on the page but the temporal process of reading. In his early work Fish did not question assumptions of New Critics about the integrity of language and the text. Moreover, close reading and the elements of literature attended to in close reading remained important. Conventional concerns of criticism (the question of intellectual background, as well as questions of literary conventions and genre) were redefined in terms of potential and probable response of readers.

From a later perspective, Fish acknowledges that his early work was not radical enough, that he had been retaining the most basic of New-Critical principles—the integrity of the text—in order to claim universality and objectivity for his method. The radical move away from New-Critical assumptions came when Fish discerned that literature is a conventional category dependent upon subjective perception. There is no basic or neutral literary language uncolored by perception and response. The conclusion is that "it is the reader who 'makes' literature." Fish qualifies this subjectivism by defining readers as members of interpretative communities (communities that differ over such matters as the nature and function of literature, for example) that determine the attention given by readers and the kind of literature made by readers.[3]

Wolfgang Iser

The work of Wolfgang Iser may be seen as mediating two positions: the position that meaning is purely and simply a content of texts (like the content of a nut) and the position that meaning is essentially a product of the reader. Iser sees the text as the product of an author's intention, with the reading of the text involving not only the intention of the author but also the intention of the reader. The necessary creative activity of the reader does not indicate (as with Fish) that literature and meaning are essentially dependent upon subjective perception. In fact, Iser's work continues a tradition in philosophy which denies that the relationship between things in the world (texts) and observers (readers) is such that things in themselves are unknowable.[4] In proper reading, the essential structures of the text (and therefore its integrity) are maintained.

Iser emphasizes that not only the actual text but also the actions involved in responding to that text must be considered in literature. A literary text is not complete in itself. "Gaps" exist—a lack of complete continuity and/or a lack of specification of relationships between the different linguistic and literary elements. Iser makes the "gaps" and completion of "gaps" by the reader the central factors in literary communication. In the linear process of reading there is movement from one literary unit to another and the bridging or unifying of the units by the reader. This process of unification requires the formation of an idea or theme (a field of reference) within which the two segments make sense. In reading, there is movement from one theme to another theme, with the earlier theme becoming the point of departure for the new theme. The same activity of unification must be carried out at the level of the entire literary work. That is, an idea must be formulated that will allow all of the linguistic and literary elements of the work to coexist so that the work will "make sense." Iser speaks of the development of an overarching idea as the "basic force" in literary communication. He calls it "negativity." It may be thought of in different ways: as the "frame" within which the relevant textual material is organized and subsumed; as the cause underlying the questioning of the world in the text; or as the unwritten base that conditions the formulations of the text by means of the "gaps" (from this perspective the term "negativity" makes sense). The idea does not come from the text alone, but it must be consistent with the text. The reader must ask, "What is the text all about?" Formulation of the idea requires the reader's observation of the world of the text (what is going on in the text). But just as important is the requirement of observation of the world of the text from outside; the reader must transcend the textual world to make sense of the textual world.

The reader becomes most fully involved as the reader is forced to become aware of norms and systems that have become a part of the literary text. These norms exist in the nonliterary life of the reader, but the reader is unaware of them—as the reader is unaware of the atmosphere in which the reader lives. In literature the norms and systems must be brought to consciousness for the text to be actually experienced by the reader. Iser sees that "the process of fulfillment is always a selective one, and any one actualization can be judged against the background of the others potentially present in the textual structure of the reader's role."[5]

Language and the Structural Tradition

The question of the integrity and determinacy of the language, texts, and the subject is at the center of the different varieties of reader-response criticism. Three positions have been noted in the essay so far: (1) the position of New Criticism and the early Fish, which maintains the integrity of language and the determinacy of the textual meaning, with the result that "informed readers" come to basically the same evaluation of literary texts; (2) the position of Iser, which demands the creative activity of the reader but which maintains the integrity of the text, with the result that in proper reading readers' intentions are determined by the text and are in continuity with the intention of the author; and (3) the position of the later Fish, which emphasizes the indeterminacy of language and texts and makes the perception of the reader within a community the creator of literature.

The argument between Iser and the later Fish on determinacy of language and literature is important for reader-response approaches to biblical texts. A strong view of integrity and determinacy of texts and meaning would maintain the internal and external relationships and references in such a way that the text could be treated essentially as a scientific document or a historical artifact and analyzed according to scientific or historical-critical criteria. An integrity and determinacy more suited to literature would maintain the broad classification of the text (e.g., comedy or tragedy) and the sorts of relationships that are involved in such a classification. But the text would not be forced at all points into some preconceived form. Readers would be allowed to sort out the potentiality of the text and the specific possibilities of the text in its uniqueness. Moreover, what a reader sees in one time and place would differ from what is seen in another time and place. When a biblical writing is classified as "gospel," for example, the idea of "gospel" will govern reading. But developments in world and church history, the history of interpretation of the Bible, and the history of individual readers and groups of readers influence the idea of "gospel" and the way that a particular writing is seen as instancing that idea.

A loosely defined sort of integrity is what has actually prevailed in literature. The text has been the occasion for varieties of readings influenced by different contexts (temporal, geographical, and ideological, for example) or reading. Past readers situated in specific times and places, with specific worldviews, have seen their particular readings as necessary and unrelated to context. Today, however, we are able to appreciate and utilize difference instead of being disabled by difference.[6] We are not required to choose between the establishment of the linguistic, or historical, or sociological meaning on the one hand and the forsaking of the possibility of meaning on the other hand.

"Formalism" is a term used to characterize movements emphasizing the analysis of literary works as self-sufficient objects, independent of reference to the world outside the text. New Criticism is a type of formalism, as is Russian Formalism and other East European movements based on linguistic theory. These Eastern European movements are often called "structuralist" because of their application of the linguistic theory of structuralism to literary study. The literary traditions formulated against the background of East European formalism have provided theoretical and practical resources for development and use of a view of textual unity or structure that is energetic and dynamic and capable of responding to cultural and individual development and valuation.[7] One basic argument and development in East European Formalism had to do with the autonomy of the literary work of art—just as in New Criticism. A severe formalist approach took the position that only structures immanent in the text are the object of literary concern. The comparison of poetics with the art of weaving by Viktor Sklovskij (a representative of the Leningrad branch of Russian Formalism) illustrates the extreme view of immanence: "I am concerned in the theory of literature only with the examination of its inner laws. To use an industrial metaphor, when studying the art of weaving, I am not interested in the situation of the world cotton market, nor in the policy of the cotton trusts, but only in the count of yarn and the techniques of weaving."[8]

The Prague formalist Jan Mukarovsky responded that the matter of weaving itself was certainly of more concern than conditions of the world market when studying the art of weaving, but he declared that the cotton market could not be entirely ignored. The needs of the market have some relation to development of the technique of weaving. The same is to be said for literature. Nonliterary factors influence literature the way that the market influences the technique of weaving, not in a direct way or in a way to change the view of literature and the literary work as a nexus of relationships. Literary structure is dynamic and not static, capable of responding to its different contexts and maintaining the nexus of internal relationships. This view of structure is adopted by Iser, for the "determinate" structure of meaning for Iser is not a static "summative whole" but "finds itself in a ceaseless stage of movement."[9]

The view of the subject (or self) is important for a hermeneutical appropriation of reader-response criticism. The view of a unified autonomous self (analogous to a unified autonomous text) capable of complete self-knowledge and knowledge of others is an Enlightenment perspective that has become problematic. The contemporary challenge to such a view of the self may either bring about efforts to validate such a view or create a nihilistic attitude toward meaning and truth (how can I understand another [or the expression of another] if that other does not completely understand himself or herself?). Just as a structural view of the literary text allows a text to retain integrity and determinacy while acknowledging change and difference, a structural view of the subject allows difference and maintains integrity. The subject is defined in part by experiences and inner and outer development. Literary experience is a part of this development and definition. It is because the subject is not a static and autonomous entity that the subject may be changed in the experience of reading.[10]

Recent Developments in the Structural Tradition

Developments in structural semiotics, poststructuralism, and deconstruction associated with scholars such as Roland Barthes, Umberto Eco, and Jacques Derrida may be reconceptualized and utilized in a reader-oriented biblical hermeneutics. Barthes sees the structure of a text as dynamic and involving the reader in a process of analysis without a final synthesis or end.[11] Eco sees the process of reading as involving moves both within the text (intentional) and outside the text (extensional). The various levels and sublevels of textual and extratextual realities are interconnected, and the reader moves back and forth within and without the text to produce meaning.[12] Derrida sets knowledge, language, meaning, and interpretation not simply within a dynamic cultural context but within a larger context of power and authority. Derrida's deconstructive approach to literature is concerned with the examination of the desire for mastery—the mastery of knowledge through language and meaning through interpretation—and the subversion of that desire through the very nature of language itself. The language and logic that form the resources of an author cannot be dominated absolutely by an author. The author uses them by being governed by them. A deconstructive reader seeks to discover relationships between what the author commands and what the author does not command of the patterns of the language used by the author.[13] Reading in the conventional mode is a synthesizing process with the subject/reader being governed (as the subject/author) by language. But a deconstructive reading gives conscious attention to the impulse toward and result of the synthesizing of the conventional reading process in order to break its "domination." The reader-oriented hermeneutical use I advocate acknowledges the dynamic and always in-process nature of the reading and the subject involved in the reading, but it emphasizes the making of sense for the reader—local, ad hoc, and partial as it may be. The unity and meaning found in a specific location and reading overlooks and/or excludes textual elements that cannot be assimilated in that reading, to be sure, but these elements become the basis for other unities and meanings.

Reader-Response Criticism and Biblical Study

Reader-oriented theories not only emphasize the reader's role in the process of achieving meaning but also see the result of reading in terms of an effect upon the reader. This is visualized in different ways. In his Oxford thesis, for example, Jonathan Culler suggested that the process of reading shows the reader the problems of the reader's condition as maker and reader of signs, and this is the meaning of the work.[14] Iser sees the process of reading as the coming together of text and imagination. It is an experience of continual modification, closely akin to our experience in life. Because of the nature of the process, the "reality" of the experience of reading illuminates the dynamic nature of real experiences.[15] Georges Poulet emphasizes the achievement of self-transcendence in reading. In reading, the object of the reader's thought is the thought of another. The reader becomes the subject of the thought (the one doing the thinking) in the act of reading. The reader thinks a thought that belongs to another mental world. "When I am absorbed in reading, a second self takes over, a self which thinks and feels for me. . . . The work lives its own life within me; in a certain sense, it thinks itself, and it even gives itself a meaning within me."[16]

Developments in Reader-Response Criticism of the Bible

Radical reader-oriented approaches are foreign to the experience of historically oriented biblical critics because of different views of the use of language and the nature of biblical literature. It is difficult to overcome this strangeness because conventional views of language and life reinforce each other. Both are governed by the Enlightenment model in which subject and object, humankind and the natural world, are distinct, with the subject—humankind—dominating. Language is a tool used by humans to refer, and the truth of the reference is validated by the human subject through establishment of correspondence between the statement and that to which it refers.

Beginnings: Literary Study of the Bible

Reader-response criticism in biblical studies began with concern with genuine literary matters, a concern that surfaced in the 1960s and 1970s and became commonplace in the 1980s. This turn in biblical studies reflected a return, in a certain sense, to concerns of the precritical period (prior to the Enlightenment). In that epoch, the cultural and intellectual distance between the biblical world and the reader's world was small. No distinction was made between the world depicted in the Bible and the real historical world. Readers had little difficulty seeing their own actions and feelings and the events of their world in relation to the biblical world. Resources of allegory and typology assisted readers to see the Bible, as a whole, as depicting the whole of historical reality. Old Testament stories referred directly to specific temporal events and indirectly (as figures or types) to New Testament stories, events, and realities. But these (both Old Testament and New Testament) also corresponded to the historical experiences of the reader. The biblical world extended to and impinged upon the present, upon the world of the reader of any age. The power of a precritical reading extending from the Old Testament to the readers' day without any rupture depended in part upon the fact that the world of Abraham, Isaac, and Jacob, the world of Moses and Jesus, was not the ultimate reality. Above and beyond the world extending from Adam to the present was a divine world that alone made sense of this world. The worldview of the ancient and medieval world did not methodologically exclude the sacred but rather made the sacred the standard.

With the Enlightenment, the historicity of literary and other cultural phenomena replaced the framework of the theological conceptualization of the ancient and medieval world. History became the standard. The realistic feature of biblical narrative was related consciously to historical reference. The role of the biblical stories was to enable readers to uncover the historical sequence of events to which they referred directly or indirectly. Undermined was the correlation between the world of the reader and the biblical world, made possible when both were seen as expressions of the preexisting divine world. This diminished the potential of the narratives to allow readers to make sense of themselves in relation to the world of the narrative in a somewhat direct fashion.

The literary turn was prepared for in the attempt of Rudolf Bultmann and the New Hermeneutic to extend the power of the biblical text into the life of contemporary readers by attention to its linguistic dimensions. Preoccupation with existential categories and the lack of interaction with secular literary criticism hindered the task. In his 1964 publication, *The Language of the Gospel,* Amos Wilder advocated a move that takes advantage of literary insights. He expounds the New Testament as "language event" (an expression used by the New Hermeneutic reflecting the idea that language and reality are inseparably connected, that reality comes into being through language) in terms of literary genre, with the conviction that "behind the particular New Testament forms [genres] lies a particular life-experience and a language-shaping faith." Wilder explicitly criticizes Rudolf Bultmann's restriction of meaning to existential concepts. The view that the New Testament "tells us about ourselves, not about 'things' and the way they are and the way they happen," according to Wilder, results in a disparagement of "the whole story of man and salvation as the Bible presents it." The literary criticism appropriate for New Testament study is not one that ignores reference and remains confined to the structures and conventions of literature. There is reference in the text, but the reference is not the same as that in conventional study of the Gospels. Students of the

New Testament can learn about its literary language and reference from students of poetry: "This kind of report of reality—as in a work of art—is more subtle and complex and concrete than in the case of a discursive statement, and therefore more adequate to the matter in hand and to things of importance."[17]

Robert Tannehill displayed concern with contemporary literary criticism of biblical texts in 1975 in *The Sword of His Mouth: Forceful and Imaginative Language in Synoptic Sayings*,[18] and in 1977 in "The Disciples in Mark: The Function of a Narrative Role."[19] Tannehill integrated narrative and reader-response criticism. Mark's evaluation of the disciples is to be found in his depiction of the concordant/discordant relationships between Jesus and the disciples, but this is also the key to readers' evaluation. Moreover, as the plot develops, readers are involved through the arousal of expectations that are either fulfilled or left unfulfilled by what ensues. In 1985 and 1989 issues of *Semeia* (a journal devoted to new and emergent areas and approaches in biblical criticism) were dedicated to reader-response criticism.[20]

The Role and Function of the Bible in Reader-Response Literary Criticism

Assumptions about the role and function of the Bible are important in reader-response criticism. The role of the Bible as literature is to be distinguished from the role of the Bible as historical "source" or literary "document." To read the biblical text as source is to read it as the container of some sort of information that may be extracted by objective procedures and validated by comparing the data obtained with data in the real world. To begin with the Bible as historical source and subject it to historical-critical analysis in order to discover the history behind the biblical texts makes movement beyond historical-critical analysis difficult. Moreover, the matter of concern to believers cannot be obtained through such analysis as such. Robert Morgan has depicted the gap that has developed between philological and historical learning on the one hand and religious engagement and theological insight on the other hand.[21] The role of the Bible as a document of ancient communication as such does not really bridge the gap. When the Bible is approached as both an ancient document with original meaning and a living message with contemporary significance, the bridge to a comprehensive and satisfying biblical hermeneutics may have been found. The reader's final focus is not upon the original circumstances but upon the text in the contemporary context of reading.

As literature, the Bible plays a role in the life of society and individuals in that society. The role of the Bible (as the role of literature) may be seen as related to knowledge that the text makes possible for the reader—knowledge extended beyond the world of the text to the world uncovered by the text. The role of the Bible is to be seen in the light of cognitive and noncognitive affective experiences of the reader in the process of making sense of the text as knowledge. It is to be seen in the light of the development of self knowledge vis-à-vis the world and the process of reading. The Bible as literature is seen as the instrument for humankind's discovering, creating, and/or making sense of world, self, and whatever world-and-self-transcending meanings and values humankind is capable of imaging.

The Bible as *religious literature* may be distinguished from other literature in terms of role and function. One way of beginning to mark the distinction of the Bible is to note that the essential shape of biblical literature is comic. That is, the Bible depicts not a reversal of fortune from good to bad (tragedy) but a movement from bad to good. Although the Bible contains examples of romance, irony, and tragedy, the thrust of the Bible is in the direction of the comic. When these other genres are present, they are to be seen in terms of the more central comic movement. Tragedy in the Bible, for example, is seen as an essential episode in the larger scheme of the divine comedy that includes restoration and resurrection.[22]

The Bible is read in the context of continuing communities of faith, and even readers who do not share the faith of those communities are influenced by that fact. The life and faith (practice and theology) of the larger communities of faith and of the local expressions of those communities play their part in the experience of reading. Most of the time this is a silent, even unconscious, influence, the result of a faith perspective that is simply taken for granted. A dialectical relationship exists between the faith perspectives of religious communities and the worldview of the encompassing philosophical and cultural world. A reader who is also a member of a religious community will operate with schemata from both worlds.

Values of Reader-Response Approaches

Whether reader-response criticism of the Bible is viewed positively or negatively depends in part upon the worldview of the reader and the role and function of the Bible in that worldview. Readers who are committed to a "modern" Enlightenment paradigm will seek to eliminate or reduce the subjective character of study. If these readers utilize reader-response criticism, it will take the form of an objective search for the implied reader or for the strategies followed by the author in influencing the reader (rhetorical criticism), which can be demonstrated as existing in the ancient world. However, this essay advocates a reader-response approach that utilizes the rich possibilities of reading for actual readers. Such an approach is valuable for a variety of reasons. First, serious interaction with the text is facilitated by reader-response criticism. This reader-response approach may do for biblical study what the New Criticism did for literature in general—free the biblical text from its domination by disciplines such as history, sociology, and psychology.

Second, this reader-response approach represents a victory for the reader. Readers are freed to make sense for themselves. This method allows readers to interact with the text in light of their own context, linguistic and literary competence, and need, as well as in light of the potentialities of the text. Confidence and further competence are developed as readers are able to make sense of the text in light of their own location and "dialect." Third, such an approach allows the obvious religious concerns of the text to impinge upon reading in a way appropriate to the concerns of the reader. The world of the reader will be seen as "like" the biblical world in some way satisfying to the reader. A type of knowledge may result from the experience of reading that is different from the knowledge gained by scientific methodologies. Levels of meaning and knowledge may be experienced that became lost with the Enlightenment paradigm. Finally, reader-response approaches are capable of accommodating and utilizing approaches followed in more conventional biblical and literary studies. Historical and sociological exegeses, for example, are not precluded in reader-response criticism. They are reconceptualized and relativized but not made illegitimate as such.

Illustration: A Reading of Luke 5:1–11

A reading of Luke 5:1–11 will illustrate the sorts of moves made by the reader in making sense of a biblical text. Two basic sorts of moves are made, one giving attention to the linear arrangement of words, sentences, and so on (paralleling the close reading of New Criticism), the other giving attention to the categories of form (genre) and content that can be assigned to those units. Relationships *within* discourse enable linguistic and literary elements to have meaning as they are *combined* or chained together in a linear and/or layered fashion. Perspectives outside of discourse as such are necessary for making sense of the combinations within discourse. The topic, reference, literary category, and function of the literary unit, for example, are not built up simply from within by words and sentences and their combinations. Formal, semantic, and other categories without discourse are imposed upon and complete the structures of discourse. Perspectives taken by readers influence the relationships discovered and created. Attention to relations outside discourse moves beyond New-Critical emphases.

Biblical texts say something, do something, and influence the reader affectively. The entry into the richness of cognitive and affective meaning and significance of biblical texts is by means of semantic content that involves topics, themes, or ideas. What texts do and how texts affect readers are related to what the texts say. At the level of every literary unit some topic must be discerned. Then, at the level of the total work, a comprehensive organizing principle or idea must be formulated in order for the identification of topics and relationships throughout the work, and, therefore, for the meaning of the work as a whole. Topics and ideas must be consistent with the literary data, but the interplay of literal, figurative, and often paradoxical meanings of words and other units makes the literary data susceptible to a variety of meanings. The same word, expression, or entire text can signify two or more distinct references and express and elicit different attitudes or feelings.

The reader comes to Luke 5:1–11 as a unit in the Gospel of Luke. The unit will be read in light of its definition as a part of a "Gospel" and in light of its part in defining the particular "Gospel" of which it is a part. A variety of nonliterary contexts also influence the reading of the text, and the reader may move to any of these to make sense of the text. The context within which reading takes place and the anticipated result of reading are important. These may be taken for granted and not considered consciously. Here, these matters are considered, for the reading is designed to illustrate the process of reading. Because of the present context of reading, all of the reader's private associations will not be shared, only those that the reader/author can make understandable to readers of this book.[23]

The reader reads until some minimal unit of meaning presents itself (can be discovered or created). Luke 5:1–3 makes up a minimal unit of meaning as it is read in light of lexical and grammatical information. It begins with the press of the people upon Jesus to hear the word of God—and the consequent inability of Jesus to teach the word—and concludes with the successful teaching of the people from a boat. The major actor in the episode is not identified in this unit (pronouns are used instead of the name "Jesus"), so the reader must identify this actor as Jesus by moving either backward or forward in the text to where the proper name is used. The reader knows that Jesus is the personal name of Jesus of Nazareth (Luke 24:19), the son of Mary (Luke 1:31), the prophet (Luke 7:39; 24:19) who is "a Savior . . . Christ the Lord" (Luke 2:11).* From the words and deeds in the unit itself, a reader constructs an image of the Jesus of the unit. He is popular and is the speaker of the word of God. He is ingenious (he uses a boat to solve the problem presented by the press of the people), and his authority is compelling. The unit shows that Jesus has a mission and indicates that the mission involves being sent by God for the purpose of teaching the word of God. This indication is confirmed and made more explicit by a movement to the earlier pericope, which has a quotation from Jesus himself indicating that he was sent to "preach the good news of the kingdom of God to the other cities also."

The text has two sentences in the first unit. The first sentence consists of two verses and gives the following information: The crowd is pressing him to hear the word of God; Jesus is standing by the lake; Jesus notices two boats left

---

*Scripture translations in this chapter are the author's own, except where otherwise marked.

unattended while the fishermen are washing the nets. A reader has to correlate the information given: "One day as he stood by the lake of Gennesaret, with people crowding in on him to listen to the word of God, he noticed two boats lying at the water's edge; the fishermen had come ashore and were washing their nets" (NRSV). The fact that the boats are at the water's edge is explained by the fact that the fishermen have come ashore and are washing the nets. We can assume that they have completed their task of fishing and are now ready to care for their gear and rest from their labors. The fact that Jesus notices the two boats results from Jesus' need and search for some way to escape the press of the crowd and to accomplish his mission.

Can we imagine some relationship between Jesus standing along the shore and the press of the crowd? Is the relationship only temporal, or does the setting of the lake of Gennesaret have some significance? The statement of Jesus in the preceding pericope indicates that he "must preach the good news of the kingdom of God to the other cities also." He has been preaching in the synagogues of Judea just before he appears beside the lake. This reader attempts to sort out information: Jesus is to preach in the cities (where the synagogues are located); in the cities (the synagogues) there is conflict; away from the cities (the "lonely place" of 4:42 and on the shore of the lake of Gennesaret) people are pressing upon him to keep him with them and to hear the word of God.

The presence of Jesus is the occasion of the activity of the crowd, and the activity of the crowd is precluding the very action the crowd desires and for which Jesus has been sent. A reader may mull over the relationship between the irony that Jesus is sent to teach in the city while it is in the country that the people crowd to hear him and the irony that in the country (and beside the lake) the press to hear Jesus precludes that hearing.

The disabling activity of the crowd causes Jesus to explore ways of carrying out his mission. Boats and fishermen are at hand. My limited knowledge of fishing in the New Testament period and of the experience of fishing in general causes me to image the fishermen using a large seine or draw net, with sinkers on the bottom and floats on the top. People fishing would wade in the waters near the shore and maneuver the net to shore in a wide semicircle. Two boats could be used to capture the fish on the lake, with the two boats (and the two ends of the net) closing in on one another instead of to the shore.

The second sentence in the unit has two coordinate clauses: "When he had gotten into one of the boats, which was Simon's, he asked him to put out a little from the land," and "when he sat down, he taught the people from the boat." For the reader who is familiar with the opening chapters of Luke (or who moves back to those chapters to make sense of the text), Simon is no stranger; it was to Simon's house that Jesus went after the healing of the demoniac in the synagogue in Capernaum. There he had healed Simon's mother-in-law. Simon is the other name of Peter, the most prominent of the apostles of Jesus.

With 5:3, the problem created by the press of the crowd has been solved. Jesus has distanced himself so as to be able to preach to the people. The reader images the scene simply: Jesus gets into Peter's boat and asks him to push off from the shore. At this point we see only Jesus and Peter in the boat, with the others washing nets on the shore. It was "a crowd" pressing Jesus to hear him at the beginning; as a result of Jesus' action he teaches "the crowds." The very last word in this unit is the plural form of the noun used in v. 1 in the singular. The reader for whom the reading of this unit is really a rereading knows about the marvelous catch of fish later in the narrative and may see such a catch prefigured at the very beginning with the success of Jesus. The meanings of the various episodes impinge upon one another and contribute to the rich meaning of the unit as a whole. But the relationships must be "seen" by the reader; they are not spelled out by the text.

What is the overall meaning of this unit? At the level of what the text is saying, the meaning seems simple: With the help of Simon and his boat, Jesus is enabled to solve the problem created by the press of the crowd and to carry out the mandate of God to teach the word. The reader is not yet prepared to go beyond the level of what is being said in the text, but a rich potentiality is present in relationships between Jesus and Simon, the lakeshore and the lake, and so on.

The next unit of meaning is Luke 5:4–7, and it deals with the catching of fish. Jesus first asks Simon to put out into the deep and let down his nets for a catch. It appears that the topic has changed from "teaching the word" to "catching fish." In a slow-motion process of reading, full attention will be given to the unit in terms of fishing. Why is Jesus concerned about fishing? Later in the same unit we discover that the fishermen have been busy all night and have caught nothing. There is need for food for the people and financial return for the fishermen! The command of Jesus moreover causes the reader to reimage the earlier events somewhat. Earlier, the reader imaged Jesus and Simon alone on the boat, with the other fishermen on shore with the nets. Other fishermen must now be included, along with a net. A rereading of earlier material may reenvision the fishermen on the shore alongside the boat, washing the net as it is spread on the side of the boat. Simon's taking the boat out would involve the net and apparently some of the fishermen also. The exchange between Jesus and Simon and Simon's action supports the view of Jesus as a person of confidence and authority. It also supports the view of Simon as obedient.[24] The success with catching brought a crisis. The mass of fish could mean failure in fishing, just as the mass of people earlier had threatened the hearing of the word by anyone. The need for help was met by the other fishermen and another boat. But the success of the help created another crisis. The boats began to sink. A slow-motion reading in which the reader attempts to finds categories of meaning and meaning-effect that will utilize the full potential of the text will give attention to the irony and contradictions in the story.

The episode of 5:1–3 has a successful ending and some ironic touches. There is a mandate to preach the word. But something must be done before that mandate can be carried out. The very presence of the crowd to whom he was to preach created the need for some sort of prior action to be carried out by Jesus. The solution to the problem involved distancing himself from the very ones to whom the word of God is to be given. The episode beginning with Luke 5:4 is more ambiguous in terms of the mood created. Initially it appears that the same sort of sequence will be repeated. There is the need for fish to be caught for the proper operation of the social and economic order. The order of society, in which fish are caught for the people, has been interrupted, but Jesus encourages and enables Simon to catch a multitude of fish in spite of Simon's earlier failures. The reader's satisfaction is premature, however. The very success of the catch invites catastrophe. The nets begin to break. The reader may see this as a repetition of the type of thing that created the lack in the first episode. Too much of what is sought spells failure! Certainly the repetition of the very same type of threat in the sinking of the boats must be seen as comic. But repetition in a tragedy may lead to catastrophe, so the emotional response of the reader must be contained until the final denouement.

The episode of Luke 5:8–11 concludes the pericope; with this unit, the reader is forced to consider the character of the whole pericope and the earlier reading in light of the decision about the meaning of the whole. Readers bring other texts with them to Luke 5:1–11, particularly those recounting Peter's call to become a disciple. Mark's account (Mark 1:16–20) followed by Matthew (4:18–22) has Jesus walking along the Sea of Galilee and calling Simon and Andrew and James and John to follow him. Jesus said to Simon and to Andrew, "Follow me and I will make you become fishers of men." Upon the call, the four left the fishing and followed Jesus. The account of Jesus' teaching from a boat because of the pressure of a crowd along the shore (Mark 4:1) and the story of the miraculous catch of fish in John 21 may influence the reading. From the perspective followed in this essay, the importance of these other texts is not historical; Luke 5:1–10 is not seen in light of some presumed literary development.

Some help may be given by these other texts in terms of the genre or the way that the text is to be read. Is it to be read as a tale? The catch of fish is clearly a wonder. Is it a myth (a story about the divine)? Mythic qualities are obviously present. Might "Depart from me for I am a sinful man O Lord" be the key? What does it mean? What is its function? How may a reader make sense? "Depart from me" alone would indicate that Simon sees Jesus as the cause of his problem. A purely spatial interpretation would emphasize that Simon wants Jesus out of the boat. With Jesus out of the boat, the problem might be solved. But the departure called for seems to be more radical, as is seen in the next statement where the focus is upon Simon's own situation vis-à-vis the divine and/or Jesus: "I am a sinful man." Is "sinful" a pleonasm? Is Simon acknowledging his humanity in face of the revelation of the sacred? Or is Simon acknowledging not merely that he is human but that he is a sinner in some specific way? In what way? In his skepticism at the power of Jesus to effect the catch of fish? At his cynical spread of the net in a fashion to be able to complete only the most limited catch? The title given to Jesus by Simon ("Lord") transforms the immediate episode to a completely different level; "Depart from me" and "I am a sinful man" constitute a confession similar to Isaiah's declaration of uncleanness in the presence of the Lord of hosts (Isa. 6:5). Jesus' response and commission of Simon, "Do not be afraid; henceforth you will be catching people," is read as paralleling the response to Isaiah's confession.

The reader is now able to begin to reconceptualize the earlier episodes. The statement of Jesus about catching people has the effect of instructing the reader to repeat all previous interpretative operations, at least from v. 4, with "people" replacing "fish." When rereading is done, the initial sequence becomes a pattern for the series of sequences with an interesting change of subjects, from God to Jesus to Peter (Peter and the others on the first boat beckon to the others to come and help). From the word of Jesus, "Do not be afraid, henceforth you will be catching people," there is not only a backward reference giving additional significance but also a forward thrust; readers of the Gospel are recipients of the word by means of the success of Simon and those to whom the word was preached. Do faithful believers not become involved in the forward movement of the Gospel? The forward thrust again forces a re-reading of the earlier narrative segments with the readers involved.

The completion of the mission of Jesus, the major theme of the entire episode, is dependent upon the successful completion of the commission given by Jesus to his followers. The subordinate episode of the catch of fish, then, as it is reinterpreted by the Christological and ecclesiastical context, serves as the model for the promise of the successful completion of both the commission given to Jesus by God and the commission given to his followers by Jesus. Luke 5:1–11 not only says something, it also accomplishes something.

The completion of the narrative finds the fishermen with their nets and boats safe on the shore. So, as a tale about successful fishing, perhaps in spite of the dangers of the success, the narrative concludes with a comic mood or tone. The reader sees this as a comic genre as opposed to the tragic genre. But this is not pure comedy. It is an ironic comedy that shows the incongruities of the world and yet that holds us to the world. The emphasis is not upon the "all too human" life, which is either oppressive or ridiculous, but neither is it the ideal comedy of "whatever you will."

A reader who is religiously mature and who has a degree of symbolic competence will center upon the episode that forms the crux of the movement from the potentially catastrophic situation of those on the lake to the safe arrival on land. From this perspective, the comic ending is not only a matter of the way the plot turns out, it is also a matter of the perspective of the reader. The reader feels raised to a position above the action. The action is seen from the perspective of a better ordered and more highly elevated world. The movement of the perspective of the reader to a point above the action, the movement away from human experience, is accomplished to the extent that the reader agrees with Simon's assessment of the character of Jesus. The text and the reader are involved in this move. The story takes on mythic qualities (in the sense of a story about the divine). The narrative is not a simple story about a divine being, however. This epiphany (manifestation of the divine in the world of human experience), if it is interpreted by the reader as such, is the occasion of Jesus' mandate to Simon and the others present, which will enable Jesus to carry out the original mandate of God. The words of Jesus that establish the mandate, "henceforth, you will be catching people," will be read as functioning the same way as Mark 1:17, "Follow me and I will make you fish for people." But in fact the statement is literally more of an institution of Simon and those others present than it is an invitation to follow Jesus. With the necessary view of God, providence, and Christology, the saying of Jesus may be read as both a mandate and as an authoritative pronouncement of final success of the mission of the disciples, the mission of Jesus, and, hence, reestablishment of the original divinely ordained society.

Limitations of the Method

Specific criticisms may be leveled at the use of reader-response criticism in biblical studies. An examination of these criticisms will show genuine limitations of the approach and ways that attitudes toward literature and toward the Bible may be modified for the development of a satisfying reader-response criticism.

1. Reader-response approaches, even taken as a whole, are not comprehensive. They do not do everything that can be done and ought to be done in biblical studies. They do not substitute for conventional approaches. In secular literary criticism as such many reader-response critics remain associated with other "schools" (formalism, structuralism, phenomenology, deconstruction,

Marxism, feminism, and speech-act theory, for example). The same is true in biblical study. Just as in literary study, however, the reader-response shift from text as product to text as process will create changes in conventional studies.

2. Reader-response approaches to the Bible may be judged from the perspectives of both religious and historical study to be inappropriate because of the literary orientation of such approaches. The Bible is not literature in the conventional sense. A reduction of the Bible to secular literature would seem to be illegitimate. Reader-response criticism, however, does not demand the conclusion that biblical writings were composed within "literary" circles or designed to be read simply for enjoyment as "literary" works of art. The literary nature of the Bible is not due to writers' concern with belles lettres but to their utilization of the same linguistic and literary realities and principles as secular literature. It is also due to the fact that biblical writers are using language to appeal to readers who will find and create meanings that involve them, that match their needs and capacity at cognitive and noncognitive levels.

3. The fact that reader-response approaches to the Bible grow out of literary study of fictional literature, primarily novels, makes such an approach suspect to some. This fact, however, may enable us to reconceive the "reference" in biblical literature as involving a truth that historical writing as such is unable to convey. A "world" is portrayed and revealed in biblical literature. It is not necessarily unrelated to what can be rediscovered historically of Israel, Jesus Christ, and the New Testament church, but it is more than that which historical criticism as such can contain.

4. Historical-critical readers will see in reader-response criticism a lack of regard for the intention of the author. This perception is valid. The conventional concern for the intention of the author has (among other things) caused biblical criticism to remain moored at the historical level of questioning of authorship and intention. And the failure to arrive at "assured results" in this regard often frustrates attention to the text itself. Reader-response criticism does not ignore the author and the intention of the author, but the construction of author and author's intention is taken to be only a penultimate strategy in reader-response criticism.[25]

5. Reader-response criticism is very unsettling and overwhelming for "modern" readers who want to control the text and discover the meaning on the basis of a secure foundation. One critic has compared historical-critical work with reader-response approaches. Historical-critical work "often left an impression of banality—monophonic interpretation of polyphonic texts." But reader-response criticism "often gave the contrary impression of an excess of critical resources . . . and of readings that outdid in complexity and creativity the texts being read."[26] This characterization is valid. But we ought to expect such complexity and creativity, given the nature and potentiality of biblical texts and the developing capacity of readers.

Notes

1. Critical theories that do not approach the theme from the perspective of the activity of contemporary readers or offer strategies of reading will not be treated in this essay. Wayne C. Booth and others speak of "implied" authors and readers as rhetorical devices of the actual author. These are to be built up by the reader on the basis of such things as the explicit commentary of the narrator, the kind of tale being told by the author, the meanings that can be extracted, and the moral and emotional content of the actions of the characters. The goal of a real reader is to become the implied reader and to find the implied author. The reader-reception criticism associated with Hans Robert Jauss is concerned with the history of readers' reception. This approach attempts to situate a literary work within the cultural context of its production and then explore the shifting relations between this context and the changing contexts of historical readers. Psychological approaches to the reader emphasize the stages of development of individual readers or (as in the case of Norman N. Holland) the role played by the "psychological set" of readers.

2. Cleanth Brooks and Robert Penn Warren, *Understanding Fiction* (New York: F. S. Crofts & Company, 1943), p. 28.

3. Stanley Fish, *Is There a Text in This Class? The Authority of Interpretative Communities* (Cambridge: Harvard University Press, 1980), p. 67.

4. The phenomenological tradition in which the work of Wolfgang Iser is situated arose as an attempt to reestablish the reality of the world by answering the philosophical theory that things-in-themselves are unknowable, that things are always perceived in terms of the one perceiving. The term "phenomenology" indicates that what is attempted in theory and practice is the investigation and description of the essential structures of the phenomena that appear in immediate experience. Two assumptions are vital: that the phenomena are constituted by consciousness through intentionality and that, although the phenomena assume accidental or nonessential forms, investigation may reveal forms that are to be regarded as essential in the sense that they cannot be removed without destroying the basic intentionality of the data. In two volumes (*The Cognition of the Literary Work of Art*, trans. Ruth Ann Crowley and Kenneth R. Olson [Evanston, Ill.: Northwestern University, 1973] and *The Literary Work of Art: An Investigation on the Borderlines of Ontology, Logic, and Theory of Literature*, trans. George G. Grabowicz [Evanston, Ill.: Northwestern University, 1973]) the phenomenologist philosopher Roman Ingarden studied the formal structures common to all works of literature and the nature of cognition that is a valid and true reconstruction of the literary work. Ingarden distinguishes between the work of art itself and a concretization of the work that is constituted during reading. The complexity of a literary work is such that the reader has too much to do at the same time and cannot give himself or herself equally to all of the components of the total apprehension. Only a few of the multiplicity of simultaneously experienced and interwoven acts become central.

5. Wolfgang Iser, *The Act of Reading: A Theory of Aesthetic Response* (London: Routledge & Kegan Paul, 1978), p. 37.

6. In his essay "Difference," (*Margins of Philosophy*, trans. Alan Bass [Chicago: University of Chicago Press, 1982], p. 8), Jacques Derrida enunciated the differential nature of language and the continual deferring of meaning. The work of Derrida has been used to support the loss of any stable meaning, linguistically and philosophically.

7. East European formalist movements ceased functioning as early as the late 1920s owing to pressure from doctrinaire Soviet Marxists, and exemplary texts of the formalists were not available in translation until the 1960s and 1970s. As movements in the structural and semiotic study of narrative, poststructuralism, and deconstruction have become influential in America, however, arguments and developments in East European formalism (structuralism) have been recapitulated.

8. Viktor Sklovskii, *O teorii prozy* [*Theory of Prose*] (Moscow and Leningrad, 1925). See Thomas G. Winner, "The Aesthetics and Poetics of the Prague Linguistic Circle," *Poetics* 8 (1973):80.

9. Iser cites Jan Mukarovsky's view of the energetic and dynamic character of the structure of the literary work: "The energy of the structure is derived from the fact that each of the elements in the overall unity has a specific function which incorporates it into the structural whole and binds it to that whole; the dynamism of the structural whole arises out of the fact that these individual functions and their interacting relationships are subject, by virtue of their energetic character, to continual transformations. The structure as a whole thus finds itself in a ceaseless state of movement, in contrast to a summative whole, which is destroyed by any change" (Jan Mukarovsky, *Kapital aus der Poetik* [Frankfort, 1967], p. 11). Cited in "The Repertoire" in *Critical Theory Since 1965*, ed. Hazard Adams and Leroy Searle (Tallahassee, Fla.: Florida State University, 1986), p. 380.

10. See Edgar V. McKnight, *Meaning in Texts: The Historical Shaping of a Narrative Hermeneutics* (Philadelphia: Fortress, 1978), pp. 24–25, 215–25, for a discussion of the role of such a dynamic structure in the hermeneutical tradition of Wilhelm Dilthey.

11. Roland Barthes, *S/Z*, trans. Richard Miller (London: Jonathan Cape, 1975).

12. Umberto Eco, *The Role of the Reader: Explorations in the Semiotics of Texts* (Bloomington, Ind.: Indiana University Press, 1979).

13. Jacques Derrida, *Of Grammatology*, trans. Gayatri C. Spivak (Baltimore: Johns Hopkins University Press, 1976), p. 158.

14. Jonathan Culler, "Literary Competence," *Reader-Response Criticism: From Formalism to Post-Structuralism*, ed. Jane P. Tompkins (Baltimore: Johns Hopkins University Press), pp. 116–17.

15. Wolfgang Iser, "The Reading Process: A Phenomenological Approach," in Tompkins, *Reader-Response Criticism*, p. 56.

16. George Poulet, "Criticism and the Experience of Interiority," in Tompkins, *Reader-Response Criticism*, pp. 46–47.

17. Amos Wilder, *The Language of the Gospel: Early Christian Rhetoric* (New York: Harper, 1964), p. 133.

18. Robert Tannehill, *The Sword of His Mouth: Forceful and Imaginative Language in Synoptic Sayings* (Missoula, Mont.: Scholars, 1975).

19. Robert Tannehill, "The Disciples in Mark: The Function of a Narrative Role," *Journal of Religion* 57 (1977):386–405.

20. Robert Detweiler, ed., "Reader Response Approaches to Biblical and Secular Texts," *Semeia* 31 (1985); Edgar V. McKnight, ed., "Reader Perspectives on the New Testament," *Semeia* 48 (1989).

21. Robert Morgan with John Barton, *Biblical Interpretation* (Oxford: Oxford University Press, 1988).

22. The literary critics Richard G. Moulton and Northrop Frye have given attention to the literary unity of the Bible. Both note the narrative unity. There is a beginning and an end, with movement involving not only narrative but also a variety of other literary forms. Both Moulton and Frye emphasize the Apocalypse and the final conception of "the kingdom of the world" becoming "the kingdom of our Lord and of his Christ" (Rev. 11:15). The kerygmatic nature of the Bible as a whole is emphasized by both writers, with Frye actually using the term. See Moulton, *Modern Reader's Bible* (Macmillan, 1926), p. viii; see also *The Literary Study of the Bible: An Account of the Leading Forms of Literature Represented in the Sacred Writings* (Boston: D. C. Heath, 1899) and Frye, *The Great Code: The Bible and Literature* (New York: Harcourt Brace Jovanovich, 1982), pp. 29–30, 224–25.

23. Because of this, the "reader" at times seems to be the reader intended by the author or even all properly prepared readers. By "reader" in this section, however, I am referring to myself. To be sure, I hope that readers of this book will be able to make sense of my reading, but I am not attempting to establish this as the only reading. I construe meanings in light of my own experiences, knowledge, and information, and other readers must do the same.

24. The reader's earlier view of the practice of fishing creates a problem. Is the reader's view of the practice of fishing in error? Could the fishermen in one boat be expected to manipulate the seine, especially with a large catch? What does Jesus have in mind? Why did Simon do what Jesus commanded when one boat with its fishermen constituted only one half of the total resources needed for successfully landing a large catch? Was Jesus intending a situation in which more help would be needed? Was Simon simply pacifying Jesus, entertaining little or no expectation of a catch of fish? A purely private reading may benefit from such speculation, but this reader is not prepared to integrate such speculation into a comprehensive reading.

25. Intentionality from a literary perspective differs from intentionality from a historical perspective. E. D. Hirsch, Jr., speaks of intentionality in terms of the "consciously willed type," and it is this that defines verbal meaning (*Validity in Interpretation* [New Haven, Conn.: Yale University Press, 1967], pp. 53–54). In *The Aims of Interpretation,* Hirsch indicates a relationship between the reader and the "type": "That which we are understanding is itself an hypothesis constructed by ourselves, a schema, or

genre, or type which provokes expectations that are confirmed by our linguistic experience, or when they are not confirmed cause us to adjust our hypothesis or schema" (*The Aims of Interpretation* [Chicago: University of Chicago Press, 1976], pp. 33–34).

26. Ben F. Meyer, "The Challenges of Text and Reader to the Historical-Critical Method," *The Bible and Its Readers*, ed. Wim Beuken, Sean Freyne, and Anton Weiler (Philadelphia: Trinity, 1991), p. 10.

For Further Reading

Reader-Response Criticism in General

Eco, Umberto. *The Role of the Reader: Explorations in the Semiotics of Texts.* Bloomington, Ind.: Indiana University Press, 1979. The first, introductory chapter discusses the basic structure of the process of text interpretation in general.

Fish, Stanley E. *Is There a Text in This Class? The Authority of Interpretative Communities* (Cambridge: Harvard University Press, 1980). Collects Fish's major essays of 1970–1980 with a general introduction, a series of headnotes, and four previously unpublished essays.

Iser, Wolfgang. *The Act of Reading: A Theory of Aesthetic Response.* Baltimore: Johns Hopkins University Press, 1978. Exemplary of Iser's practice of close reading in a phenomenological mode.

Suleiman, Susan, and Crosman, Inge, eds. *The Reader in the Text: Essays on Audience and Interpretation* (Princeton, N.J.: Princeton University Press, 1980). Contains sixteen original articles. In her introduction, Suleiman surveys six approaches to "audience-oriented criticism": rhetorical, structuralist-semiotic, phenomenological, psychoanalytic, sociological-historical, and hermeneutical. She (unlike Tompkins) treats European critics who were important in the development of reader-oriented theory and practice.

Tompkins, Jane P., ed. *Reader-Response Criticism: From Formalism to Post-Structuralism.* Baltimore: Johns Hopkins University Press, 1980. Contains eleven key texts signifying the culmination of the move from text-centered to reader-oriented criticism in literary study in American universities. Also contains an introduction and conclusion by Tompkins herself.

Reader-Response Criticism in Biblical Studies

Brown, Schuyler. "Reader Response: Demythologizing the Text. " *New Testament Studies* 34 (1988):232–37.

Detweiler, Robert, ed. "Reader Response Approaches to Biblical and Secular Texts." *Semeia* 31 (1985). Offers a theoretical orientation and examples of reader-response criticism, illustrating that reader-response criticism is an aggregate of approaches that interact with one another.

Fowler, Robert M. *Let the Reader Understand: Reader-Response Criticism and the Gospel of Mark*. Minneapolis: Fortress, 1991. A synthesis of over a decade of work directed toward the actual experience of reading.

McKnight, Edgar V. *Postmodern Use of the Bible: The Emergence of Reader-Oriented Criticism*. Nashville: Abingdon Press, 1988.

McKnight, Edgar V., ed. "Reader Perspectives on the New Testament." *Semeia* 48 (1989). Contains essays growing out of the work of a seminar of the Society of New Testament Studies inaugurated in 1984 to deal with the theme of "The Role of the Reader in the Interpretation of the New Testament."

Moore, Stephen D. *Literary Criticism and the Gospels: The Theoretical Challenge*. New Haven, Conn.: Yale University Press, 1989. Surveys the field of biblical literary scholarship with particular attention to narrative criticism and reading of the Gospels.

Van Iersel, B. *Reading Mark*. Edinburgh: T. & T. Clark, 1989. A commentary on Mark that gives particular attention to the insights of structural linguistics, especially to the nature of narrative structures and the way they function in communication.

12

POSTSTRUCTURALIST CRITICISM

William A. Beardslee

I

POSTSTRUCTURALIST criticism includes several ways of reading a text. We concentrate here on deconstructive criticism or deconstruction, since other poststructuralist methods appear elsewhere in this book. Deconstructive criticism is a way of reading that involves both discovering the incompleteness of the text and finding a fresh, if transient, insight made possible by the "free play" or indeterminacy of the text. These formal moves are not arbitrarily chosen as simply one possible form of criticism; they are dictated by the sense that "not only is 'Truth' fatally embroiled with power; it is inseparable from and dependent on historical change."[1] Deconstruction is distinguished from other sorts of poststructuralist criticism by its focus on the dismantling of existing patterns. Other poststructuralist approaches such as much feminist and Third World criticism, in contrast to deconstruction, offer a positive program to counter the structures they criticize.

The first move of deconstructive criticism, the strategy of uncovering the inconsistencies or gaps in the vision or argument of the text, has quite understandably been the focus of most of the attention in the attempt to evaluate its contribution. Deconstructive criticism insists that if we are to read any text fruitfully, we need to be aware of several aspects of language: its incompleteness, that is, the way in which the hearer or reader has to fill in the picture that is suggested by speech or writing; its enclosure within itself, that is, the way in which the immediate connection of words is not with "reality," but with other words in a pattern that gives them meaning; and the unfixed, flowing quality of language, that is, the way in which meanings are continually being enlarged or shifted as a reader moves through a text. Hence the emphasis on "deconstruction," which is the most characteristic form of poststructuralist criticism, with its disassembling the structure of language, even language that seems to convey a clear and unequivocal meaning.

But the deeper importance of this kind of reading is in its second move, which affirms that significant reading is not "reproduction," not the reactualizing of a meaning that was once expressed by the author of the text or that is resident in the pattern of the text. Rather, it is reading that challenges the reader, throws open the reader's world to creative discovery, to new associations that may be suggested as much by irrational or chance associations as by the logical relations so carefully studied, for instance, by the structuralists. A central example of this kind of reading is discovery through the pun, or paronomasia, which juxtaposes two elements of language that have no logical relation, and not necessarily any emotive relation either, but are brought close simply by similarity of sound. Thus Jacques Derrida plays with the similarity between "Hegel" and "eagle" (even closer in French, *aigle*),[2] and we might play with the pun between "here" and "hear" to shock the reader into awareness of the ambiguity of "presence," that is, present meaning in spoken language. But the emphasis on "play," so well illustrated by the pun, should not distract attention from the function of this kind of poststructuralist interpretation: to deliver the interpreter from the repression of limits and traditions, so that fresh interpretation may take place.

Poststructuralist criticism, and its specific and most rigorous form, deconstruction, are at home in the culture of Western Europe. Kant and Hegel provide the remoter background—Kant with his argument that we cannot know the "thing in itself," since the forms of our knowing are so deeply shaped by the processes of thought themselves, and Hegel, with his conception of spirit as unfolding in the history of the human mind. But there is a long path from Kant and Hegel to deconstruction. Deconstruction represents one of the various currents of thought that have eroded what Kant and Hegel, after their critical work, believed they could still affirm as the bases on which culture and society were founded. Gone now are Kant's conviction that a sense of obligation is a universal component of human existence and Hegel's view that the history of the unfolding of Spirit is marked by a teleology, a purposive direction. Both of these fundamental convictions, which guided so much nineteenth-century European thought, have been abandoned by much late twentieth-century European culture, and this abandonment marks deconstructive criticism's approach to language and texts. This sort of critique of the bases for stability in culture was first sharply formulated by Friedrich Nietzsche. Marx and Freud in their different ways were also important forerunners of "deconstruction," for they showed that the deceptively consistent surface-level logic of discourse actually functioned to express power relations at the economic (Marx) or psychological (Freud) level.

Martin Heidegger, with his critique of Western metaphysics, is another important forerunner of deconstruction. But Heidegger, for all his criticism of metaphysics, was reaching for an ontology, a statement about "Being." Deconstruction recognizes that we are perpetually entwined in the quest for an order that stands behind our language and experience but holds that no "closure," no final, and indeed, no real result is possible in this quest. Rather, we work with "traces," marks left by earlier quests, none of which can lead us out of our imprisonment in language and the worlds that language creates, to any higher or transcendent vision.

Existentialism, well-known in biblical studies especially through the work of Rudolf Bultmann, provides an important background for poststructuralism and deconstruction, since existentialism abandoned the belief that there is an ordering in the world. But existentialism retained a vision of a centered self, a self that was still very Kantian in its sense of obligation. In the face of the destructive social forces of our century, the existentialists were able to affirm the "centered" self, which they drew from a long Western tradition, by seeing the self as isolated, as creating its own meaning and world. In poststructuralism in general and specifically in deconstruction, the centered self is replaced by a self that is a node in a network of relations. At times, in this perspective, the relatedness of the self tends to erode the sense of responsibility.

Structuralism is also deeply important for understanding deconstruction. Structuralism's turn away from the referential or descriptive view of language to a picture of language as a system of relations, so that each part is defined by its role in the linguistic network, is also taken up by deconstructive poststructuralism. Structuralism and poststructuralism are both, in different ways, suspicious of the seemingly clear surface meaning of a text. The difference is that most structuralism looks for a determinate deeper structure in the linguistic network, while deconstructive poststructuralism emphasizes the openness, the play, of the network of relations, the imperfections in the text that disallow any thoroughly consistent patterns, with the aim of freeing the reader or hearer to make her or his own creative discovery of transient meaning.

Michel Foucault and Jacques Derrida are the two figures particularly associated with deconstructive poststructuralist criticism. Foucault's emphasis on the ways in which texts express power relations is taken up in much poststructuralist criticism.[3] But the figure usually in mind when one speaks of deconstruction is Jacques Derrida. To introduce this difficult thinker, we will cite from an excellent introduction to his thought:

> If in this process of deciphering a text in the traditional way we come across a word that seems to harbor an unresolvable contradiction, and by virtue of being one word is made sometimes to work in one way and sometimes in another and thus is made to point away from the absence of a unified meaning, we shall catch at [atten-

tively seek out the nuances and connections of] that word. If a
metaphor seems to suppress its implications, we shall catch at that
metaphor. We shall follow its adventures through the text and see
the text coming undone as a structure of concealment, revealing
its self-transgression, its undecidability. It must be emphasized
that I am not speaking simply of locating a moment of ambiguity or
irony ultimately incorporated into the text's system of unified
meaning but rather a moment that genuinely threatens to collapse
the system.[4]

Often deconstructive writing uses a formidable special vocabulary in the
attempt to stimulate us to think differently. Some key terms are *undecidability,*
the openness of meaning that is often concealed by the seeming closure of the
text; *differance,* a revised spelling of "difference" (originally, of course, in
French), which indicates, in a form that appears only in writing, both differing
and deferring (meaning is found in difference, but it is never really *found,* it is
deferred; the quest is endless); and *deconstruction* (see below). A key term is
logocentrism, which is criticized and dismissed as the assumption that language
communicates the presence of an order or logos that is beyond language.

The often hidden assumption of a metaphysical consistency at least partly
expressed by language is abetted by the assumption that spoken language,
with its seeming immediacy of "presence," the presence of the speaker's
meaning through the presence of the speaker, is the primary form of language. On the contrary, according to deconstruction, *writing* is primary,
since writing makes clear the impossibility of full presence in communication, and also makes much more evident that all language is a reworking of
previous language, not a fresh and impartial presentation of a translinguistic
referent. Thus *intertextuality* is a fundamental feature of writing; any given
"text" or structured communication either simply repeats or else modifies
(perhaps "deforms") earlier conventionally established patterns in forming
its own structure. Deconstruction considers any form of communication as a
text, a configuration interwoven ("textured") with previous communications, in contrast to a *book,* which is thought of as a coherent whole, an
organized statement in which the parts support one another because they
are all supported by a coherent system that comes to a conclusion, a closure.
And contrary to what has often been assumed, deconstruction asserts that
there is no connected pattern in the historical shifts of meaning that intertextuality produces.

Deconstruction, the commonest term in this vocabulary, means dismantling
the seeming coherence of the text and reading it in a way that resists "closure." In contrast to most earlier forms of interpretation, including structuralism, poststructuralist reading looks for the "gaps," the incoherences, the

points where aspects of the text pass by one another, in order to show that the text does not communicate a definitive or closed meaning.

Deconstructive criticism does not speak much about ethics; traditional ethics is seen as narrow and repressive. But this kind of criticism is no detached intellectual exercise. It has strong ethical implications. The reaction against the traditional ethics of obligation is grounded in the assumption that rule-making is a form of violence or coercion. The emphasis on undecidability, on the plural meaning of texts, is intended to challenge reigning orthodoxies and dominant social groups. Deconstruction is an attack upon the social and institutional powers that justify their power and authority by appeal precisely to a structured world in which they hold a recognized and often dominating place. From this point of view the various forms of Marxist critique of culture form an important background to and preliminary form of deconstruction, by virtue of their pointing to the ideological functions of theoretical systems and of religion. The difference between the various Marxist critiques and deconstruction is that classical Marxism, at least, offered a "true" vision to supplant the false and power-driven ideological visions it criticized. (The "true" vision was qualified in some forms of later Marxist thought.) Deconstruction, on the other hand, offers no such resolution. Each dismantling of a cultural or religious expression can be a valid critique of social power, but it cannot provide a clear-cut alternative. Its function is rather to lead readers to live without absolutes, in a world of process that is not directed to a goal.

Thus poststructuralism identifies with the "marginal." At times there may be a romantic glorification of the martyr-position of the marginally situated critic. And the resistance to choice, the emphasis on keeping one's options open, is difficult to maintain indefinitely. Yet this resistance has to be recognized as itself an ethical claim, a protest against the power of established interpretations.[5]

Deconstruction is highly critical of traditional religion and theology, which are seen as falsely believing in the "presence" of a transcendent reality. Though the approach can well be combined with a variety of religious and theological positions (and thereby relativized), its affinities are with "negative theology."[6]

II

A major way in which New Testament scholarship was prepared for deconstructive criticism was the fresh approach to the parables of Jesus that is especially associated with the names of Robert W. Funk and John Dominic Crossan. Traditionally, parables have been read as reinforcing some aspect of the overall Christian story, but Funk and Crossan reread key parables to show that they are better understood as challenging or subverting the world of the hearer (including the way in which that world is shaped by the tradition of faith). Funk emphasized the element of *risk* in listening to a parable; one has to let go of the structured world that one brings to hearing it.[7] Crossan contrasted organizing stories with disorganizing stories; the parable is the classic type of the latter. It shatters the hearer's world. As Crossan put it, parabolic religion (he could have said, "parabolic language") "continually and deliberately subverts the final words about 'reality' and thereby introduces the possibility of transcendence."[8] Others, including the present writer, have seen a similar function in some of the proverbial sayings in the Gospels.[9]

These interpreters looked within the text for moves toward dismantling the reader's world, and thus they anticipated deconstructive criticism. They were not agreed about the key point of whether the parables or proverbs of the Gospels also implied the possibility of rebuilding a vision of the whole after it had been jolted by the saying's immediate impact. Crossan was closest to deconstructive interpretation with his recognition that the force of parabolic language ran counter to the force of what he called "mythic" language that structured the world of the hearer—"myth" (including Gospel narrative) establishes world, while "parable" subverts world.[10]

From this example, it is clear that one may approach a text in a deconstructive way with an eye to finding how aspects of the text that are "intended" by the text work against one another—in the illustration of the parable, how the organizing narrative of a Gospel is countered by the shattering of world by a parable. Equally characteristic of such criticism is the effort to work with oppositions in the text that are not "intended" by the text or the author, as in Derrida's breaking traditional connections and making unexpected new ones through the use of the pun, as noted above.

A direct encounter between biblical studies and deconstruction is a mark of contemporary New Testament studies. We need cite only one work: Stephen D. Moore's *Literary Criticism and the Gospels: The Theoretical Challenge.*[11] Moore carefully analyzes narrative criticism, which is perhaps the most widely used form of literary criticism in biblical studies, looking especially at those forms of narrative criticism that deal with the response of the reader. One of his techniques is to show how varied and even contradictory are the results that different scholars achieve by using the same or very similar methods. His conclusion is that the texts do not sufficiently determine the interpretation for traditional narrative criticism to be successful. Moore offers a challenge to those forms of literary criticism that look for coherent meanings in a text by showing that in order to achieve such an interpretation one has to find a privileged position "above" the text or above the world created by the text. Poststructuralism or deconstructive criticism is the rejection of the attempt to find such a position. Since the reader or critic has no such superior position, the results of criticism are necessarily part of the flux.[12] Moore gives an example of a deconstructive reading of a symbol in the Gospel of John, but he also discusses at length the narrative criticism of Luke.

Luke-Acts, or, for that matter, despite their interrelationships, either Luke or Acts taken separately, is very much a rounded whole, a "book," in the language of deconstruction. So we find a text that cries out for deconstruction. We should remember that a kind of dismantling of the internal order of biblical books has been practiced for a long time, namely, historical source criticism. In method and perspective coming from an immensely different world from that of deconstruction, this more traditional criticism nonetheless has a similar effect on a text: breaking up its seeming unity. The very important difference is that traditional source criticism, though often finding a complete work to be a patchwork of points of view, nonetheless assumed that the scholar could work from a coherent point of view, "above" the text, so to speak.[13]

Our deconstructive reading will focus on the first of Luke's beatitudes: "Blessed [perhaps better, 'Happy'] are you who are poor, for yours is the kingdom of God" (Luke 6:20).

The first beatitude is a powerful focal statement of what in Luke-Acts is at the heart of the "new" that Jesus brings—a "new" that remains active in the new community of the church. Jesus' inclusion of outsiders, outcasts, or marginal people among those whom he drew into community with himself is a central thread of Luke-Acts. Correspondingly, Jesus challenges the rich, not only because of the danger of riches for the wealthy but also because of the need of the poor. The rich, it should be said, are not simply condemned but are sharply challenged (Luke 6:24; 12:13–21; 16:13; 18:18–25).[14]

This is a theme that runs throughout Luke-Acts. From the Magnificat ("[God] has brought down the powerful from their thrones, and lifted up the lowly; [God] has filled the hungry with good things, and sent the rich away empty," Luke 1:52–53), into the central part of the Gospel, with the early scene of Jesus in the synagogue at Nazareth speaking of bringing "good news to the poor" (Luke 4:18), and with its many encounters of Jesus with the poor and marginal, and his sayings about them on into Acts, according to which in the Jerusalem community "no one claimed private ownership of any possessions, but everything they owned was held in common" (Acts 4:32), to Paul's last visit to Jerusalem, which included the purpose of "bringing alms to my nation" (Acts 24:17), the theme of openness to the "otherness" of the poor is a major theme of the two-volume work.

Robert Tannehill summarizes the position well:

> We see, then, that Jesus preaches good news to the poor not only by announcing that they will share in God's reign and by healing the poor beggars but also by creating disciples who are pledged to share with the poor and by seeking to transform grasping rich peo-

ple into persons who will give their wealth to the poor. Later the
narrator will suggest that Jesus' call has the power to create a community that cares for the poor so that there are no longer needy
persons among them (Acts 4:34). Jesus' mission to the poor,
claimed by him in the Nazareth synagogue, becomes a major
theme in the narrative of Jesus' words and deeds in Luke.[15]

Later, in commenting on Acts 4:34, Tannehill adds:

> The community of goods is mentioned only in connection with the
> early Jerusalem church. It is part of the narrator's picture of the
> ideal church at the beginning. Already at the time of writing there
> was probably a clear difference between this ideal picture and the
> actual practice of Christians. Nevertheless, this ideal is empha-
> sized. We need not suppose that the narrator expected later
> churches to be transformed into the ideal community described.
> Such an expectation is not required for the ideal to be relevant.
> The ideal can function as a critique of a complacent church with
> narrow vision, content with its own obedience, and this construc-
> tive criticism may find a response among individuals, if not in a
> church as a whole. If Jesus' call and this ideal picture of the church
> lead some Christians with assets to recognize that they can and
> should give those assets to the poor, something important has hap-
> pened. Such responses by individuals may not in themselves pro-
> duce the ideal community of the narrator's vision, but they do
> recognize the needs of the poor as a moral claim, as did the early
> church, according to Acts.[16]

The immediate thrust of the text of Luke-Acts is to integrate the concern
for the poor into the practice of the community. The global concern for "the
poor," and the bold proclamation that they are "happy" because the kingdom
of God is theirs, is structured into the practice of the church, and even there it
becomes an ideal that, we may agree with Tannehill, was at best only very
imperfectly practiced. The pressure of the saying, with its reversal of our ordinary standards, can be bent to fit the narrative pattern if one keeps in mind
that for this text (1) there was a stronger presence of salvation during the time
of Jesus than later and (2) a final eschatological resolution would bring about
that aspect of God's will which is not realized in the present.

We do not have to ask any historical questions to become aware of the
tension between the saying and its context. In our actual study of the Gospels,
we may indeed assume that the strong power of the beatitude represents the
early stage, the time of Jesus, while the more calmly organized text of Luke
reflects a later, more institutional time. But deconstructionist criticism brack-

ets such questions and looks at the tensions in the text as it stands. It asks, Can the parabolic, reversing power of "Happy are you who are poor" be so smoothly integrated into the story of the church that Luke created? Can the hearer's identification with the poor, which the beatitude calls for, be so readily expressed in the limited moves for the poor that Acts describes? In our discussion above, we have emphasized the integration of the saying into the narrative pattern. But it resists integration! Tannehill recognizes that this is a saying of reversal,[17] but he correctly sees that the text intends to domesticate this reversal into the narrative. The narrative pattern does just what the saying resists. It organizes a structure into which life fits, in the sense that one can expect a meaningful result from one's acts. In this case, the structure is one in which limited acts on behalf of a specific small segment of the poor are enough and are all that can be expected, and in which the poor tend to become the objects of generosity rather than being themselves subjects. This is true even though the church has many times brought people of differing social strata together effectively, so that marginal people could indeed become subjects. Of course, we suppose that an author ("Luke," whoever he was) drew the beatitude from tradition and worked to fit it into the overall story of the book. But deconstructive criticism as such is not concerned with the question of the author's intention, or with the historical question whether the beatitude represents Jesus better than the Lucan narrative does. We will have to add that the distinction between the text, the proper focus of deconstructive criticism, and the author and the author's world is harder to maintain than many deconstructive critics admit. When Derrida writes about Rousseau's work, a vivid Rousseau appears.

To return to the beatitude about the poor, the radical thrust of the saying has often been noticed. For instance, James Dawsey comments about the Lucan Sermon on the Plain as a whole, that it has "much more the flavor of a statement about how God is reversing the order of society."[18] If we bracket out the eschatological framework of the saying, the statement is deeply disconcerting, since it seems to be out of touch with reality as we know it. And how can we not bracket out or at least transform the eschatology that the saying presupposes, since the poverty of the poor, after so many centuries, is still so unbearable? Deconstructive criticism starts with the present reader, not with an attempt to reconstruct a historical picture of an "original meaning."

What happens when we listen seriously to the statement "Happy are you who are poor" is exactly the opposite of finding a place for the poor in a structured society. The structure is broken; the line between the hearer and the poor is erased; we find ourselves open to, at times perhaps even identified with, the subjects of the saying. A vivid, shattering awareness of the possibility that there, among the poor, is the place of happiness or blessedness does not produce a plan of action (not even giving away all that one possesses, to say nothing of a plan for restructuring the means of production or the rules of property ownership). It does break the established lines of relatedness by opening up a new and hitherto unrecognized relatedness to the poor. It challenges the structure of power that establishes a place for the poor. Such a listening is a deconstruction of the way in which the text integrates the saying into its overall narrative pattern, a pattern admirably interpreted by Tannehill in the quotations that we have cited above and in his chapter, "Jesus' Ministry to the Oppressed and Excluded."[19]

The broken structure and our exposure to identification with the poor are not timeless insights. They are the fragile opening to a glimpse, or to use a favorite deconstructive word, a "trace," of that which we cannot grasp. The encounter leaves us shaken, but we will have to turn elsewhere if we are to do precisely what deconstruction is so loath to do, namely, find a new pattern in which to act in order to try to do something purposeful as a response to the glimpse.

III

Since Jacques Derrida, the leading thinker of deconstruction, has insisted that he does not present a method, and that he does not want people simply to copy what he is doing, it would be mechanical to set out rules for developing a deconstructive way of reading. What is required is a way of listening. If the perspective sketched at the beginning of this chapter makes sense, one can listen to texts from that perspective. We do not have to accept the total historical relativity of truth, or hold that its involvement with power deprives truth of any assertiveness, to find that there is a large persuasive element in the convictions that are the presuppositions of deconstructive criticism. We do not have simply to jettison the coherent readings of a text, such as Tannehill so ably works out in the case of Luke-Acts. What we do have to do to read deconstructively is to set beside a traditional way of reading a radical questioning of the pattern into which the text seems to fit.

One could test one's reading with another important theme in Luke-Acts: the text's view of the Jewish people. As Luke-Acts presents the matter, is it too late for the Jewish people? Are they included in the ongoing work of God, or has their time passed?

Fortunately for the student, a very useful volume of essays on this question is available: *Luke-Acts and the Jewish People*, edited by Joseph B. Tyson.[20] A student could review Luke-Acts with an eye to how it deals with the relation between Jesus and the emerging church on the one hand, and the Jewish people on the other. Then one would sample the essays in Tyson's book, for instance contrasting Jack T. Sanders's contention that the Jewish people are consistently rejected with Robert C. Tannehill's view that salvation is still open to them.[21] (But the whole volume is well worth attention.) Then one would confront the question, Does the text succeed in being consistent on this point? If not, can the contradiction be dealt with under a mediating heading like irony, in which two points of view are held in tension, or is a more radical deconstruction appropriate, which would show that the approach of Luke-Acts on this point is incoherent and unsatisfactory?

IV

Poststructuralism in general is a way of recognizing that our visions of reality are historically situated and that the exercise of power plays a large, though often unnoticed, role in shaping what we think of as truth. Deconstruction is a particularly rigorous form of poststructuralism, because taken by itself it does not offer any alternative structure to the pattern it deconstructs, other than a transient flash of new insight. The thrust of deconstruction is critical, disclosing the incoherences and the implications of domination in accepted patterns and thus depriving them of their power.

The discussion above has shown that deconstruction has a very important role to play in biblical studies. Many biblical books and many, if not most, modern readers and scholars tend to accept uncritically the move of organizing the world, and to a degree at least, also God, into an at least partly comprehensible pattern, an ordered whole. Most commonly, in the Bible, the world is "organized" by telling a story in which the community and the believer can find a place. All of the Gospels serve this function in different ways. For instance, Matthew's emphasis on the believer's place in the church and John's exploration of what it means to believe in a hostile world are what is here termed organizing the world. Yet the deconstructive move is also found in biblical texts, as our references to the parables and to Luke's first beatitude have shown. Deconstruction shows how broken and imperfect the organizing patterns are, as in the example chosen above of the poor. In this function it is related to a major thrust of prophetic faith. But taken by itself, deconstruction does not effectively move toward the kind of "application" that has long been recognized as an important part of interpretation. This is equally true whether one focuses on the sheer deconstructive act or whether, as in the example of the first Lucan beatitude worked out above, the emphasis shifts to the rhetoric of discovery, the shock of the unexpected.

Thus deconstruction does not have the self-sufficient adequacy as a critical method that is often claimed for it. Or rather, it can be taken as adequate only if one agrees that human existence and the world as a whole are as directionless as the wandering or "erring" that is sometimes presented as the sober postmodern alternative to the dominating purposiveness of the modern world.[22] That this is not the whole story is shown by the way in which the shock of insight often requires a subsequent move to act, a move that in turn needs a framework, if not an absolute one. A recognition of this is part of the reason that college and university departments of literature and philosophy are moving away from deconstruction toward neopragmatism. We cannot here discuss neopragmatism. Like deconstruction, it is thoroughly relativisitic, but it makes a place for purposive action.

One way of using deconstruction would be to deconstruct the "public" or "natural" patterns of religion and society and then affirm a "confessional" or revealed pattern that, it would be claimed, was self-authenticating and did not need to be subjected to deconstruction. We may expect to see this route followed, but it is ultimately unsatisfactory, since it leaves the competing confessional perspectives with no way of communicating with one another. No perspective is exempt from deconstruction. But that does not undermine the strength of religious faith or of religious communities; it requires that they see that they, too, are part of the process.

If deconstruction is taken to be an academic method, unfriendly to the life of religious communities, its prophetic potential may easily be lost. Serious interpretation of biblical texts must engage both the religious and the academic communities. The illustration of "the poor" shows how the method of deconstruction can be relevant to both. Academic reflection about how language "works" (such as we have suggested above, showing how the beatitude about the poor is in conflict with the setting in which it is found) can lead the reader beyond academic circles to an actual engagement with the poor such as religious communities often speak for. Also, from the other side, as base communities in Latin America have found, the intuitive insights of religious communities, as their members reflect about them, call for a dialogue with the work of biblical scholars; in this case, the kind of study of the first Lucan beatitude that we have explored here can lead a religious community to see that the ways in which we fit "the poor" into our institutional structures is not enough. But as noted above, the disassembling of a structure, in this case a way of fitting the poor into the picture, is a prelude to a fresh engagement with all the ways in which the reader deals with this issue. Deconstruction calls for a reengagement in a more inclusive frame. That requires a search for a new structure and work to make it actual. The reluctance of some deconstructionist thinkers to deal with this stage can be understood as a reaction against the "totalizing" nature of so many "solutions."[23]

Thus the presuppositions of deconstruction are not to be accepted uncritically.[24] We can indeed accept its "nonfoundationalism," that is, the claim that we do not have a clear and certain way of knowing by which we can build up our knowledge and our values. But that does not mean that our language is as fully out of touch with the larger reality within which we live and speak, or as fluid and bereft of any determinate meaning, as deconstructionists have claimed.

For one thing, despite their indeterminacy, which deconstruction has emphasized, texts nonetheless do set limits to interpretation. The very form and language of a lament, for instance, prevents its being taken as a joyful lyric. Here the structuralists, who strive to be more rigorous in establishing an ancient and widely held insight, are right. The structures in a text may indeed be in conflict, but this is not always a destructive conflict. The interplay of structures may keep conflict within such limits that it does not become destructive, or it may also release new creative insight.[25] For example, the central illustration on which this chapter focuses, the conflict between the "Lucan" structure that incorporates the poor into a pattern of institutional life and the disruptive structure of the first beatitude, is at the heart of the creative life of the Christian community. No final resolution of this conflict is possible, yet it has repeatedly released new energies and new activities in the life of the church.

More than that, the reach of language beyond its own network—the referential dimension of language—is not as formless as it is often pictured. Our commonsense intuition that language is "about" something, something that is at least partially given, has not been canceled by deconstruction. On the contrary, starting in the midst and without any fixed foundational method of knowing, we nevertheless can know something about reality, including values and the reality with which religious language deals. What deconstruction does is to remind us of the limitations of any particular perspective. That recognition can open the way to a reengagement with the quest to know, in a more inclusive frame.[26]

Thus this writer sees promise for deconstruction as it is used as one tool and not the sole way of reading. A good example would be David Jobling's combination of deconstruction with liberation theology; Jobling also indicates how deconstruction and feminist theology work together.[27] The present author has practiced a kind of deconstruction while reframing a patterned way of viewing the scripture made possible in part by process theology.[28] An evaluation of deconstructive reading that is more positive about making it the central focus can be found in Stephen D. Moore's *Literary Criticism and the Gospels*.[29]

Notes

1. Helen Vendler, commenting on the postmodern vision of the poet Frank Bidart in *The New Yorker*, June 10, 1991.

2. Jacques Derrida, *Glas*, 5, cited in Gayatri Chakravarti Spivak, "Translator's Preface," in Jacques Derrida, *Of Grammatology* (Baltimore: Johns Hopkins University Press, 1974), p. lxxxiv.

3. See, for instance, Michel Foucault, *Power/Knowledge: Selected Interviews and Other Writings, 1972–1977* (New York: Pantheon, 1980).

4. Spivak, "Translator's Preface," in Derrida, *Of Grammatology*, p. lxxv.

5. On ethics in poststructuralist criticism, see especially Tobin Seebers, *The Ethics of Criticism* (Ithaca, N.Y.: Cornell University Press, 1988).

6. See John Dominic Crossan, "Difference and Divinity," *Semeia* 23 (1982):29–40.

7. Robert W. Funk, "The Good Samaritan as Metaphor," *Semeia* 2 (1974):76. See also Robert W. Funk, *Language, Hermeneutic, and Word of God* (New York: Harper & Row, 1966), pp. 124–222; *Parables and Presence* (Philadelphia: Fortress, 1982).

8. John Dominic Crossan, *The Dark Interval: Towards a Theology of Story* (Allen, Tex.: Argus Communications, 1975), p. 128.

9. William A. Beardslee, "Uses of the Proverb in the Synoptic Gospels," *Interpretation* 24 (1970):61–71, reprinted in Beardslee, *Margins of Belonging: Essays on the New Testament and Theology* (Atlanta: Scholars, 1991), pp. 13–24.

10. Crossan, *Dark Interval*, pp. 57–62, referring to the work of Sheldon Sacks.

11. Stephen D. Moore, *Literary Criticism and the Gospels: The Theoretical Challenge* (New Haven, Conn.: Yale University Press, 1989).

12. Ibid., pp. 174–75.

13. See the comments of Moore, *Literary Criticism*, p. 165.

14. Robert C. Tannehill, *The Narrative Unity of Luke-Acts* (Philadelphia: Fortress, 1986–1990), vol. 1, p. 129.

15. Ibid.

16. Ibid., vol. 2, p. 46.

17. Ibid., vol. 1, pp. 109–10.

18. James M. Dawsey, *The Lucan Voice: Confusion and Irony in the Gospel of Luke* (Macon, Ga.: Mercer University Press, 1986), p. 146.

19. Tannehill, *Narrative Unity*, vol. 1, pp. 101–39.

20. Joseph B. Tyson, ed., *Luke-Acts and the Jewish People* (Minneapolis: Augsburg, 1988).

21. Jack T. Sanders, "The Jewish People in Luke-Acts," in Tyson, *Luke-Acts*, pp. 51–75; Robert C. Tannehill, "Rejection by Jews and Turning to Gentiles: The Pattern of Paul's Mission in Acts," in Tyson, *Luke-Acts*, pp. 83–101.

22. As by Mark C. Taylor, *Erring: A Postmodern A/theology* (Chicago: University of Chicago Press, 1984).

23. For a startlingly fresh approach to our economic structures, see Herman E. Daly and John B. Cobb, Jr., *For the Common Good: Redirecting the Economy Toward Community, the Environment, and a Sustainable Future* (Boston: Beacon, 1989). For many, a shock of "deconstruction" of our present system will be needed before they can confront the new possibilities that Daly and Cobb offer.

24. See, from a somewhat different point of view, the similar point of Wesley C. Kort, "'Religion and Literature' in Postmodern Contexts," *Journal of the American Academy of Religion* 53 (1990):575–88.

25. See Chapter 9 in this volume and Henrikus Boers, *Neither on This Mountain nor in Jerusalem; A Study of John 4* (Atlanta: Scholars, 1988).

26. See the important but difficult book of Robert C. Neville, *Recovery of the Mea-*

sure: Interpretation and Nature (Albany, N.Y.: State University of New York, 1989); for an introduction to this topic, see my review of Neville in *Process Studies* 19 (1990): 138–40.

27. David Jobling, "Writing the Wrongs of the World: The Deconstruction of the Biblical Text in the Context of Liberation Theologies," *Semeia* 51 (1990):81–118.

28. William A. Beardslee, "Vital Ruins: Biblical Narrative and the Story Frameworks of Our Lives," *Southern Humanities Review* 24 (1990):101–16, reprinted in Beardslee, *Margins of Belonging*, pp. 219–36.

29. Moore, *Literary Criticism*, pp. 171–78.

For Further Reading

Derrida, Jacques. *Of Grammatology*. Trans. Gayatri Chakravarti Spivak. Baltimore: Johns Hopkins University Press, 1974. An important work by Derrida, translated with a long and perceptive introduction by Gayatri Chakravarti Spivak.

Detweiler, Robert, ed. *Derrida and Biblical Studies*. *Semeia* 23 (1982). Essays in the interpretation of biblical texts by reading them "as systems of difference rather than privileged channels of an extra-textual transcendent" (p. 1).

Moore, Stephen D. *Literary Criticism of the Gospels: The Theoretical Challenge*. New Haven, Conn.: Yale University Press, 1989. Moore's survey of literary criticism moves toward showing the limits of coherence in New Testament texts and concludes with a presentation of deconstruction.

Phillips, Gary A., ed. *Poststructuralist Criticism and the Bible: Text/History/ Discourse*. *Semeia* 51 (1990). A variety of poststructuralist approaches, "concerned with institutional control and power" (p. 2).

Taylor, Mark C. *Erring: A Postmodern A/theology*. Chicago: University of Chicago Press, 1984. A major work of theological deconstruction.

Ulmer, Gregory. *Applied Grammatology: Post(e), Pedagogy from Jacques Derrida to Joseph Beuys*. Baltimore: Johns Hopkins University Press, 1985. Ulmer moves poststructuralism to a focus on the rhetoric of discovery, contrasting linear thought to discovery quickened by unexpected juxtapositions.

13
READING THE BIBLE IDEOLOGICALLY: FEMINIST CRITICISM

Danna Nolan Fewell

I myself have never been able to find out precisely what feminism is. I only know that people call me a feminist whenever I express sentiments that differentiate me from a doormat or a prostitute.—Rebecca West*

Indeed, if I were to try to articulate very succinctly what feminist criticism, as a way of thinking about literary texts, wants philosophically, I would say that at its most ambitious it wants to decode and demystify all the disguised questions and answers that have always shadowed the connections between textuality and sexuality, genre and gender, psychosexual identity and cultural authority.
—Sandra M. Gilbert**

It was as her life was departing—for she was dying—she called his name Son of my Sorrow. But his father called him Son of the South.—Genesis 35:18†

Stein says we no longer have the words people used to have so we have to make them new in some way but women haven't had them at all and how can you deconstruct a language you never constructed or it was never constructed by others like you, or with you in mind?—Frances Jaffer[1]

ECAUSE feminist theory insists that singular definitions are misleading and limiting, I confess to a certain amount of confusion about how to explain what feminist criticism is. Basically, feminist criticism concentrates on the political, social, and economic rights of women. Beyond that description, I dare not venture to speak for all. Instead, I begin with the above quotations to make several interrelated observations about feminist criticism.

First: Feminism as an ideology is difficult to date since women's historical records tend to be in short supply. As a critical discipline, however, feminism came into its own with the rise of the women's movement in the 1960s. It is a secular discipline, unapologetically political, that is gradually infiltrating all areas of the humanities and the sciences.

Like all new critical approaches, feminist criticism is born of a dissatisfaction with other means of inquiry and, like most new critical approaches, it has been greeted with skepticism and, in some quarters, even condescension. Feminist criticism, however, has met with more hostility than most, probably because it questions the very presuppositions of Western scholarly tradition, a tradition that has been, until quite recently, exclusively male-oriented in posture. Like other ideological criticisms (Marxist or African-American criticisms, for example) and unlike traditional forms of analysis, feminist criticism makes no pretense to objectivity; it challenges the notion of universals; it is more interested in relevance than in so-called absolute truth. In short, it resists the categories and definitions that male scholars and artists have set forth, in particular their definitions of women. When women speak "uncategorically," when they, as West so adroitly puts it, fail to fit the mold of doormat or prostitute, many men become uncomfortable, partly because such resistance to categorization signifies a deficit in the male reservoir of knowledge (in other words, the world is not as men have pictured and depicted it) and partly because the issue of gender difference is as personal as it is academic.

Second: Feminist critics work in a number of fields and use an assortment of methods to pursue their subjects. Their specific goals, their self-identities, are as varied as the critics themselves. Diversity is considered to be a major strength of the movement. If there is, however, any one thing that most feminist critics are likely to agree on, it is that texts of all kinds, whether creative or critical, are gendered. It has commonly been thought that women's writings are clearly feminized while men's writings are neutral. Feminist critics would claim rather that all of Western culture's classics—the literature, the histories, the paradigmatic philosophical, psychological, and sociological theories—

---

*Rebecca West, *The Young Rebecca*. Ed. J. Marcus. London: Macmillan, 1982, p. 219.

**Sandra M. Gilbert, "What Do Feminist Critics Want? A Postcard from the Volcano," in *The New Feminist Criticism: Essays on Women, Literature, and Theory*. Ed. Elaine Showalter. New York: Pantheon, 1985, p. 36.

†All scripture translations in this chapter are the author's own.

reflect and promote a gendered perspective. There is no universal norm from which women writers deviate. The writings of men are just as masculinized as those of women are feminized.

Gender, however, is more than simply a matter of sexual difference. Gender is a matter of power. There are few, if any, cultures today where men and women are equal. Men have power over women socially, politically, and economically. Race and class further complicate the hierarchy of dominance. Such hierarchy is inscribed in our classic texts, presupposed as if it were natural law rather than cultural construct. One of the tasks of feminist criticism is to expose the culturally based presuppositions embodied in classic discourse.

Third: Throughout the course of history, women have rarely been allowed to name their experiences. Just as Rachel's child and Rachel's ordeal are renamed by her husband, so women's experiences have countless times been inscribed or reinscribed by men. Women's sufferings, joys, and concerns have been "written over," altered, and even negated in subservience to what has been of significance to men. What has the world looked like to women? How have women felt about their assigned roles in society? How have women perceived men? How have they viewed one another? The history, the perceptions, the wisdom of half the human race have been lost. Another of feminism's critical tasks is to recover and to reclaim these lost lives and voices and values.

Fourth: While the task of reclaiming often involves rediscovering women's texts and encouraging women to experiment with and to produce new texts, more often the task and its results in the historical disciplines are less promising. Sometimes, as in the case of biblical studies, there are no new texts to be rediscovered. We must, instead, read behind what men have written. We must deal with texts that are not ours, texts that were not written for us or by others like us. We work with a feeling of estrangement, reading between the lines of alien texts, looking for invisible women, listening for muted voices.

The Bible, for the most part, is an alien text, not written by women or with women in mind. Some feminist critics have asked why we should be reading the Bible at all. For some, reading is a matter of religious tradition. For others, the issue is more diffuse. The Bible has prescribed our gender, dictated our sexuality, and defined our social roles even to this day and this culture. Genesis 2–3, perhaps more than any other biblical text, has been the biggest influence on the way men and women relate to one another in the Western world. Cited most often as "proof" that women are inferior to men and as support for male dominance over women, Genesis 2–3 has hardly been a liberating text. Consequently, this story has attracted a wide variety of feminist critiques.

Some would contend that *readings* of Genesis 2–3—not the text itself—have contributed to the present inequality between the sexes. Closer attention to the details of the text, some feminist critics argue, yields a more positive portrait of woman and woman's plight.

Phyllis Trible, among the first to publish on this story in contemporary feminist criticism, points out that the history of interpretation has shown more misogynist tendencies than does the actual text.[2] Rather than a justification of woman's inferiority, Trible discerns in the text a remarkable equality between the sexes in the original creation of humankind, arguing that it is only after the "fall" that hierarchy becomes a part of human existence as a consequence (not a "punishment") of the disobedience.

Using rhetorical analysis, she argues that God created the first human without gender. Her interpretation has merit. The *'adam*, literally, the "human," is created from the *'adamah*, the "humus," the earth. Though a masculine pronoun is used for this "earth creature" (Hebrew has no neuter pronoun), it is not until the woman is differentiated from this creature (made from its side) that the original human being acquires a gender. (This line of interpretation is actually not new. The famous tenth-century Jewish commentator, Rashi, suggested that the first human was male on one side and female on the other and that God simply divided the creature in half.) The interpretation may not be supported by the grammar of the text, but it appeals to our sense of binary logic. We know things by their opposites: We only know light because we know darkness; we know hot because we know cold; we know male because we know female.

Trible offers further arguments. She interprets the woman as the crown of creation rather than God's afterthought. She argues that the word "helper" (*ezer*) used to describe the woman is most often used in reference to God and therefore denotes a superior rather than an inferior being, and she observes that the woman is assertive and decisive while the man is passive and compliant. Read in this light, the text affirms women in ways the history of interpretation never imagined.

More recent work on Genesis 2–3 has been less idealistic about the egalitarian nature of the text but has nonetheless attempted to rehabilitate the character of Eve. For Mieke Bal, another feminist literary critic, Eve develops into a character of great power.[3] Her decision to eat the fruit from the tree of the knowledge of good and evil is the first act of human independence and puts the human creatures on a more equal footing with God. For Bal, this is not a negative thing because now the human and the divine are in a real relationship of give and take rather than an artificial relationship of puppet and puppeteer. Eve did not "sin"; she opted for reality. She chose real life, and her choice marks the emergence of human character.

Text-affirming or character-affirming readings are not exclusive to literary criticism. Carol Meyers, a feminist historical critic, in an attempt to reconstruct the social situations of ancient Israelite women,[4] has also understood this text to be less misogynist than its subsequent interpretations have allowed. For Meyers, the story of Eden must be set against the backdrop of the premonarchical agrarian society of the Palestinian highlands. Eden is indeed paradise because it depicts an existence very different from that of the ancient Israelite farming family. The garden's trees are already well established, there is no need to plant backbreaking field crops, and water is in steady supply. The repetition of the words "food" and "eat" suggest that the people who would have told this story, the farm community in the highlands of Palestine, understood the sustenance of life to be a central concern, overriding the theme of disobedience and its consequences. For Meyers, Genesis 2–3 is not a story of "the fall" (no word for "fall" or "sin" is ever mentioned) but a wisdom tale dealing "with the meaning of the paradoxes and harsh facts of life" (p. 91).

Crucial to her argument is a retranslation of Gen. 3:16, God's judgment upon the woman, which she renders as follows:

> I will greatly increase your toil and your pregnancies;
> (along) with travail shall you beget children.
> For to your man is your desire,
> and he shall predominate over you. (p. 118)

The plight of women described is not pain in childbirth but increased agrarian toil in addition to multiple pregnancies. The ancient Israelite woman, due to the mortality rate of women in their childbearing years (life expectancy for a woman was around thirty years, while a man could expect to live to forty), would have understandably been reluctant to endure repeated childbirths. But because of her own sexual desire and the propensity of men to insist on sexual intercourse, she would have faced the additional risks of pregnancies and childbirths along with the hard work she would have shared with her man.

For Meyers, then, the text's emphasis on female subordination lies only in the realm of sexual activity. The reference is to the man's overpowering sex drive rather than to any general social hierarchy. Men and women in an agricultural society would have, according to Meyers, lived a more egalitarian existence than would have been the case in later urban culture.

While the preceding critics have attempted to rehabilitate the text's gender code, making the story more palatable to modern women, others have viewed the biblical text with more suspicion. Could the ancient writer(s) have intended for Eve to be so equal and admirable? Was Even truly meant to be portrayed as bold, decisive, and wise? Can the centuries of interpreters who have read her to be gullible and stupid be so far off the mark? Suppose the text is implying that she is inferior, the first to sin, and responsible for the fallen state of humankind—who has cast her in this light?

In other words, some critics are asking, if all writing is gendered, then what about the sexual politics of biblical composers? Who has defined positive and negative female qualities? Are the womanly assets commended in the Bible (beauty, submissiveness, obedience, fecundity, industriousness, for example) merely those characteristics deemed valuable by the patriarchy? And what about less than admirable female characters—the Jezebels and the Delilahs? Are they being portrayed thus because of some political strategy at work to control women's self-understanding?

Gender is, after all, a social construction. Unlike biological sexual difference, gender identity is socially defined. People are born male or female, but they become men and women through adhering to cultural constructions of what men and women are supposed to be like. As Myra Jehlen[5] writes, "Femininity is a performance and not a natural mode of being" (p. 269).

Genesis 2–3, as a story of origins, is, among other things, in the business of constructing gender roles and fitting them into accepted social hierarchy. The man does name both genders—and according to him, the woman is derivative of the man. God relates the woman to the man as his "helper." The narrator defines their sexual orientation to be heterosexual. God designates the labors assigned to each gender. The man stipulates that the woman's primary role in life is to be the "mother of all living." The narrative establishes a particular kind of life-style for men and women. In whose interests is this description? Who would have promoted this construction of gender?

The appeal to authorial intention has led recent commentators to counter the reading of sexual equality. Susan Lanser, applying the principles of speech-act theory to the text,[6] argues that inference and context are as important to the production of meaning as the formal characteristics of language. When a character is introduced into a story, that character is assumed to have a gender. Even though the first human is not identified as male, argues Lanser, *ha'adam* would have been, and should be understood to be, a male human. There is nothing in the text to indicate otherwise. Furthermore, inference and context suggest that when the man calls the new creature "woman," this, like the naming of the animals, is an act that defines her. It is not, as Trible would contend, simply a recognition of sexual difference. Finally, context dictates that the accusatory formula "Because you did this," addressed to the serpent in 3:14, also carries over to the woman. Thus God's pronouncement in 3:16 is in fact punishment and not simply a statement of consequences as Trible and Bal would allow. When the context of production is foregrounded against the context of reading or reproduction, Genesis 2–3 remains very much a text of the patriarchy.

David Clines[7] has argued at length that the word "helper" does not, as Trible has suggested, designate a superior being. While a helper may have superior status, she or he is, nevertheless, secondary to the project of the one who is being helped. Eve is, in Clines's reading, unalterably subordinate to

Adam. Citing Gen. 1:28 and finding support among the church fathers, Clines concludes that Eve is necessary to help Adam do the only task he cannot accomplish by himself, namely, procreate.[8]

Despite its androcentricity ("man-centeredness"), however, the text is not completely a lost cause. Clines insists that it still has much to offer us:

> The authority of a text has to do with its nature; we want to be saying things about the Bible that have to do with its *function*. We want to be saying, not so much that the Bible is right, not even that the Bible is wrong, but that it impacts for good upon people. Despite its handicaps, despite the fact that it has misled people and promoted patriarchy, it has an unquenchable capacity—when taken in conjunction with a commitment to personal integrity—to inspire people, bring out the best in them and suggest a vision they could never have dreamed of for themselves. Think of it as dogma and you will at times, as over the matter of men and women, either be wrong or get it wrong. Think of it rather as a resource for living which has no authority but which nevertheless manages to impose itself powerfully upon people. (p. 48)

Recognizing the androcentric nature of the text but taking a more compromising tack is Phyllis Bird's attempt to examine Genesis 1–3 as a source for a theology of sexuality.[9] The first human is admittedly male, but though "he bears the appellation of the species, he does not fully represent it" (p. 38). The remainder of the chapter, suggests Bird, is devoted to overcoming this problem of singularity. As far as woman's status as helper is concerned, Bird considers closely the narrative context: "Although the help which the woman is meant to give to the man is undoubtedly help in procreation, the account in Genesis 2 subordinates function to passion. The attraction of the sexes is the author's primary interest, the sexual drive whose consummation is conceived as a re-union" (p. 38).

The subordination of woman to man is not part of the created order. Rather, says Bird, the equality of the sexes in Genesis 2 is the "prelude to its negation in Genesis 3" (p. 39). Alienation and estrangement are the result of sin. This is still a message of relevance: "It is the Yahwist's contribution to remind us that the good gift of sexuality may become the means and the sign of alienation within the species, that what was intended for fulfillment and self-transcendence may become the occasion and instrument of deprivation and oppression" (p. 44).

Pamela Milne[10] is less optimistic about any helpful message coming from Genesis 2–3. If men created the text, then Adam will always dominate Eve. And as long as men read the text, Eve comes out the loser. No feminist reformation of surface elements, suggests Milne, is going to disguise the fact that

Genesis 2–3 is essentially male mythology and has been consistently perceived as such by male scholars who have analyzed it. She somewhat despair-
ingly points to the fact that feminist work on Genesis 2–3 has consistently
been ignored by male scholars dealing with this text.

Readers who look to the Bible for spiritual direction and yet disagree with
the values found there face a dilemma. In Milne's judgment, our alternatives
are few:

> We can either accept the patriarchal biblical text as sacred and con-
> tent ourselves with exposing its patriarchy . . . or we can expose its
> patriarchy and reject it as sacred and authoritative. But if we are
> looking for a sacred scripture that is not patriarchal, that does not
> construct woman as "other" and that does not support patriarchal
> interpretations based on this otherness, we are not likely to find it
> or to recover it in texts such as Genesis 2–3. If we want an authori-
> tative sacred scripture that does not make it possible to believe that
> women are secondary and inferior humans, it appears that we need
> to make new wine to fill our new wineskins. (p. 22)

Feminist criticism has had the tendency to focus on the roles and characterization of women in the biblical text. While inevitable and crucial to the project, such study is not without its drawbacks. Paradoxically, the focus on
women has, to some extent, slipped into the patriarchal syndrome of defining
women as "other." Women, because they differ from *men*, are the subject of
investigation. Whether women emerge as positive figures, as in the analysis of
Trible, or are hopelessly minimal, as in Clines's view of the text, the implication is the same. Men and men's interests somehow remain the unquestioned
standard. Even the recognition that writing itself is gendered—that is, that it
reflects gendered experience—has often occasioned little more than observation in biblical criticism.

As has been noted above, gender is not simply a matter of difference but a
matter of power. Thus to say that a text is androcentric or racist, as if that were
an ideological perspective equal to any other, and to leave it at that, may sound
scholarly, but it is not neutral. It is according some value, if only by default, to
certain oppressive relations of power between people. How critics write of
gender, then, is a matter of grave responsibility. Categories like gender, race,
and class hierarchically structure our lives and our texts, but not without troubling tensions and contradictions. To say that a text is androcentric, even when
taking a clear stand on the question of value, and to leave it at that, may be
missing an opportunity to deal with inherent tensions and contradictions in
androcentrism's disposition of power.[11]

Scholars who are scrutinizing the power relations both within texts and in the writing of texts are producing readings in which tension and contradiction are part of the text's meaning. David Jobling,[12] employing structuralist methodology clearly informed by Marxist and feminist ideology, finds several conflicts at work in Genesis 2–3. First, there is the conflict between two narrative programs. On the one hand, the story explains the creation and fall of humankind—this is the program traditionally recognized. On the other hand, this plot agenda competes with a more basic agenda—explaining how there came to be a man to till the earth, the problem or need set forth at the beginning of the story.[13] Conflict also exists on the ideological level. The patriarchal tendency of the story is to subordinate the woman in the social order and to blame the woman for the misfortune that has befallen humankind. In tension with this agenda are the undeniable positive characteristics of the woman in the text.

There is, Jobling insists, asymmetry in the creation of the man and the woman and in their subsequent offenses. Yet while the patriarchal culture that produced and received this text would have assumed the first human to be male, an assumption grounded in the grammar of the text, the logic, Jobling admits, is on Trible's side: "Male" is meaningless without "female." While the woman sins first and is implicated in the man's sin, the woman is (as Trible has also observed) active and intelligent while the man is passive and oblivious. How do such characterizations come to be in patriarchal text?

> They are inevitable expressions of the logic of the myth: woman and sexuality belong to the same semantic configuration as knowledge. Part of the price the male mindset pays is the admission that woman is more aware of the complexity of the world, more in touch with "all living." And finally, at the deepest level of the text, where the fall myth as a whole is in tension with "a man to till the earth," the possibility is evoked that the human transformation in which the woman took powerful initiative was positive, rather than negative, that the complex human world is to be preferred over any male ideal.
>
> But these "positive" features are not the direct expression of a feminist consciousness. . . . Rather, they are the effects of the patriarchal mindset tying itself in knots trying to account for woman and femaleness in a way which *both* makes sense *and* supports patriarchal assumptions. (pp. 42–43)

Bal recognizes the same phenomenon. The text reveals a problem with man's priority and domination.

> The reason for this situation is obvious. The burden of domination is hard to bear. Dominators have, first, to establish their position, then to safeguard it. Subsequently, they must make both the domi-

nated *and* themselves believe in it. Insecurity is not a prerogative exclusively of the dominated. The establishing of a justifying "myth of origin," which has to be sufficiently credible and realistic to account for common experience, is not that simple a performance. Traces of the painful process of gaining control can therefore be perceived in those very myths. They serve to limit repression to acceptable, viable proportions. (1987:110)

Consequently, the story may be designed to communicate male priority and natural superiority over women and to justify thereby the social dominance of men over women, but the more vehement their claim, the more fragile their case. Texts do more than they say. In fact, they often do quite the opposite of what they intend to say.[14]

We are dealing here, however, not simply with instability or indeterminacy within texts but with a particular way of reading. "Reading against the grain" is, in Gerald Graff's terms, "a method which does not take the texts' apparent contexts and intentions at face value, but looks at the doubts they repress or leave unsaid and how this repressed or 'absent' element can undermine or undo what the text says" (p. 171). It is, in short, choosing to question the priorities and hierarchies of a text, to deconstruct the text, if you will.

In the case of Genesis 2–3, the questioning of hierarchies might extend beyond the roles of man and woman. The divine, the human, and the animal realms also fall into a prioritized order. The divine character, YHWH Elohim, not surprisingly, is heavily engaged in the business of authority. He is the "author" of the garden and all that is in it. He creates not only the man but also the woman and the serpent, who are traditionally blamed for the "fall." And it is he who places that momentous tree in the midst of the garden and circumscribes it with arbitrary prohibition.

Most commentators, for obvious theological reasons, want to "protect" God, to remove this character from scrutiny, much as God pronounces the tree of the knowledge of good and evil to be off-limits to the humans in the garden. Some readers, however, are willing to pluck the fruit, eager to learn what the knowledge of good and evil is all about. Tensions and contradictions within the text, and between text and reader, may challenge us to reenter the garden with our eyes opened, even if that means eventually running up against the contradictory, unstable character of God.

David Jobling's structural analysis reveals that YHWH Elohim is both the initiator and the opponent of the action. God creates what the earth needs, a man to till it, but then acts as villain by retaining the man to keep his own private garden. Furthermore, YHWH counteracts his own villainy by creating the tree of knowledge, the serpent, and the woman, who converge to foil the divine conspiracy.

In a more recent attempt to "read against the grain,"[15] David Gunn has suggested that certain characteristics of God, established in Genesis 1 and transferred to the humans who were created in the divine image, keep the text from completely succeeding in shifting the blame of the fall onto the woman and the serpent. God's desire for dominion (evident in such language as "rule" [1:16], "subjugate [1:26], and "subdue" [1:28]), for dividing and naming, for creating self-likeness, and for discovery color both God and humans with a mixture of control and freedom. Domination, categorization, labeling, and ensuring sameness or conformity are all manifestations of the need to control. The capacity for discovery, however ("And God saw that it was good"), undermines control, valuing exploration and venture. Further-more, as the divine pronouncements of "good" reveal, God can differentiate between good and evil. In the slippage between plural self-reference and sin-gular verbs ("Elohim [plural] said [singular], 'Let us make humankind in our image . . . ' "), God admits differentiation within the divine self.

The contradictions in the creator are manifested in the creature. We see the first human categorizing and naming the animals. We see the man labeling the woman, declaring her likeness and yet her difference. We see the woman's curiosity and love of discovery, her desire to be "like" God, to know good and evil. And we see humankind divided among itself, aware of and attempting to conceal its differences. The man blames the "other" one and eventually subju-gates her.

The language of the text allows the blame to shift from man to woman to serpent, and there the buck-passing stops, because "the serpent's mouth is stopped with dust." But as hard as the words try to locate fault in humans in general, and women and their animal counterparts specifically, the silences, the tensions, the contradictions whisper that, ultimately, God is responsible for the "fallen," or perhaps more to the point, the "realistic" state of creation.

It should be clear by this catalogue of readings that feminist criticism is not a monolithic enterprise. Granted, all of these critics, in one way or another, are asking about the status of women in Genesis 2–3. They are nonetheless also asking other questions, using a variety of methods, and arriving at different answers. Although I have suggested some affinities and dissimilarities among these readings, it should be quickly noted that feminist work on other biblical texts may or may not fit these heuristic categories. Even these particular critics do not always employ the same critical stance.

As I have tried to indicate in this outline, there are many explicit and im-plicit interchanges taking place among scholars working in this critical mode. An energetic internal critique is occurring among feminist readers.

These dynamics raise some troubling questions about the nature of the Bible and its authority. Should we be looking with Bal and Trible for role models (whether male or female) in the Bible?[16] Is the Bible really in the business of providing us characters to emulate, people after whom we can pattern our lives? Or are biblical messages more complex than that?

If interpretation is to be guided by context and inference, as Lanser suggests, how precise can we be? Is "precision" even the right word to describe the goals of reading? If we all are to "infer" the same things, to understand contexts in the same way, do we not run the risk of returning to the univocality of patriarchy?

Can we depend on reconstructed historical and sociological contexts to inform our reading? Do the Bible's stories simply reflect the life-styles of a particular community, as Meyers contends? Or are there some sexual politics at work that are meant to promote a specific way of life?

If we conclude that the Bible is androcentric, should we completely reject it as sacred scripture, as Milne suggests? If we hang on to it as sacred scripture, what do we do with its androcentrism? Is the androcentrism, as Clines argues, an unfortunate but not necessarily an insurmountable problem? Can we truly distinguish between a text having authority and a text "imposing itself powerfully upon people"? Can we indeed rely on "personal integrity," knowing that church fathers such as Augustine and Aquinas no doubt read with integrity, yet constructed *and promoted* debasingly misogynist interpretations?

Given that the text is androcentric, is there not always a danger in using it as a resource for a theology of sexuality, even for careful readers like Phyllis Bird? Can we accept how the Bible defines gender roles? And what about the deconstructionists—how comfortable are we when the character of God becomes the subject of deconstruction? After all, in the biblical story world God allows, if not promotes, patriarchal hierarchy. What are Jewish and Christian believers to do with that?

While some might construe these questions and others like them to indicate weaknesses in the critical approach, I tend to think they are a sign of great vitality. More voices are engaging the question of gender, helping to create a language, a body of critical discourse. What we are discovering is that the conversation cannot stay in or with the text. Inevitably, it leads to questions about how we live and how we should live. It cuts through to the heart of our values, challenging us to dismantle oppressive structures in our world.

Postscript

Because of its diversity, I find it difficult to pinpoint major weaknesses in feminist criticism in general. Nevertheless, I do think that anyone wishing to employ feminist criticism should be forewarned: Feminist criticism is not always taken seriously. Considered by some to be "faddish" or "trendy" or downright trivial, it is often ignored, or in some situations even ridiculed. Its results sometimes make people angry, and that anger is almost always directed toward the interpreter.

One need not be surprised by this response. Feminist criticism undermines ingrained worldviews and cherished beliefs. It suggests that the Bible offers something other than universal truth, and for many Jewish and Christian believers that is a difficult notion to accept.

Nevertheless, for readers who are open to the complexity, the plurality, and even the indeterminacy of the biblical witness, for readers who are comfortable with the notion that the Bible shows us a broken world more often than it does an exemplary one, for readers who recognize that not all people experience life in the same way, feminist criticism is an effective and stimulating mode of analysis for men as well as women. Not only does it have the potential to transform the way we look at the Bible, it also has the power to transform the way we look at ourselves and the way we live in our society.

Notes

1. Unpublished lecture. Quoted by Rachel Blau DuPlessis in "For the Etruscans" in *The New Feminist Criticism: Essays on Women Literature and Theory*, ed. by Elaine Showalter (New York: Pantheon, 1985), pp. 271–91.

2. First argued by Trible in "Depatriarchalizing in Biblical Interpretation," *Journal of the American Academy of Religion* 41 (1973):30–48 and "Eve and Adam, Genesis 2–3 Reread," *Andover Newton Quarterly* 13 (1975):251–58. Later appearing in "Genesis 2–3 Revisited" in *Womanspirit Rising: A Feminist Reader on Religion*, ed. Carol Christ and Judith Plaskow (New York: Harper & Row, 1975) and in *God and the Rhetoric of Sexuality* (Philadelphia: Fortress, 1978).

3. Mieke Bal, "Sexuality, Sin and Sorrow: The Emergence of Female Character [A Reading of Genesis 2–3]," in *The Female Body in Western Culture*, ed. Susan Rubin Suleiman (Cambridge: Harvard University Press, 1986), pp. 317–38; reprinted in *Lethal Love: Feminist Literary Readings of Biblical Love Stories* (Bloomington, Ind.: Indiana University Press, 1987), pp. 104–130.

4. Carol Meyers, *Discovering Eve: Ancient Israelite Women in Context* (New York: Oxford University Press, 1988).

5. Myra Jehlen, "Gender," in *Critical Terms for Literary Study*, ed. Frank Lentricchia and Thomas McLaughlin (Chicago: University of Chicago Press, 1990), pp. 263–73.

6. Susan Lanser, "(Feminist) Criticism in the Garden: Inferring Genesis 2–3," *Semeia* 41 (1988):67–84.

7. David Clines, "What Does Eve Do to Help? and Other Irredeemably Androcentric Orientations in Genesis 1–3," in *What Does Eve Do to Help? and Other Readerly Questions to the Old Testament* (Sheffield: Journal for the Study of the Old Testament, 1990), pp. 25–48. It should be noted that though Clines shows sympathy for feminist concerns and a "mastery" of the discussion regarding this particular text, he also main-

tains a certain detachment and is careful not to refer to himself as a feminist. For some pertinent observations on male feminist criticism, see Elaine Showalter's "The Rise of Gender," in *Speaking of Gender*, ed. E. Showalter (London: Routledge, 1989), pp. 1–16, especially pp. 5–8 and 10.

8. Note that Meyers would, in all likelihood, dispute this claim. She would have no problem seeing Eve (Everywoman) helping with gardening/farming duties.

9. Phyllis Bird, "Genesis 1–3 as a Source for a Contemporary Theology of Sexuality," *Ex Auditu* (1987):31–44.

10. Pamela Milne, "The Patriarchal Stamp of Scripture: The Implications of Structuralist Analyses for Feminist Hermeneutics," *Journal of Feminist Studies in Religion* 5 (1989):11–22.

11. Susan Lanser is moving in this direction when she asks, "Might not the tension between inference and form signify a deep ambivalence on the part of the Jahwist writer or his society about the place of woman? Might such a disease not signify the dissonance within early Judaism between the status of woman in traditional patriarchal society and the theologically egalitarian impulse manifested more openly in the later Genesis 1? Might this not make Genesis 2–3 the document of a patriarchy already beginning to be uncomfortable with itself?" (79).

12. David Jobling, "Myth and Its Limits in Genesis 2.4b–3.24," in *The Sense of Biblical Narrative II* (Sheffield: Journal for the Study of the Old Testament, 1986), pp. 17–43. Many of his arguments were first published in "The Myth Semantics of Genesis 2:4b–3:24," *Semeia* 18 (1980):41–49.

13. Note here the similarity to Meyers's position that the real issue in the story is not "the fall" but sustenance of life.

14. Gerald Graff writes, "The point here is that language attempts to build up positions of authority which language itself calls into question. . . . The very expressions by which we claim . . . credibility betray how fragile and challengeable [that credibility] is" ("Determinacy/Indeterminacy," in Lentricchia and McLaughlin, *Critical Terms for Literary Study*, p. 170).

15. David Gunn, "Shifting the Blame: God and Patriarchy in the Garden," unpublished paper presented at the midwest regional meeting of the Society of Biblical Literature (1990). This paper provides the basis for a jointly authored chapter of the same name forthcoming in Danna Nolan Fewell and David M. Gunn, *Gender, Power, and Promise: The Subject of the Bible's First Story* (Nashville: Abingdon, 1993).

16. Let me reiterate that Bal and Trible do not take such a stance in all their work. See, for example, Trible's more recent *Texts of Terror: Feminist Literary Readings of Biblical Narrative* (Philadelphia: Fortress, 1984) and Bal's *Death and Disymmetry: The Politics of Coherence in Judges* (Chicago: University of Chicago Press, 1988).

For Further Reading

Collins, Adela Yarbro, ed. *Feminist Perspectives on Biblical Scholarship.* Chico, Calif.: Scholars, 1985.

Day, Peggy L., ed. *Gender and Difference in Ancient Israel.* Minneapolis: Fortress, 1989.

Exum, J. Cheryl, and Bos, Johanna W. H., eds. *Reasoning with the Foxes: Female Wit in a World of Male Power. Semeia* 42. Atlanta: Scholars, 1988.

Newsom, Carol A., and Ringe, Sharon H., eds. *The Women's Bible Commentary.* Louisville, Ky.: Westminster/John Knox, 1992.

Russell, Letty M., ed. *Feminist Interpretation of the Bible.* Philadelphia: Westminster, 1985.

Tolbert, Mary Ann, ed. *The Bible and Feminist Hermeneutics. Semeia* 28. Chico, Calif.: Scholars, 1983.

Trible, Phyllis, ed. "The Effects of Women's Studies on Biblical Studies." *Journal for the Study of the Old Testament* 22 (1992).